AMERICAN
COLONIAL GOVERNMENT
1696-1765

At the Council Chamber Whitehall
the 9th day of February 1749

By the Right Honourable the Lords of the Committee
of Council for the Affairs of Guernsey and Jersey &c

Present

Lord President   Lord Chief Justice Willes
Lord Sandys

Guernsey

Committee Report on the Petition of Thomas Le Cocq Senr. agt the Royal Court

Their Excellencys the late Lords Justices having been pleased by their Order in Council of the 13th of October 1748 to referr unto this Committee the humble Petition of Thomas Le Cocq Senior of the Island of Alderney Esqr in relation to his carrying into Execution Your Majestys Order in Council of the 10th of June 1747 obliging all Ships coming from Sta Cruz or places adjacent in West Barbary to perform Quarantine and his causing William Samford to be arrested for obstructing the Execution of the said Order, And complaining of two Orders made by the Royal Court of the Island of Guernsey the One dated the 26th of September 1747 for the Petitioner to appear in person before the said Royal Court to Answer the Complaint of Mr John Le Mesurier Farmer of His Majestys Revenues in Alderney in relation to the arresting the said Samford; And the other Order dated the 28th of January 1747 for the Provost of Alderney to Seize the Petitioner and carry him Prisoner to Guernsey And humbly praying that the said two Orders may be annulled and set aside and that the Petitioner may be otherwise relieved in the Premises ── The Lords of the Committee upon Consideration of this Petition on the 24th of November 1748 thought it proper to direct that a Copy thereof should be transmitted to the Bailiff and Jurates of Your Majestys Royal Court of Guernsey requiring them to return their Answer thereunto to this Committee with all convenient Speed; And that in the mean time all proceedings should be stopt with regard to the personal Appearance of the Petitioner upon his Appearing by his Agent or Attorney And the said Bailiff and Jurates having accordingly returned their Answer to the said Petition; The Lords of the Committee this day proceeded to take the whole Matter into their Consideration and having heard Counsel thereupon on both sides Do Agree humbly to Report as their Opinion to

Your

A PRIVY COUNCIL COMMITTEE MEETING

Note the method of handling appeals. Appeals from Virginia and Minorca were
also disposed of at this meeting

AMERICAN COLONIAL GOVERNMENT
1696-1765

A study of the British Board of Trade in
its relation to the American Colonies,
Political, Industrial, Administrative

BY

OLIVER MORTON DICKERSON, Ph.D.
Professor of History, Western Illinois State Normal School

CLEVELAND, OHIO
THE ARTHUR H. CLARK COMPANY
1912

CONTENTS

ILLUSTRATIONS

PREFACE

The period covered by this volume, 1696-1765, is one of the most important in the growth of the American nation. It was during this period that the original colonies developed their traditions of political liberty, and acquired by steady encroachments on the part of the assemblies practically complete self-government. The year 1700 found the colonies outside of New England weak dependencies under the direct control of the crown or of proprietors: in each colony an appointed council exercised the full legislative powers of an upper house, an appointed governor held the executive power unlimited by any written constitution, the elected lower house was timid and inexperienced. By 1765 the councils had been robbed of their chief legislative powers, judges and other officers had become dependent upon the lower house, and the governors had been reduced to inefficient figureheads, dependent upon the assemblies for their daily bread, and impotent to obey the orders they received from England. There are few stories more fascinating than the account of this gradual subversion of the old colonial constitution by our stubborn forefathers, and the substitution in its place of a government which could be controlled independent of the mother country. On account of the steady evolution which was taking place, no period affords a better opportunity than this to study British colonial administration in action, nor is the study of any other period likely to throw more light upon the origin of political institutions which are peculiarly American.

The Board of Trade was the department of the British government which, during this period, was officially charged with colonial affairs and which united the colonies administratively with the rest of the empire. It was constantly in touch with the various plantations, learning their special needs, considering their grievances, advising their officers, encouraging their development, and examining and criticising their laws. It is difficult to estimate the influence which the Board of Trade exerted upon American history because it touched so many things and yet did its work so quietly; but beyond question it played a most important part in shaping colonial institutions at a time when they were most susceptible. Notwithstanding the close relations between this bureau and the colonies, and regardless of the fact that its records comprise the most important single collection of manuscript material in existence for a study of early American history, the Board of Trade has hitherto received but scant notice and the story of its activities has remained untold. This has left a serious gap in the literature of American history. How the colonial office was organized, its plans, its success in carrying them into operation, its methods of handling colonial business, and the difficulties it encountered should be known. This volume is intended to supply that information.

The theme of this book is definitely stated in its title. It is a study of the British Board of Trade and the machinery of imperial control: what it was, the men who directed it, their ideas of the relations of the mother country to the colonies, the relations of the colonial office to other branches of the government, and the conditions under which colonial affairs were administered. The study has inevitably included economic and industrial questions; transportation, money, and means of communication profoundly affected administration in the colonies and have been discussed from that point of view. Some of the larger questions of colonial policy, such as boundaries, the westward movement of population and the attitude of the British government towards it, Indian relations and Indian problems, and commercial and trade policies, have been discussed at considerable length. A special effort has been made to trace the development of the Board of Trade's imperial ideas and its schemes for making colonial government more effective, and to determine how successful these plans were in operation.

It has been impossible to discuss the above questions without pointing out in considerable detail how, athwart all the schemes for the enlargement of imperial control, rose the colonial assemblies with their resistless, creeping encroachments upon the prerogative; and how, as a result of the rise of the assemblies, the center of gravity of colonial administration was shifted from England to America. As is shown in the body of the text, that was the most important condition confronting those who attempted to rule the colonies, and was the factor which spelled failure for so many of their plans.

Another phase of the relations of the colonies to the home government which has never received adequate consideration, and which is dealt with at some length in the present volume, is the treatment of colonial legislation. Who directed the royal veto? What laws were vetoed and for what reasons? Were such interferences with colonial legislation the result of the arbitrary action of an irresponsible monarch, or that of a conservative judicial body? What was the effect of such vetoes upon colonial legislation? Has our own judicial practice inherited anything from colonial precedents in such matters? These are some of the questions which have been considered, and upon which, it is believed, light has been thrown.

As there is no treatise which discusses in adequate detail the changes in the English constitution during the eighteenth century, it has been necessary to investigate rather carefully the operation of the Privy Council and the work and development of its committees. This has led to conclusions somewhat novel, and perhaps at variance with commonly accepted ideas; but it is believed that these conclusions will stand criticism and be fully sustained by more complete investigation. The subject is one which properly belongs within the field of English constitutional history; but as an understanding of the matter is necessary to an intelligent account of the organs of colonial administration, there was no alternative but to include a rather detailed description of the committee system and its operation.

As the field covered is one which has hitherto remained undeveloped, the subject matter has of necessity been drawn to a preponderant extent from original sources. In the first place, these have been the manuscript records, formerly in the possession of the Board of Trade, but now deposited in the Public Record Office in London; secondly, the Privy Council *Register* at Whitehall and the British Museum *Additional Manuscripts*, sources which generally have been neglected by former writers of this period; and finally, very careful use has been made of the readily accessible printed copies of colonial records, colonial laws, and the correspondence of colonial governors. Secondary material has proved unusually disappointing, although a small percentage of it was of real service. No use has been made of transcripts, but in all cases where manuscripts are cited, the reference is to the original documents in London. In general these citations follow the present classifications and are by number instead of name: a glance at the table in the bibliography, however, will make clear the nature of all papers cited.

The author wishes to express his appreciation of the unfailing courtesy of the officials at the Privy Council Office at Whitehall and of those at the Public Record Office in London, especially Mr. Hubert H. Hall whose vast knowledge of the material in the records under his care is placed so unstintingly at the disposal of American students. To Professor Edward Channing and Professor Evarts B. Greene special acknowledgments are due. Help and advice have also been received from Professor Charles M. Andrews, Herman V. Ames, and Clarence W. Alvord.

OLIVER MORTON DICKERSON.

Macomb, Illinois, June, 1911.

I. ORGANIZATION AND PERSONNEL OF THE BOARD OF TRADE

Colonial Administration prior to 1696

The first half of the seventeenth century had been a period of beginnings and experiments in colonial administration. The planters on the continent of America had not been numerous enough nor wealthy enough to invite very serious attention from the British government until after the great Puritan migration was well under way. What little control there was came from the Privy Council; but in 1634, Archbishop Laud was delegated to head a commission for foreign plantations with almost royal powers over political, judicial, and ecclesiastical affairs in the colonies. This commission seems to have been created as a result of the steady Puritan emigration to New England with the object of enforcing the royal will beyond the sea, but it accomplished practically nothing and came to an end when Parliament seized control of the central government.[1]

The periods of the Civil War, Commonwealth, and Protectorate produced no new organs of colonial administration; in fact the colonies were left pretty much to their own devices. What control was exer-

---

[1] Andrews, Charles McL. *British Committees, Commissions, and Councils of Trade and Plantations, 1622-1675*, chap. 1; Osgood, Herbert L. *American Colonies in the Seventeenth Century*, vol. iii, chap. 1; Egerton, Hugh E. *Short History of British Colonial Policy*, 74.

cised centered either in Parliament directly or in the later Council of State where the protector's will was dominant.   The advent of Cromwell, however, had instilled a new spirit of efficiency and aggressiveness into every department of the government and pervaded other phases of the nation's activity.   Colonial commerce attracted able and wealthy merchants and soon acquired such importance that the administrative machinery for both trade and plantations became plainly inadequate.   This led Martin Noell and Thomas Povey, two merchants who had considerable financial investments in the colonies and in colonial commerce, especially in the newly acquired West India plantations, to lay before the protector a scheme for colonial control which would weld the isolated governments in America into a single government under the control of a central board in England.[2]

Noell's plan was not put in operation during Cromwell's rule, but with slight alterations it was presented to the advisers of Charles II soon after the Restoration and became the basis for the scheme which they adopted in 1660.   Instead of a single committee, however, two were created: one to deal with trade, and the other with the plantations, although each assisted the other.   Both committees included in their membership privy councilors and merchants, and neither acted independently of the Council, but reported their findings to that body.   The Committee for Foreign Plantations was given very extensive powers, including control over commercial, governmental, and religious conditions, and anything else which might concern the existing colonies or those which should

[2] Andrews, C. *British Committees, Commissions, and Councils,* 24-58.

be acquired. Most of these powers were never exercised and the committee seems to have come to an end about 1665, although its commission does not appear to have been suppressed at that time.[3] In one form or another the dual arrangement of separate committees for trade and for the plantations continued until 1672 when they were merged into a single committee,[4] which in turn was suppressed, and in 1675 the entire control of trade and foreign plantations was transferred to a committee of the Privy Council.[5]

This body is known as the Lords of the Committee of Trade and Plantations, or simply Lords of Trade, a name which continued to be used for the members of the later Board of Trade.[6] Aside from changes in membership this committee continued to be used for the control of both trade and colonial affairs until 1696, when the Board of Trade was created. Under James II this committee became very energetic, especially in its efforts to suppress the proprietary and charter colonies and to establish in New England a single consolidated government modeled after that in New York. It was the period of Andros and his somewhat arbitrary methods and of the *quo warranto* proceedings against the charters of Massachusetts Bay, Rhode Island, and Connecticut.[7] For the first

[3] Andrews, C. *British Committees, Commissions, and Councils,* 61-95.

[4] This committee had even greater powers than its predecessors. See: Andrews, C. *British Committees, Commissions, and Councils,* 97-110; *Colonial Self Government,* 25.

[5] New York *Colonial Documents,* vol. iii, p. xiv; Andrews, C. *British Committees, Commissions, and Councils,* 111-113.

[6] New York *Colonial Documents,* vols. iii, iv, v, vi, vii, *passim.*

[7] Osgood, H. L. *American Colonies,* vol. iii, chap. ix-xiv; Andrews, C. *Colonial Self Government,* 26-40; Egerton, H. E. *British Colonial Policy,* 92-112.

time a serious attempt had been made to carry out a definite plan of administration in the colonies, and it came so near succeeding that direct control by the crown acquired a most unsavory reputation in America. The Revolution of 1688 interrupted the plans for colonial government and led directly to the restoration of the charters, but it produced no change in the existing machinery for managing the colonies. William III followed closely in the footsteps of his predecessor and appointed a new committee of the Privy Council to take up the work of colonial administration where it had been laid down. With slight changes in membership, this body continued to be employed by him for all questions concerning commerce or the plantations until opposition in the House of Commons forced him to abolish it and establish the Board of Trade.[8]

Organization of the Board of Trade

The merchants had suffered severe losses during the great continental war, and the opposition in the House of Commons took advantage of the dissatisfaction caused by these losses to attack the administration. There was a bitter debate in the committee of the whole. Some even asserted that the administration had neglected the needs of English merchants and had openly connived at the destruction of English trade so that the Dutch traders and merchants might be the gainers.[9] As a result of the debate in the committee, a series of fourteen resolutions were reported to the house.

---

[8] New York *Colonial Documents*, vol. iii, p. xiv.

[9] Burnet, Gilbert. *History of his own Time*, 621; Cobbett, Wm. *Parliamentary History of England*, vol. v, 977.

These resolutions provided for the creation, by act of Parliament, of a council of trade whose members should be named by that body and which should have the power to control commerce, even to the extent of appointing convoys for outgoing vessels. It was also to take charge of the plantation and other trade of the kingdom, supervise the administration of poor relief, and could enforce its authority by examining persons on oath.[10] Some of the resolutions, specifying an oath of allegiance for members of this committee, prohibiting the appointment of members of Parliament, and directing the council to take steps to improve the balance of trade, were rejected by the house. The others were approved, January 31, 1696, and a bill ordered brought in.[11]

William III was opposed to any such body as the bill would establish, as it contemplated a serious encroachment upon the royal prerogative. Many

Apprehended that, if the Parliament named the persons, how low soever their powers might be at first, they would be enlarged every session, and from being a council to look into matters of trade, they would next be empowered to appoint convoys and cruisers. This in time might draw in the whole admiralty, and that part of the revenue or supply which was appropriated to the navy;

and those who pushed the measure the most vigorously

Did not deny that they designed to ingraft many things upon it.[12]

Sunderland surprised many people by pushing the

[10] *Journal of the House of Commons*, vol. xi, 423-424; Burnet, G. *History of his own Time*, 621; Cobbett, Wm. *Parliamentary History*, vol. v, 977.

[11] *Journal of the House of Commons*, vol. xi, 424.

[12] Cobbett, Wm. *Parliamentary History*, vol. v, 978; Burnet, G. *History of his own Time*, 621.

bill, and William is said to have come near breaking
with him because of this fact.   In spite of the king's
opposition, the bill passed its second reading, but was
afterwards dropped.[13]   Burnet says this was done
because of the threatened invasion of England and the
discovery of the plot against the life of William.[14]
Perhaps that was the real reason, but it should also
be noted that the bill became unnecessary because of
the prompt issue of an Order in Council creating a
board to exercise almost the same functions as the
council of trade proposed by the bill.

The last action of the House of Commons on the
bill was March 3, 1696; [15] and the commission under
the privy seal which created the Board of Trade is
dated May 15, 1696.[16]   That the clamor in the House
of Commons had hastened the measure seems evident;
an examination of the terms of the commission corrob-
orates that opinion.   The commission created a board
similar to other boards of the British government:
there were the real and the nominal members.   The
real members were eight in number and were paid
annual salaries of one thousand pounds.[17]   The pres-

---

[13] Granville introduced the bill, February 12, 1696, when it was read
for the first time.   February 18, it was read a second time and referred to
the committee of the whole house.   See: *Journal of the House of Commons*,
vol. xi, 440, 454.

[14] This is very probable, as the plot was discovered between the first and
second postponements of the consideration of the bill in the committee to
which it was referred.   See: Burnet, G. *History of his own Time*, 621.   Cf.
Andrews's *British Committees, Commissions, and Councils*, 113-114.

[15] *Journal of the House of Commons*, vol. xi, 488.   On that day the consideration of the bill by the committee was postponed to a fixed date, but
apparently it was never again taken up.

[16] New York *Colonial Documents*, vol. iii, p. xv.

[17] Privy Seal for payment of salaries, June 29, 1697.   See: Board of
Trade *Miscellanies*, vol. ii, 34-38.   Other payments are the same.

ident usually received an additional five hundred pounds,[18] but this was paid by the secretary of state and so does not appear in the annual privy seal.[19] All of the chief officers of state were ex officiis members, but were excused from attendance upon the ordinary meetings of the Board.[20] They were not merely sham members, however, as are similar officers in the case of the so-called administrative boards of the present time. They often met with the Board, sometimes at the request of the latter, sometimes without special request, and sometimes the Board was called upon to attend cabinet meetings.[21] On all ordinary occasions, however, the eight paid members constituted the

---

[18] Bedford in offering the position to Halifax, September 3, 1748, says: "Mr. Pelham informs me that the salary of ye first Lord of Trade is the same as to all the rest, viz. £1000 a year, but that the first Lord has always been paid by him £500 a year additional." — British Museum *Additional Manuscripts*, 32716, f. 337.

[19] Nearly all of the privy seals for the payment of the salaries of the Board are entered in Board of Trade *Miscellanies*.

[20] The commission itself provides that the principal secretaries shall not "be obliged to give constant attendance at the meetings of our said commissioners, but only so often and when the presence of them or any of them shall be necessary and requisite, and as their other public service will permit." — New York *Colonial Documents*, vol. iv, 148.

[21] A few of the many cases of the attendance of some or all of the principal secretaries of state are cited below:

April 19, 1700. Indian affairs and the danger of an uprising. Board of Trade *Journal*, 13, pp. 10-11.

June 12, 1700. Proposed treaty with the French as to the bounds of the Hudson's Bay region. *Ibid.*, pp. 70-73.

May 17, 1709. Board requests Sunderland to confer with them about provisions for some poor Germans. *Ibid.*, 21, p. 98.

February 18, 1712. Great officers summoned to consider the trade to Africa. Attended on February 25, February 28, and March 3, 1712. *Ibid.*, 23, pp. 100-113.

April 7, 14, 20, 29, May 4, 11, 19, 1726. African Trade. *Ibid.*, 36, pp. 84-225.

July 12, 1749. Troubles in New Jersey. *Ibid.*, 57 (pages not numbered).

Board; and of these three or five constituted a quorum, according to the nature of the business. Ordinary questions of trade or matters touching the plantations could be considered by three members, but formal representations on plantation affairs to the king or the council had to be signed by five members.[22]

The new board was given an imposing array of duties. In the first place, it was charged with the care of the trade of England in general and with that of particular countries. It was to consider plans for improving such trade as was deemed beneficial; to devise means of fostering manufactures that were "useful and profitable;" and to determine how "new and profitable manufactures may be introduced." [23] These were the inevitable duties imposed by the general mercantilist doctrines of the time. Secondly, the Board was charged with the care of the poor and the duty of employing them so as not to burden the kingdom. The third, and for our purpose the most important function of the Board, was the care of the plantations. Even here, however, the commission shows the same general subordination of colonial administration to mercantile ends. The whole question of proper government for the colonies was considered a matter of minor importance. That alone would not have precipitated the discussion in the House of Commons,[24] nor was it the principal function of the new organ of central control. The most

---

[22] Copy of the commission in New York *Colonial Documents*, vol. iv, 146.

[23] — *Ibid.*

[24] It is an interesting fact that, so far as the debates on the proposed bill are reported, there is not a single word about proper administration in the colonies. The vital question was commerce and its protection.

important duty of the Board was to make the colonies commercially profitable to the mother country. To this end it was to consider what naval stores could be secured from them, and how to people them so they could furnish the raw materials which "our subjects of England are now oblidged to fetch and supply themselves withall from other princes and states." [25] It was also to find out what manufactures the colonies already had, which ones were capable of development, and which ones should be discouraged in the interests of the home manufacturers.

In order to carry out this general task of colonial supervision, the Board was given control of the governors' instructions, with the duty of conducting the correspondence with them, and was expected to embody in its reports to the king the important information gleaned from this source. The Board was not given control of the colonial patronage, but it was to consider and recommend to the king for appointment proper persons for governors, deputy governors, members of the provincial councils, secretaries, and other colonial officers. This was a power of nomination, but not of appointment, as all final action had to be taken by the king in council. All colonial legislation was intrusted to the care of the Board: it was to examine the laws passed by the colonial assemblies, decide which ones were fit to be confirmed and which ones should be disallowed, and report its opinions to the king in council. Likewise it was made the organ for hearing all complaints of oppressions and maladministration in the colonies and reporting to the king

---

[25] See the Commission, New York *Colonial Documents*, vol. iv, 147.

in council what should be done in each case.[26]   It was also to require strict accounts of all funds raised by the colonial assemblies and expended for public purposes.   Finally, in order to make the grant of powers and duties effective, the Board was authorized to send for persons and papers, to examine persons on oath,[27] and to "execute and perform all other things necessary or proper for answering our royal intentions in the premises."   If the Board desired legal advice on any point of law, it could apply to the attorney- and solicitor-general, either or both; or it might employ any other crown attorney.[28]

The body which was to perform these various duties was not a sham board, as are the present so-called "Boards" of the British government; it was a real collegiate body, as all of its actions required the sanction of three or five members.   That was one of its defects in organization, because responsibility was divided; yet it was always possible for an able president to assume responsibility, completely dominate the Board, and raise himself to the position of secretary of state, which is what finally happened.

Another criticism is that the Board lacked independence.   Those who make this charge seem to mean by the word independence something akin to the independence of the civil service officer, or an executive officer with independent functions such as we are

---

[26] New York *Colonial Documents*, vol. iv, 148.

[27] The only occasions I have found of the exercise of this power were in connection with the charges against Surveyor of the Woods Armstrong in 1722, and a case from St. Christophers which came before the Board for investigation, when several witnesses were sworn before testifying. See: Board of Trade *Journals*, 22, p. 227, and 56, pp. 148-193.

[28] New York *Colonial Documents*, vol. iv, 148.

accustomed to in the United States.[29]   The first condition is one of dependence, and the second is impossible under the parliamentary form of government.
That man must finally shape the policy of the administration who is responsible to the House of Commons.
If he must answer for the actions of a board in his
department, that board cannot claim independence.
In such a government as that of England, important
administrative policies are the result of compromise
among those who are to assume responsibility for
them, and in reaching that compromise, that man's
opinion has most weight who can muster the greatest
support in the House of Commons.   Thus the question of independence is a personal one; and the members of the Board of Trade could be independent only
so far as their support was necessary to the stability
of the existing ministry.

The terms of the commission are by no means so
important as the personal relations of the president
of the Board to the chief ministers.   If the minister
were powerful enough he could, and sometimes did,
give the Board to understand that it should not presume to exercise some of the most important of its
commission powers.   Under such circumstances the
will of the minister, not the terms of its commission,
determined what it could do.   If, on the other hand,
the president of the Board secured his position because of the support which he commanded in the

---

[29] Miss Kellogg, in her article on the "American Colonial Charter," in
discussing the defects of the Board and after comparing it with the earlier
committees of the Privy Council, adds: the powers given to the Board "indicate an unwillingness to render the colonial administration independent of
the control of the crown and of its chief ministers." — American Historical
Association, *Report for 1903*, vol. i, 217.

House of Commons, he became, by virtue of that fact, one of the important crown officers and could insist upon carrying out his own policies. All of these conditions are illustrated in the history of the Board of Trade.

The personnel of the Board

As the Board had been created largely to silence criticism, its first list of members was designed to inspire confidence. John Egerton, Earl of Bridgewater, was made president.[30] He was not especially noted for his knowledge of colonial affairs, but he had the confidence of the country and especially of William, was a member of the Privy Council, a staunch supporter of the Revolution, and a close personal friend of the king.[31] He was assisted by men who were familiar with colonial affairs; the most noted of whom was John Locke who had enjoyed the best possible training for such a position, as he had long been interested personally in trade affairs and had written on various economic questions. He had been associated with Lord Ashley, had drawn up the elaborate constitution for Carolina, was made secretary of the reorganized Council of Trade and had held that position until he was forced to leave England because of his complicity in the Monmouth plot. Returning to England with William, he had been made one of the commissioners of appeals and, on the creation of the Board of Trade, was induced to become a member. Although he was old and in failing health, he attended

---

[30] New York *Colonial Documents*, vol. iii, p. xv.

[31] *Dictionary of National Biography*, vol. xvii, 1578; New York *Colonial Documents*, vol. iv, 103, 146; Macaulay, Thos. B. *History of England from the Accession of James the Second*, vol. v, *passim*.

the meetings very regularly until he resigned in 1700.[32]
John Pollexfen was another man who had special
knowledge of the colonies and of colonial affairs. He
had served as one of the Lords of Trade in 1675, and
was a man of great influence. He was noted as a
writer on economic subjects, and belonged to the moderate school of mercantilists, who believed in state
regulation of industry but also in freedom of trade,
and was especially opposed to such monopolies as that
of the East India Company.[33] Another, and by no
means the least important of the men with colonial
experience, was William Blathwayt, a man of great
ability,[34] who had been secretary to the old committee
of the Privy Council, and had retained his position
after the Revolution.

Of the other members of the Board, Ford Grey,
Earl of Tankerville, who was second in the commission, had played a prominent part in politics. A man
of much parliamentary ability, he had voted for the
conviction of Strafford, was commander of the cavalry
in Monmouth's rebellion, and escaped punishment
only after giving excessive bonds, he had taken an
active part in the Revolution as one of the Convention
Lords, and was made a member of the Privy Council.

[32] *Dictionary of National Biography*, vol. xxxiv, 27-36; Fowler. *Life of
John Locke*, 22-112; Cunningham. *Growth of English Industry*, vol. ii, 380,
381, 385, 426.

[33] *Dictionary of National Biography*, vol. xlvi, 62; Cunningham. *Growth
of English Industry*, vol. ii, 280-291, *footnote.* See also the *Discourse of
Trade, Coyne, etc.*, by Pollexfen.

[34] Because of his linguistic skill he was also a great favorite of William
III and was with him in the campaign in Flanders. See: *Dictionary of
National Biography*, vol. v, 206; Macaulay, Thos. B. *History of England*,
vol. ii, 378-381; Privy Council *Register*, "George I"; Pepys, Samuel. *Diary
and Correspondence*, vol. iv, 243, 295.

He was also a close friend of William and, on the absence of that sovereign in 1700, was one of the Lords Justices.[35] Abraham Hill was a man of science, a member of the Royal Society, and was, for many years, treasurer of that organization.[36] John Methuen, one of the prominent Whig members of the House of Commons, was a politician and a diplomat and after his withdrawal from the Board of Trade was sent to Portugal on important diplomatic duties.[37]

From the above account, it is seen that the first Board was of a very representative character. Two of its members, and these the first two names in the commission, were members of the Privy Council, which made the Board in a certain sense a committee of that body, as the older organization had been. Two other members occupied seats in the House of Commons; in that respect it recognized the demand for popular control. Three of the members had served on the earlier Council of Trade, consequently the expert knowledge gained by experience and the strong government tendencies of the preceding reign were represented. In politics, however, the Whigs were the only party represented.

Great results were expected from the work of a Board which apparently had very generous powers and was composed of such able men; and, on the whole, it cannot be said that the Board disappointed these expectations. It organized at once at Whitehall, the papers and records of the old Council for Foreign

[35] Burnet, G. *History of his own Time* (ed. of 1857), 321, 352, 359, 405, 411, 414; *Dictionary of National Biography*; New York *Colonial Documents*, vol. iv, 146, 628.

[36] *Dictionary of National Biography*, vol. xxvi, 389-390.

[37] — *Ibid.*, vol. xxxvii, 310.

Plantations and of the Committee of the Privy Council were transferred to its offices, and it entered upon its duties with vigor.[38] Meetings were held at first three, and later five times a week.

So far as colonial affairs are concerned, the action of the Board shows efficiency at all points down to the accession of George I. The acts of trade and navigation were enforced, able men were sent out as governors, piracy was suppressed, and the Indians kept in alliance. It exercised a careful supervision of colonial laws, and assailed the independence of the proprietary and charter colonies so vigorously that the power of the crown over them was considerably extended. Their governors not only had to be approved by the Board, but they were also required to accept the instructions of that body for the enforcement of the acts of trade and navigation, and were compelled to give bonds for observing them.[39] Had it not been for lack of ministerial support and the pressure of more weighty matters, all the proprietary governments would have been resumed by the crown, and possibly the existing charters seized by *quo warranto*. In view of the actual accomplishment of the Board during the first twenty years of its history, it cannot be accused of impotence or of not having justified its existence.

The personnel of the Board remained efficient until 1714, although there was a gradual change in mem-

---

[38] The first session was held at Whitehall, June 25, 1696. See: Board of Trade Papers, Journal A. (cited by Miss Kellogg, in "American Colonial Charter" in American Historical Association *Report for 1903*, vol. i, 217). The commission required the Board to take charge of the existing records. See: New York *Colonial Documents*, vol. iv, 147.

[39] See the correspondence of Bellomont with the Board in New York *Colonial Documents*, vol. iv, *passim*; Penn-Logan correspondence, *passim*; North Carolina *Colonial Records*, vol. ii, 51 and *passim*.

bers, Sir Philip Meadows alone remaining of the original appointments. The Earl of Bridgewater was replaced in 1699 by Thomas Grey, Earl of Stamford, a rigid, narrow-minded Whig who had been one of the active opponents of the policy of the Stuarts, had been a member of the Privy Council during a part of William III's reign, and continued to serve under Anne. The work of the Board during his administration shows him to have been an able officer. On the accession of Anne, he was dismissed from all his offices, but was soon restored to the presidency of the Board, and continued in that position until the Tories acquired the ascendency in 1711.[40] The interim between his two periods of service was filled by William Legge, Lord Dartmouth, a moderate Tory and also a member of the Privy Council. He was afterwards secretary of state for the Northern Department and was influential in bringing about the downfall of Marlborough.[41] The change that swept Stamford and Marlborough out of office brought in the Earl of Winchelsea as president of the Board, only to be replaced after two years by Lord Guilford, who in turn lost office at the death of Queen Anne.[42]

Aside from the presidents, many prominent men served on the Board between the years 1696 and 1715.

[40] The lists of changes in the personnel of the Board in New York *Colonial Documents*, vol. iii, p. xv, does not show the dismissal of Stamford and the promotion of Dartmouth, but the statement is made in the biographical notice of him in the *Dictionary of National Biography*, vol. xxiii, 207-208. Miss Kellogg in the "American Colonial Charter" also accepts this statement. See: American Historical Association, *Reports for 1903*, vol. i, 220.

[41] Burnet, G. *History of his own Time* (ed. of 1857), 856; *Dictionary of National Biography*, vol. xxxii, 416.

[42] New York *Colonial Documents*, vol. iii, p. xvi.

George Stepney, who succeeded Methuen in 1697, was a diplomat and a poet, and his wide knowledge of foreign affairs was of much assistance to the Board in framing some of its policies.[43]   Locke, who retired in 1700, was replaced by Matthew Prior,[44] who had been an under secretary of state, and who later was one of Bolingbroke's secret agents in negotiating the Treaty of Utrecht.   He was a Tory and, because of his active relations with that party, was removed from the Board in 1706.[45]   Lord Herbert of Cherbury, who served from 1706 to 1710, was another man of considerable prominence, active in the affairs of the House of Lords and frequently chairman of its committees.[46]

The Tories acquired control of the government during the last years of Queen Anne's reign, and the Board of Trade reflects the change in politics.   The Whig members were gradually retired after 1710, and Tories took their places.   By 1713 the Board had become almost entirely Tory, several new men being added that year.   The most prominent of these were John Hynde Cotton,[47] a famous Jacobite politician, and Arthur Moore.   Of the latter, Burnet says he had

> Risen up, from being a footman without any education, to be a great dealer in trade, and was the person of that Board in whom the lord treasurer confided most;

and Mr. Speaker Onslow tells us he was a man

> Of extraordinary talents, with great experience and knowledge of the world, very able in Parliament, and capable of the

---

[43] *Dictionary of National Biography*, vol. xliv, 190.

[44] Board of Trade *Journal*, July 17, 1700, 13, p. 114.

[45] Burnet, G. *History of his own Time* (ed. of 1857), 872 and *footnote*. See also Johnson's *Lives of the Poets*; and *Dictionary of National Biography*, vol. xlvi, 397.

[46] *Dictionary of National Biography*, vol. xxiv, 193.

[47] — *Ibid.*, article "Cotton."

highest parts of business, with a manner in it, and indeed in his general deportment, equal almost to any rank.[48]

He was, however, accused of having sacrificed the commercial interests of England in the Treaty of Utrecht.

The accession of George I, with its complete change of ministry, caused a sweeping change in the personnel of the Board. As the last Board under Anne had been Tory, the new one was completely Whig. The new members had little or no previous experience in colonial affairs, whatever their knowledge of trade might have been. Many of the members of the Board for the next three decades were either placemen of the ministers in power or needy members of the House of Commons, to whom the salary of a thousand pounds a year was a sufficient inducement to secure their support of the ministerial policy. Too often, these men looked upon their positions as sinecures and rendered little or no real service. The whole period from 1714 to 1748 is characterized by the insignificance of the men who served on the Board of Trade. There were really no members, during this time, who made lasting reputations for themselves in the colonial field.

The first president under George I was William, Lord Berkeley of Stratton. In a few months he was superseded by Henry Howard, Earl of Suffolk and Bindon, who held the position from 1715 to 1718.[49] In that year, Robert D'Arcy, Earl of Holderness, assumed charge but he continued in office only one year, when Thomas Fane, Earl of Westmoreland, was ap-

[48] Burnet, G. *History of his own Time* (ed. of 1857), 898 and *footnote*; *Dictionary of National Biography*, vol. xxxviii, 340.

[49] New York *Colonial Documents*, vol. iii, p. xvi; Burke, Sir Bernard. *Genealogical and heraldic Dictionary of the Peerage and Baronetage*, 1402.

pointed. There was no further change until 1735,[50] when Benjamin Mildmay, Lord Fitzwalter, became president and served for two years. He in turn was succeeded by Sir John Monson, one of Marlborough's soldiers and a close adherent of Newcastle and Bedford, who continued in office for eleven years. There is no evidence that he ever evinced any desire to make his office anything but a sinecure,[51] and it is during his administration that the Board shows its least activity.

[50] A letter written by Robert Hunter Morris, who was in London at that time, to James Alexander offers a possible explanation for this change. Governor Cosby had removed certain members of the council in New Jersey for opposing him. His letter, stating his action and asking the home government to confirm it, was in the office of the Board and the confirmation was opposed by the colonial agent, Mr. Paris. On account of this opposition the Board delayed action. Morris says, "the governour's letter was dated in December last and was committed to the care of the Duke New Castle who has been all this time striving to get the report of the board of trade upon it, and could not do it before. My Lord West Moreland was much against it, as being unjust to condemn the parties unheard and without giving them an opportunity to justifie their conduct, especially when there was a caveat enter'd in their office against such a removal. Blagdon [Bladen] and Dockmineque were also against it but my Lord West Moreland being removed from the Board and Dockmineque being dead, my Lord Fitzwalter and another new member made in the room of Dockmineque were fond of obliging the secretary of state and so got a report in favour of Mr. Cosby." — New Jersey *Archives*, vol. v, 431-433.

[51] Some idea can be formed of how much of a sinecure some of the members made of their positions and how regularly others attended the Board from the record of attendance [Board of Trade *Journal*, 50, 51] during the three years, 1741-1743.

	1741		1742		1743	
	PRESENT	ABSENT	PRESENT	ABSENT	PRESENT	ABSENT
Monson	80	40	101	37	92	27
Bladen	100	20	123	15	101	18
Plumer	112	8	128	10	118	11
Brudenell	58	62	79	59	45	74
Ashe	46	74	49	89	38	81
Croft	8	112		138		
Herbert	4	116	8	130	4	115
Pelham	12	108	45	93		
Keene	46	74	97	41	98	21

Governors and other persons interested in colonial affairs found little heed paid to their communications addressed to the Board: they also learned that if it refused to take any desired action the remedy lay in an appeal directly to Newcastle. Under Monson's [52] care, the Board became little more than a bureau of information, and it was not even efficient in fulfilling that function.

The records on their physical side show that the Board was little more than a joke during his administration. The *Journal* had formerly been a very bulky folio volume of several hundred pages. Each succeeding volume grew steadily thinner after the ascendency of Newcastle, and after 1737 they were reduced to quartos, and in some cases only one hundred fifteen pages of this were used in a year.[53] The records for each province show the same dearth of business. This change is not directly chargeable to the personnel of the Board, but must be ascribed to the pernicious interference of Newcastle. The powers of the Board were nominally the same as before; but, as Halifax says, the Board had been given to understand

---

[52] *Dictionary of National Biography*, vol. xxxviii, 196. For the neglect of colonial affairs, see the New York *Colonial Documents* for the period. The absence of any correspondence worth noting speaks for itself. It was such periods as the above which justified Pownall's comment, "at one time it hath had the powers, and held the part of a minister's office; and at another, hath become a mere committee; inefficient as to execution; unattended to, as reporting. The colonies, and the officers of the colonies, have one while been taught to look up to the Board, as the minister for their affairs: and at another, have learned to hold it in that contempt, which inefficiency gives; which contempt, however, hath not always stopped there." — *Administration of the British Colonies*, vol. i, 27.

[53] *Journal for 1738*. The average from 1737-1748 was about one hundred thirty of the small pages. The earlier volumes contain four hundred or five hundred pages of folio.

that the chief business was to be referred to the secretary of state's office.[54] That remained the situation until 1751 when Halifax insisted upon doing the full work assigned to the Board by the commission.

During the foregoing period, there were a few men of real ability who served as individual members. One of the best known of these was Daniel Pulteney, who served during the years 1717-1721. He had been envoy to Denmark in the reign of Queen Anne, and had displayed marked ability as a diplomat and, after his service on the Board, was transferred to the admiralty office. He was a member of Parliament and in politics a close supporter of Sunderland.[55] Paul Docminique (1714-1735) was another very active member. Having been an early member of the West Jersey Society, he always took a lively interest in New York and New Jersey affairs, was nearly always present when the Board considered matters of interest to those colonies, and his name is found on nearly all the documents which concern them.[56]

The most active member, however, was Martin Bladen, who has the distinction of enjoying the longest continuous service of any man who ever served on the Board. For nearly thirty years, he discharged his

[54] Halifax to Newcastle, August 25, 1751. "Those powers in the commission of the Board of Trade, contained in the first and second clauses of ye inclosed extract, of representing to the king upon all matters relating to trade and plantations, of recommending what may be proper to be passed in the Assemblies, of hearing complaints of oppressions and male-administration and representing thereupon, have not for many years been exercised, the Board having been given to understand that they should represent only on such points as should be referred to them by ye secretary of state or the council." — British Museum *Additional Manuscripts*, 32725, f. 91.

[55] *Dictionary of National Biography*, vol. xlvii, 24.

[56] New Jersey *Archives*, vol. iii, 51 and *note*, and *passim*.

duties faithfully, both as a member of the Board and
as a member of Parliament. He was very regular in
his attendance at the Board meetings, and his name is
affixed to most of its representations.[57] He frequently
spoke on questions of trade, commerce, and colonial
affairs in the House of Commons; and because of his
attention to business, he was known as "Trade," while
his colleagues were referred to collectively as the
"Board." In politics he was a close adherent of Walpole.[58]

Joseph Addison (1715-1717) was another very well
known member during the early part of the period;
but his period of service was too short to enable him
at all to mould the policy of the Board, even if he had
displayed any particular interest in colonial affairs.
His appointment must be looked upon, not as a reward
for merit, but as a reward for political service.[59]
Thomas Hay,[60] Viscount Dupplin (1746-1754) was
a much abler man in administrative matters. He had
great parliamentary influence, was especially interested in Nova Scotia, usually spoke on money matters,
and is said to have refused the position of chancellor
of the exchequer in 1757. He was much talked of as
a successor to Halifax as head of the Board, and
helped to form the Newcastle ministry of 1758.

[57] During the ten years, 1732 to 1742, he was present at nine hundred
seventy-eight different meetings of the Board and on seventeen occasions he
was the only member present. His absence when it occurred was usually
consecutive, indicating sickness or pressure of other duties. — Board of Trade
Journals, 42-51.

[58] *Dictionary of National Biography*, vol. ii, 154; New York *Colonial
Documents*, vol. iii, pp. xvi, xvii; Cobbett, Wm. *Parliamentary History.*

[59] *Dictionary of National Biography*; New York *Colonial Documents*,
vol. iii, p. xvi.

[60] *Dictionary of National Biography*, vol. vi, 762.

With the year 1748, the Board enters upon a new period in its history. The change was due to the appointment of George Dunk, Earl of Halifax, as president. On the death of Monson, Newcastle sought to have his brother-in-law, the Duke of Leeds, appointed to the vacancy, as he was anxious to have him in some office which required little attendance and less application. In this, however, he was balked by Bedford who insisted upon having an able man at the head of the Board.[61] His choice was Halifax and an arrangement was finally made satisfactory to all. The Duke of Leeds took the position of chief justice in eyre, which Halifax then held and which required little or no work, and Halifax came to the Board.[62] Bedford admits that his reason for desiring Halifax was partly selfish, as the Board was under the Southern Department of which he was secretary. Another reason, however, was the pretty definite conclusion on the part of both Newcastle and Bedford that the colonial situation was such as to require the attention of an able man.[63]

---

[61] Bedford to Newcastle, August 11, 1748, British Museum *Additional Manuscripts*, 32716, f. 38.

[62] His commission bears the date of November 5, 1748. Board of Trade *Journal*, 56, p. 269. He was sworn to the Privy Council, January 11, 1749. See: Privy Council *Register*, "George II," vol. iv, 137.

[63] After referring to the conditions described above, Bedford in offering the position to Halifax says: "I took the liberty (tho' I had not had an opportunity of knowing ye sentiments upon it) to mention your Lordship to Mr. Pelham as one whom I thought, on account of ye application to, and abilities in business the proper person to be put at the head of a board which has under its care and inspection business of the highest national concern, and which has always had at its head, and more particularly in ye last instance, persons of great consideration and worth.

"There were two other reasons which induced me to take the liberty — to mention you as ye properest person I could think of for this employment, the

Halifax came into his new office with little or no knowledge of colonial affairs or of trade; but his energy and zeal, together with his ambition, soon supplied the deficiency. He belonged to the new generation of opponents of Walpole. Although he allied himself with Newcastle, he had sufficient wealth and parliamentary influence to make his position one of more than usual independence; and in the shifting politics of the next few years his support became more and more essential to that politician. When he accepted the position as head of the Board, he exacted no promises as to the power which that body should exercise, nor were any given him.[64] He was hardly familiar with his new duties, however, before he began to insist upon an extension of his power, and so far as conditions permitted, made his influence felt.[65] The settlement of Halifax, Nova Scotia, in 1749 by discharged sailors and seamen was largely due to his

one was, that I look upon it as a post of business and useful business and a good qualification for better and greater things; and the other (which I own has a little the air of selfishness) was my desire to have a person of ye Lordship's weight and consequence and for whom I have so true a regard, at the head of a Board with which in my present situation as Secretary of State for ye Southern Department I must have so close and frequent correspondence. I am now authorized by His Majesty's command to offer this employment to your Lordship, which if you shall think proper to accept, the king designs the Chief Justice in Eyre for ye Duke of Leeds.

"Mr. Pelham informs me that the salary of ye first Lord of Trade is the same, as to all the rest, viz. £1000 a year, but that the first Lord has always been paid by him £500 a year additional. He is willing either to continue it on this footing or to make £500 addition to the salary which ever you shall chuse." — Bedford to Halifax, September 3, 1748, British Museum *Additional Manuscripts*, 32716, f. 337.

[64] Halifax to Bedford, September 7, 1748, British Museum *Additional Manuscripts*, 32716, f. 339.

[65] Letters of F. J. Paris to James Alexander, New Jersey *Archives*, vol. vii, 295.

most secret

My dear Lord

      I am now to acknowledge your Graces private letter to me of the 31st of last month, which I received at Woburn, on Saturday last. It gives me great pleasure to find that the Steps I have taken, in regard to the vacancy that it was apprehended, was likely to happen in the University of Cambridge, by the death of the Duke of Somerset, has met with your Graces approbation, and I am much obliged to you for your having obtained his Majesties approbation of my conduct. I can assure you, my dear Lord, I will omit nothing in my power, in case that Event should happen, before the King's return, to bring every thing there to such a Conclusion as I flatter my self will be agreable to his Majesty, and honourable to your self. I am glad to find you have hopes (I suppose by what Sr Thomas Robinson has told you) that the Court of Vienna may be brought to conclude <u>all at once</u> which I take for granted

Duke of Newcastle   you

BEDFORD'S MOST SECRET LETTER TO HALIFAX
[_British Museum Additional Manuscripts, 32716, f 38_]

you mean, that they will join with us in concluding in one general definitive Treaty with France and her Allies. I must own that has during the whole Course of the Negotiation appeared to me to be the likeliest (not to say the only) way to obtain a solid and lasting Peace.

To come now to affairs more immediately at home, I have talked with Mr Pelham about the vacancy in the Board of Trade occasioned by the death of Lord Monson, in whose loss I do most sincerely condole with your Grace. I think both your Graces and Mr Pelham's idea is, in which I do most truly concur, that it would be highly improper, considering the present Situation of things, to have a non efficient Man at the head of that Board, and therefore I must take the liberty to differ from you in the Arrangement you have proposed to Mr Pelham, in order to make room for the Duke of Leeds to come into a Post suitable to his Quality. To convince your Grace that no one wishes the Duke of Leeds better than myself, I will now mention an Idea, but which I must own my self entirely unwarranted to suggest, having never mentioned it, to one single Soul, but your Lordships, and that is, if Lord Halifax could be prevailed upon to exchange from what he now has to the Board of trade (for which I should think him perfectly well qualified) the Duke of Leeds might succeed him as Chief Justice in Eyre. As I am entirely ignorant of Halifax's Sentiments on this Subject, I only mention this in confidence to your Grace, as a means of getting the Duke of Leeds into an employment suitable for him, and at the same time putting an efficient Man at the head of the Board of trade. If your Grace should like this proposal, Sandwich would be the properest man to find out whether it would be agreeable to Halifax or not. I should rather incline to think it would as a Post of business seems to me to be the properest thing for one of Lord Halifax's turn. I hope soon to receive a letter from your Grace to be forwarded to Mr Keene, with directions to him

6

39

to set out immediately for Madrid, if his health will permit him. I am sure
I shall make no objections to H.R.H.' commands about Lord Rochford. I
hope soon to hear from you whether Mr Cayley gives over all thoughts of going
to Cadiz, as I only wait for that, before I begin to prepare the Commissions for
Consuls in order to be laid before the King for his approbation and signature.
Mr Pelham and I were talking to day about Sr Thomas Robinson's
appointments, and whether he was not to be put on the same foot as
Lord Sandwich in relation to Plate &c. and £100 & Week, as was
the case both at Cambray and Soissons. Mr Pelham desired me to
mention this to you, as a thing we both thought reasonable. I
question whether he has had time to write to you to day as he
proposed, as he was obliged to set out at 1 o'clock to day for
Halland, in order to attend his Constituents at the Lewes Races
to morrow. My Lord Chancellour sets out for Whimple on Monday
next, so I shall be left almost alone. I have two other long Letters
to write to your Grace by to morrow's Mail, on seperate Subjects,
so will take up no more of your time than to assure you, that
I am, with the truest regard

Your Graces

most faithfull
humble Servant
Bedford

enterprise, and his services were recognized in naming the new city. Colonial affairs everywhere received more attention than they had for years. Affairs in New York and in New Jersey were in a chaotic condition and had been steadily growing worse. A careful investigation was undertaken of the dispatches which had been left unnoticed in the office during the preceding years, and the true condition of affairs in those provinces was laid before the ministry. All the work and records of the Board show new life and vigor, and everything indicates that for the first time in years an efficient man was at the head of affairs.[66]

No energetic man, however, could have been induced to remain long at the head of the Board under the conditions existing when Halifax was appointed. The commission conferred upon the Board full power over colonial affairs, but for years it had been given to understand that all questions of importance should be referred to the secretary of state and that no report or representation was to be made on any matter which had not been definitely referred to it either by the secretary of state or by the council.[67] That rule left the Board only a shadow of its real powers, and, however efficient a president was, he could accomplish nothing so long as that condition persisted. Halifax determined to have conditions changed or to resign, and wrote to Newcastle that he wished to be released from the very disagreeable situation in which he found

---

[66] New York *Colonial Documents*, vol. vii, 745, *footnote* and *passim*; *Dictionary of National Biography*, vol. iii, 363; Walpole, Horace. *Letters*, vol. i, 137, 181, 324, vol. ii, 367, vol. iii, 49, 58, 373; Mahon, Lord. *History of England from the Peace of Utrecht to the Peace of Versailles, 1713-1783*, vol. iv, *passim* and vol. v, 28; *Grenville Papers*, vol. ii, 427, vol. iii, 221-222.

[67] See footnote 54.

himself.[68] As his support could not be dispensed with, this resignation was not accepted, and Newcastle began to arrange terms which Halifax could accept.

Halifax was frankly ambitious for a seat in the cabinet or even higher honors, and made full use of his position as head of the Board to secure the coveted prize. The political situation in England contributed to his success, as his support was becoming more and more necessary to Newcastle. When the ministry was reorganized in 1751, Halifax asked that he, as president of the Board, be made a secretary of state for the West Indies, or at least that he be admitted to the cabinet, and that the Board should be permitted to act up to the full measure of its commission powers.[69] There was considerable delay in arranging the terms upon which Halifax would continue in of-

---

[68] Halifax to Newcastle, November 28, 1750, British Museum *Additional Manuscripts*, 32723, f. 312.

[69] "There is no doubt but that the first Commissioner of Trade, being admitted to frequent access to the king on all plantation matters would be ye most eligible method. I therefore hope your Grace will propose it, and that it will not be objected to.

"But if this method should fail and your Grace should agree in opinion with my Lord Granville that ye publick end may be answer'd by ye Commissioners of Trade being suffer'd to act up to the letter of their commission, by presenting to the Council the names of proper people to be employ'd as governors, deputy governors, secretarys, etc., and by taking cognizance of the government of the colonies, (for which end two new instructions to the governors will be necessary).

"That I may neither seem impracticable nor bigotted to my own opinion, I am willing to submit to His Majesty's pleasure, and to try whether I can serve with publick utility and satisfaction to myself on this new footing.

"Provided I have the honour of being appointed a Cabinet Counsellor, with such additional salary as His Majesty shall think proper; and that it be fully understood by His Majesty's ministers that I shall have the same weight in all plantation matters as if by my post I had frequent access to his Majesty." — Halifax to Newcastle, August 6, 1751, British Museum *Additional Manuscripts*, 32725, f. 1.

fice. Newcastle says the king opposed his admission to the cabinet because that body was already too large.[70] Finally Halifax agreed to accept the powers of a secretary of state without the honor of a portfolio, and dictated the provisions of the Order in Council which transferred all colonial business, including the patronage, to the Board.[71] He had now secured the powers of a secretary of state, and he at once demanded [72] and received the salary of one,[73] but he was still denied the public recognition he coveted, and which he was still determined to have.

Newcastle evidently promised to aid him in his ambitions, but failed to keep his promises; consequently

[70] Newcastle to Halifax, November 7, 1751, British Museum *Additional Manuscripts*, 32725, f. 378.

[71] The proposals which formed the basis for the Order in Council are included in a letter of Halifax to Newcastle, January 5, 1752. These were laid before the Privy Council, went through the regular course, and appeared as an Order in Council, March 11, 1752. Admiralty and revenue officers were not included in the patronage of the Board. See: British Museum *Additional Manuscripts*, 32726, f. 22; Privy Council *Register*, "George II," vol. xiii, 467, 511; Board of Trade *Journal*, 60.

[72] If my friends had succeeded in the application to His Majesty that I might be called to the Cabinet Council, it must have been understood that a cabinet councillor's salary would have attended it. The honour, however, was the principal thing I had in view, and I would have accepted it (as Mr. Pelham knows) without any additional pecuniary emolument. His Majesty was pleased to object to my being a cabinet councillor; but from the refusal of this mark of His Majesty's favour, it cannot, I apprehend, be inferred that I am of course to be refused every other. Some sort of one is necessary for my credit in the execution of the office, with which His Majesty has entrusted me; and no mark of the royal favour is more obvious than such an augmentation of salary as would have been given, if I had been called to the Cabinet Council. — Halifax to Newcastle, March 26, 1752, British Museum *Additional Manuscripts*, 32726, f. 338.

[73] A paper in the Newcastle correspondence entitled "Considerations with Respect to the Matter of appointing a Secretary of State for Plantation Affairs" states that the salary of Halifax as president of the Board was £3850 a year. See: British Museum *Additional Manuscripts*, 33029, f. 104.

Halifax resigned in 1756,[74] but was again induced to remain in office. The next year he refused to serve any longer under such unsatisfactory conditions [75] and, as his services were indispensable, he was admitted to the cabinet. This made him virtually a secretary of state for the colonies, in which capacity he continued to serve until 1761, when he resigned to go to Ireland as lord-lieutenant. His dominating influence in colonial affairs is noticeable, however, for some years afterward. During his presidency the Board occupied a very different position from that which it had ever before held in its history. Although it was still nominally a collegiate body, the president was either a secretary of state or exercised all or most of the powers of one. This change had been brought about by two causes: the increased importance of colonial affairs, and the energy and ambition of one man, backed by the political influence he was able to wield in Parliament. It is a striking fact that this revolution in the Board's position was accomplished without any change in the terms of the commission.

Halifax was assisted by some able colleagues, a few of whose appointments dated back to 1746. One of these was Dupplin, already mentioned. Another was James Grenville, an adherent of William Pitt and a brother to George Grenville and Richard, Earl of Temple, who continued on the Board till 1755. Still another able man was the former attorney for the Board, Francis Fane. From his long years of experience as legal adviser on colonial laws, he should

---

[74] Walpole, Horace. *Letters*, vol. iv, 11, 64, 66.

[75] Halifax to Newcastle, June 16, 1757, British Museum *Additional Manuscripts*, 32871, f. 323.

My dear Lord
Plantation Office
June 16th 1757

Your Grace must think me an Idiot, if you imagine me insensible to the Treatment I have received; but, I thank God, I am above Complaint; & shall therefore make no Remarks on the Singularity of my Case, in not having been able to obtain of my Friends what I was ... other Day by those I had no Reason to rank as such. The only Reason of my troubling your Grace now, is to inform you that I find it impossible for me to think of continuing in the Employment I have at present the honor to hold, of which in the present arrangement of things it may be of some use to your Grace to be apprised.

I am My dear Lord
Your Grace's
Most obedient
humble Servant
Dunk Halifax

HALIFAX RESIGNS THE PRESIDENCY
[British Museum Additional Manuscripts, 32871, f 323]

have been especially well qualified to give efficient service.

Halifax also brought in men who were his own followers, among whom Charles Townshend was the ablest and best known. He had entered Parliament in 1747, and had from the first attached himself to Halifax. When the latter came to the Board, Townshend was soon given a place and continued in office for nearly five years. He was ambitious, and a man of remarkable ability. Halifax relied much upon him and with reason, for he was one of the few men who really made a name for himself as a member of the Board. On his retirement, he found a place on the admiralty board. He continued to rise in parliamentary power and was president of the Board of Trade for one month in 1763. Three years later, he was chancellor of the exchequer and head of the ministry. It was in the last capacity that he made dangerous use of the knowledge he had gained of colonial affairs, and brought forward the unfortunate bills which have ever since borne his name.[76] William G. Hamilton, known as "single speech Hamilton," was another of the able personal followers of Halifax. He served from 1756-1761 and retired with Halifax, accompanying the latter to Ireland.[77]

Even during the ascendency of Halifax, however, all the members were not especially able men, nor necessarily his own lieutenants. Newcastle's influence

[76] Walpole, Horace. *Letters, passim*; New York *Colonial Documents*, vol. iii, pp. xvii, xviii; *Dictionary of National Biography*, vol. lvii, 117; *Grenville Papers*, vols. i, ii, iii, *passim*; Mahon, Lord. *History of England*, vol. iv, 27, 218, 249, vol. v, *passim*; Lecky, Wm. *History of England*, see index.

[77] Walpole, Horace. *Letters*, vol. iii, 367, 403, vol. v, 76, 86, 391; *Dictionary of National Biography*, vol. xxiv, 232.

was sufficiently great to secure appointments when he
wished them, and several of the members continued to
be Newcastle's favorites. Andrew Stone (1749-1761)
was probably the best of these. He had been private
secretary to Newcastle and was a most active man in
politics, although he worked behind the scenes. He
had been an under secretary of state, and is famous
as the tutor of George III. It is said that it was due
to his unfortunate influence that the prerogative took
on the new growth which it did. Stone later became
notorious as one of the party known as "the king's
friends." [78] Other able men who represented the
Newcastle influence were Edward Bacon (1759-
1765) and George Rice (1761-1770). The less
worthy satellites of leading ministers were present
during the entire period: Richard Rigby [79] (1755-
1760), an unblushing placeman, who supported various interests and so managed to maintain himself in
some position of profit; Edward Elliott [80] (1760-
1776), who owed his position to the fact that he had
vast borough influence at his command; and John
Roberts [81] (1761-1762), formerly secretary to Henry
Pelham and dispenser of the secret service money
which was used so largely for corrupt purposes, were
the most noted of these.

On the retirement of Halifax in 1761, Samuel

---

[78] Walpole, Horace. *Letters*, vol. i, 318, *footnote*, vol. ii, 257, 259, vol. iii,
46, 104, 135, 137, 140, 213; Mahon, Lord. *History of England*, vol. iv, 21,
22; New York *Colonial Documents*, vol. iii, p. xvii, vol. vi, 753, *footnote*;
Dictionary of National Biography, vol. liv, 405.

[79] Walpole, Horace. *Letters*, see index; *Grenville Papers*, vols. iii, iv,
passim; Mahon, Lord. *History of England*, vol. iv, 126, vol. v, 40, 259;
Dictionary of National Biography, vol. xlviii, 302.

[80] *Dictionary of National Biography*, vol. xvii, 184.

[81] — *Ibid.*, vol. xlviii, 384.

Sandys was made president of the Board and continued in office for two years. He was a man of little
real ability, had risen into importance only because
of his opposition to Walpole, and his influence rapidly
waned after that statesman's fall. Horace Walpole
speaks of him as a member of a dish-clout ministry,[82]
and adds that the Board of Trade was to be reduced to
its former insignificance and that he was not to get
the extra thousand pounds a year which had been
granted to Halifax.[83] This was carried out only in
part.[84] Colonial affairs were too important, at that
particular time, for the Board to be reduced to its
former impotence; although the most important business was transferred to the secretary of state's office,
and orders to that effect were sent to the colonial governors.

Sandys was replaced by Townshend who, within a
month, gave way to William Fitzmaurice Petty, Earl
of Shelburne. The latter had acted as peacemaker in
the negotiations which brought Bute and Fox together, had helped form the Grenville ministry, and would
have been made secretary of state for the colonies at
that time had Grenville not opposed it. He finally
accepted the presidency of the Board as a substitute,
and with it was given a seat in the cabinet. He soon
quarreled with his colleagues, resigned from the

[82] Walpole, Horace. *Letters*, vol. iii, 379.

[83] Walpole, Horace. *Letters*, vol. v, 36, also see index; *Dictionary of
National Biography*, vol. l, 293; Mahon, Lord. *History of England*, vol. iii,
68, 110, 112.

[84] The Order in Council was issued, May 15, 1761, and repealed so
much of the rule of 1752 as vested appointments in the Board, but directed
that correspondence between the Board and colonial governors should continue as directed in 1752. See: Board of Trade *Journal*, vol. lxxix, 265.

Board, attached himself again to Pitt, and on the latter's return to office was made secretary for the Southern Department, August, 1766. As such, he again had charge of colonial affairs and did all he could to conciliate the colonies, being always opposed to coercive measures. Hillsborough, who had followed Shelburne as president of the Board, was replaced for a brief time by Dartmouth, but again came into office at the time Shelburne was made secretary of state. At Hillsborough's own request, however, the Board was again shorn of its executive powers and reduced to one of report only;[85] thus the entire responsibility for the American policy was thrown upon Shelburne. As the latter was unable to get on well with his colleagues, and as they were out of sympathy with his American policy, he was relieved by raising Hillsborough to the full rank of secretary of state for the colonies, thus ending Shelburne's control over colonial affairs. Very soon after that event Shelburne resigned from office and joined the opposition (October, 1768).[86]

Hillsborough's colonial policy during his first term of service (1763-1765) was marked by more than usual rigor, and colonial laws had to be transmitted

[85] "I resolved to accept, provided the Board should be altered from a Board of Representation to a Board of Report upon reference only; that the order of the governors in America to correspond with the Board of Trade only, should be rescinded; and that every executive business that has by degrees crept into the Board should revert to the proper offices, particularly all treasury business; and that I should not be of the cabinet (which was also offered me). In this manner, which has been agreed to I have accepted the office." — Letter of Hillsborough to Grenville, August 6, 1766, *Grenville Papers*, vol. iii, 294-296.

[86] Fitzmaurice, Edmund. *Life of Shelburne*, vol. i, 239, 241, 243, 245, 259, vol. ii, 2-3; *Grenville Papers*, vol. ii, 5, 38, 51; Mahon, Lord. *History of England*, vol. v, 27, 29, 41, 159, 203, 209, 235; *Dictionary of National Biography*, vol. xlv, 119.

with a promptness hitherto unknown.[87] As secretary of state for the colonies, Hillsborough stood for the fullest exercise of the prerogative, was responsible for the aggressive policy of the British government toward the colonies, and demanded the most vigorous repressive measures.[88]   He resigned his position as secretary of state in 1772 because he could not consent to the settlement of the Ohio country; hence he must have looked upon his western policy as essential to the proper carrying on of colonial affairs.[89]

Political position and terms of service of members

Under the English parliamentary system, the Board of Trade was very naturally subject to change with the change in ministries.   It has already been pointed out how Stamford was dismissed from office on the accession of Anne.   On the change of ministry in 1705, three additional members were changed, and the same was true when Sunderland replaced Hedges in 1706.   Stamford again went out of office in 1711 for political reasons, and when Bolingbroke acquired the

---

[87] See Calvert's letters to Governor Sharpe of Maryland urging him to transmit copies of the laws passed in that colony, in Sharpe's *Correspondence*, vol. iii.

[88] This attitude is well summed up by Junius, vol. iii, 172. "In his new department, I am sorry to say, he has shown neither abilities nor good sense. His letters to the colonies contain nothing but expression equally loose and violent. . . This treatment of the colonies, added to his refusal to present a petition of one of them to the king (a direct breach of the Declaration of Rights) will naturally throw them all into a flame. . . The other ministers were proceeding in their usual course, without foreseeing or regarding consequences; but this nobleman seems to have marked out by a determined choice the means to precipitate our destruction." — *Grenville Papers*, vol. iii, pp. lii-liii.

[89] *Grenville Papers*, vols. iii, iv, *passim*; Mahon, Lord. *History of England*, vol. v, 41, 185, 236-240, 320; *Dictionary of National Biography*, vol. xxvi, 437.

ascendency two years later, the Board was almost reorganized, no fewer than four members being changed. It also has been pointed out that at the close of Queen Anne's reign the Board had become just as exclusively Tory as the first one had been exclusively Whig.   On the accession of George I and the return of the Whigs to power, there was an entire change in the personnel of the Board.[90]   After that, changes were a little less sweeping, but the reason is evident: changes in ministries were essentially changes within a single political party and usually meant only a readjustment of personal followings, and men who had been in a discharged ministry frequently found comfortable berths in the one that succeeded to power.

Every important change in ministry meant considerable changes in the Board.[91]   Thus in 1742 when Walpole was finally forced to resign, three members of the Board followed him out of office, and none of these was the president.[92]   When the ministry was reorganized in 1755, three new men became members of the Board; John Pitt was dismissed, James Grenville resigned, and Richard Edgecombe was transferred to the admiralty board.[93]   There were no more radical changes in the ministry until 1761; but, along with the numerous ministerial changes of that year, one half the members of the Board of Trade were

[90] New York *Colonial Documents*, vol. iii, pp. xv-xvi.

[91] Miss Kellogg in her monograph on the "American Colonial Charter," in the American Historical Association *Report for 1903*, 220, says: "But while the fortunes of the presiding officers varied with the rise and fall of political ministries, the active working members of the board were seldom changed for such reasons." It is impossible to reconcile this statement with the facts.

[92] New York *Colonial Documents*, vol. iii, p. xvii.

[93] — *Ibid.*; Walpole, Horace. *Letters*, vol. iii, 379-381.

changed. Halifax resigned to go to Ireland; and John Yorke, Edward Thomas, and George Rice replaced Thomas Pelham, William G. Hamilton, and William Sloper, respectively.[94] In the readjustment of the minor offices in 1763, three members of the Board, including the president, were changed; and in 1765 with the formation of the Grafton ministry, one half of the Board including the president again lost office.[95] Such changes continued to occur until the Board was finally abolished in 1782. It is thus seen that the Board of Trade was considered ministerial so far as the men who directed its policy were concerned, and that the positions of the ordinary working members were regarded as either ministerial or the legitimate spoils of victory; consequently they were also subject to change with the change of party.

Although the positions on the Board were political, the tenure of office was not so precarious as might be supposed. Between the years 1696-1765 inclusive, there were, in all, ninety-five separate appointments. Disregarding fractions of years of service, the average tenure during this time was just about five years for each appointment. The average tenure for the presidents of the Board was not greatly different. There were in all eighteen different administrations, counting interrupted administrations, like that of Stamford and that of Hillsborough, as distinct periods of service and not as constituting a single administration. This gives, as the average term of service, four and nine-tenths years. If the broken administration

[94] New York *Colonial Documents*, vol. iii, p. xvii; Walpole, Horace. *Letters*, vol. v, 36-37.

[95] New York *Colonial Documents*, vol. iii, p. xviii.

of Stamford be considered as a single administration, the average is a little more than five years, which is almost the average tenure for the other members of the Board.[96]

There were, however, some remarkable periods of service on the part of some of the members. Four men, during the period covered by this volume, served continuously for periods of more than twenty years. These were Paul Docminique, twenty-one years; Thomas Pelham, the elder, twenty-five years; Edward Ashe, twenty-eight years; and Martin Bladen, twenty-nine years. These periods of service are rivalled by that of Soame Jenyns, who had already served ten years in 1765, and who continued to serve for fifteen years after that date. Long tenure in office does not necessarily mean efficiency. It should be noted that only one of these men was especially faithful in the performance of his duties; [97] and he has not left a single measure of his own, which can be called his contribution to the colonial policy of the English government.[98]   The men of brains and ideas, the men who had definite opinions regarding proper colonial policy, men like Townshend or Shelburne, enjoyed comparatively short terms in office. The very fact that they were active and influential men meant their removal when a ministry, to which they were opposed, came into office. The longest term of office of the president was that of Westmoreland, who served for sixteen years; Halifax, with a tenure of thirteen years, comes

[96] In computing the above averages use was made of the data given in the New York *Colonial Documents*, vol. iii, pp. xv-xviii.

[97] Martin Bladen.

[98] Possibly an exception should be made in favor of his proposal for a stamp duty in 1726.

second; and the next is Monson, who served for only eleven years, and accomplished nothing in all that time.

Periods of varying activity

The most casual examination of the printed colonial records discloses that the Board of Trade was very much more active in its correspondence at some times than it was at others.[99] No satisfactory explanation of this has been given, nor can any be had from an examination of the printed records alone. The manuscript sources, however, throw some light upon the matter.

As has been stated, the Board had other duties imposed upon it in addition to those of looking after the government of the continental American colonies.[100] There were the other colonies, especially the West Indian group, which required even more attention than did those on the continent. Then there were the great trading companies, and the merchants who had complaints or demands to present. Last of all the Board was charged with the consideration of England's trade with the various countries. This was not a merely nominal duty, but involved a great deal of hard work. The various representatives of the British government reported to and corresponded with the Board in much the same way as our consular officers report to our government today. This material alone comprises many volumes, known as the *Commercial Series I and II*.[101] If one can judge from their bulk and from the

---

[99] See the colonial records of New York, North Carolina, and New Jersey for illustrations of this.

[100] See page 24.

[101] Series I is made up of in-letters, memorials, and enclosures. Series

entries in the *Journal*, the business involved required much time and labor. To meet these constant demands upon its time, the Board arranged regular schedules for the business of each week. Thus in 1707, Tuesdays and Thursdays were set aside for the use of merchants and others "trading to America" who desired personal interviews with the Board.[102] Ten years later the program had become much more definite: viz., Mondays for reading letters, memorials, petitions, etc.; Tuesdays and Wednesdays for plantation business; Thursdays for trade; and Fridays for the consideration of laws passed in the plantations.[103]

It would seem that the regular routine business was more than enough to keep one set of officials busy, especially as some of the public hearings required several days; but the Board was frequently called upon for extraordinary work of the most exacting character. As it had charge of all trade and commercial relations, it was required to consider all the various commercial treaties that were negotiated,[104] was called upon to prepare instructions for the envoys who drafted these treaties,[105] and in some cases members of the Board were themselves sent as envoys to negotiate treaties

II includes entry books of out-letters, representations to the king or Council, instructions to envoys, etc. Both are in the Public Record Office in London.

[102] Board of Trade *Journal*, 19, p. 137.

[103] November 20, 1717, Board of Trade *Journal*, 26, p. 438.

[104] See the treatment of the commercial treaties with Sweden and the States General in 1702, in Board of Trade, *Trade Entry Book*, 15, pp. 419, 427-444 *et seq.*; the proposed commercial treaty with France in 1712, in Board of Trade *Commercial Series II*, 647, pp. 3-84; the proposed commercial treaty with Spain in 1713, *Ibid.*, pp. 404-411; that with Portugal in 1714, *Ibid.*, 648, pp. 206-240. Many other references could be cited.

[105] See the call for information, June 2, 1709, C.O. 324, 9, pp. 294-394; the letter from Bolingbroke to the Board for instructions for the commissioners to treat with those of France, July 28, 1714, Board of Trade *Journal*,

of this character.[106]   As these treaties are among the most important any nation makes, and as they are the most liable to be complained of by the merchants, the Board found its task onerous at times.[107]

Other treaties which were very important and required a great amount of care and research to supply the envoys with proper information in drafting were those dealing with boundaries.   When any treaty which affected boundaries or British claims to territory was being made, the Board was required to furnish instructions, documentary proof of claims, maps, etc., in many cases very voluminous, for the use of the envoys.[108] In one important case, that of the bounds of the Hudson's Bay Company, the southern limit of 49° as stated by the Board has become the northern boundary of the United States.[109]

25, p. 297; also instructions prepared by the Board for Daniel Pulteney and Martin Bladen, envoys to France, August 13, 1719, *Ibid.*, 29, p. 135. The following letter is perhaps most representative of all:

"Her Majesty having given directions for the immediate dispatch of my Lord Bingley to Spain, I am commanded to give your Lordships this notice of it, in order to your preparing such draughts of instructions as you may judge necessary to be given his Lordship, as well on the Treaty of Commerce lately concluded between Her Majesty and the Catholic King as on any other matter relating to the trade of this Kingdom." — Bolingbroke to the Board, April 27, 1714, in Board of Trade *Commercial Series II*, 648, p. 189.

[106] Daniel Pulteney and Martin Bladen were envoys to France 1719-1720. The latter's letters to the Board furnish a very interesting account of the speculation in Paris at the time and of current gossip and rumor as to the operation of Law's company in the Mississippi country. See: Board of Trade *Journal*, 29.

[107] See the numerous consultations with merchants in the references cited above.

[108] Note what was done in 1700 in the negotiations with France in Board of Trade *Journals*, 13, pp. 19, 70-73; in 1709 when a treaty was contemplated with the same country, C.O. 324, 37, pp. 294-394; and when the treaty was made in 1714, Board of Trade *Journal*, 24, p. 277.

[109] August 26, 1719, the following instructions for the envoys to France

The work of supplying information for envoys and the consideration of old treaties with the object of negotiating new ones was, of necessity, badly distributed, as it came in the form of sudden demands. Wars abrogated most commercial treaties, consequently at the close of a war there was a great deal of this treaty work to be done. Especially was this true after the War of the Spanish Succession, when so many commercial treaties had to be prepared and so much information of one kind and another supplied that the Board was literally swamped with work of this kind for two years or more. This, together with the confusion and accumulation of business resulting from war conditions and the change in sovereigns, is sufficient to explain the dearth of correspondence with the royal governors between 1713 and 1718. Letters were not answered for the simple reason that the Board could not get to them, and, as they continued to arrive, a considerable number of unanswered letters accumulated in its office.

The correspondence was neglected for some time after 1713, but this was not wholly due to the inefficiency of the Board, as its work along other lines testifies. During this period the Board wrote about one letter a year to each of the governors, and stated that

were agreed to by the Board. "And further that a line be drawn from the south westward of the Island of Griminston or Cape Perdria (so as to include the same within the limits of the bay) to the great Lake of Miscosinke, at Mistovenny, dividing the said lake into two parts, and that where the said line shall cut the 49th degree of northern latitude, another line shall begin, and be extended westward from the said lake upon the 49th degree of northern latitude, over which said line so to be described as above mentioned, the French and all persons by them employed shall be prohibited to pass to the northward of said 49th degree of latitude." — Board of Trade *Journal*, 29, p. 135.

his letters had not been answered because of the pressure of other business immediately referred to it by the king.[110] No doubt these statements are essentially true. Another reason for the unusual delay is suggested in one of the letters to Governor Spotswood; namely, that the Board lacked direction as to what it should do in the case of some of the colonies.[111]

As soon as the most pressing work in regard to treaties was out of the way, the Board took up the accumulation of correspondence. As current business had to be taken care of, only a small portion of the Board's time could be devoted to unanswered letters. Those which had been received most recently were considered first, and the earlier ones taken up as opportunity offered.[112] In most cases it had been so long since the letters were written that they did not require an answer. It was not until 1718 that all the letters received by the Board about the close of the war were

[110] Secretary Popple to Governor Spotswood, January 14, 1714, C.O. 5, 1364, p. 23.

Alexander Spotswood, one of Virginia's most famous governors, served from 1710 to 1722. He was greatly interested in the development of his colony, assisted in improving the culture of tobacco, aided the cause of education, and favored the westward movement of population.

[111] Board to Spotswood, August 18, 1715, C.O. 5, 1364, p. 236. In this letter the receipt of eight letters from Spotswood bearing the following dates is acknowledged: December 13, 1713; March 9, 1714; October 25, 1714; December 5, 1714; January 27, 1715; March 28, 1715; June 4, 1715; and November 26, 1715. None of these was answered at that time.

[112] June 21, 1715, the Board considered the following letters from Governor Hunter: September 10, 1713; May 7, 1714; August 27, 1714; October 18, 1714; October 18, 1714; November 8, 1714; November 8, 1714; November 25, 1714; March 28, 1715; March 28, 1715; April 9, 1715. See: Board of Trade *Journal*, 25, pp. 135-138. November 27, 1717, the following were considered: June 8, 1711; June 8, 1717; October 2, 1716; February 3, 1717; April 8, 1717; May 3, 1717; May 27, 1717, and one undated. See: *Ibid.*, 27, pp. 1-4.

Correspondence from the other colonies was considered in about the

read.[113]   After that, correspondence was attended to with reasonable regularity for a time.

same way. None of this delay can be ascribed to slowness in transmission, as the following table of letters from Governor Spotswood [C.O. 5, 1317] shows:

DATED	RECEIVED	READ
November 16, 1713	January 4, 1714	May 16, 1716
October 25, 1714	December 10, 1714	" " "
November 25, 1714	January 28, 1715	" " "
December 5, 1714	January 28, 1715	" " "
January 27, 1715	April 6, 1715	" " "
March 28, 1715	June 27, 1715	" " "
June 4, 1715	January 16, 1716	" " "
February 16, 1716	April 18, 1716	" " "
May 9, 1716	June 28, 1716	July 10, 1716

On June 1, 1716, the Board wrote to Spotswood that it had just had under consideration his letters of the following dates: June 2, August 17, September 14, November 16, and December 29, 1713; March 29, October 25, and December, 1714; January 27, March 28, June 4, July 15, August 9, and October 24, 1715; and January 16, 1716, making fifteen letters in all, many of them containing enclosures, which were considered and answered at one time. C.O. 5, 1364, p. 376.

[113] On June 25 and 26, 1718, the Board cleared up the following list of letters from New England [C.O. 5, 915, pp. 120-158]:

FROM	DATED
Lieutenant-governor of Mass.	December 30, 1712
Governor Dudley of Mass.	August 24, 1713
Secretary Addington of Mass.	August 24, 1713
Governor Dudley of Mass.	August 25, 1713
" " " "	November, 1713
" " " "	December 1, 1713
" " " "	July 13, 1714
Secretary Addington of Mass.	August 16, 1714
Governor Dudley of Mass.	August 9, 1714
" " " "	August 19, 1714
" " " "	October 3, 1714
Colonel Shute of Mass.	July 23, 1717
Lieutenant-governor of N. H.	August 16, 1716
Governor Dudley of Mass.	July 5, 1715
" " " "	June 27, 1715
" " " "	May 7, 1715
" " " "	May 2, 1715
Council of Mass.	March 2, 1714
Governor Dudley of Mass.	November 29, 1714
" " " "	November 18, 1714

The lack of force in the action of the Board, which gradually appeared and culminated in 1737, was due to the steady transfer of business from the Board to the secretary of state's office and to the gradual decay which resulted from lack of authority. A good part of the delay in answering the letters of the royal governors after 1730, however, was due to downright indifference and neglect by the Board. There was no period of excessive pressure of other business, such as there was immediately after 1713; consequently there is no valid excuse for letters lying in the Board's office for a year or more before they were read, neither is there any reason why it should allow a period of three years to elapse between its own letters to the governors of the most important colonies. Nevertheless these things are common in the Board's records for the period.[114] Its other duties were neglected about as badly, especially after 1737, and in no field did it show vigor or efficiency.

The change which appears after 1748 is due wholly to the energy and ambition of Halifax, who recovered the powers which had gradually been usurped by the secretary of state, and even acquired new ones which the Board had never before exercised; such, for instance, as the power to appoint colonial officials and to perform other executive functions.

[114] A letter from Lieutenant-governor Wentworth of New Hampshire bears the following endorsement: "Written April 2, 1730; Rec'd. June 2, 1730; Read, June 9, 1731." — C.O. 5, 872. No letter was written by the Board to Lieutenant-governor Gooch of Virginia from September 13, 1732, to September 4, 1735. See: C.O. 5, 1336, p. 131. A letter from the Board to Governor Belcher of Massachusetts, dated September 10, 1735, acknowledges the receipt of eighteen letters from him, covering a period of two years. See: C.O. 5, 917, p. 138.

Office force

To transact the voluminous work of the Board there was at first a modest office force of a secretary and five clerks.[115] As all the work had to be done with the pen, this force must have been kept very busy preparing the many letters, representations, commissions, instructions, and other documents for which the Board was responsible, to say nothing of the numerous entry books which had to be kept up. Although the task was a heavy one, it was very well done, as the records themselves testify. This office force was gradually increased until, in 1708, there were, besides the secretary, eight clerks, one door keeper, two messengers, and a "necessary woman." The salaries paid were small, ranging from five hundred pounds for the secretary to forty pounds for the lower clerks and doorkeeper. The total pay roll was one thousand one hundred fifty pounds.[116] Even these small salaries

---

[115] Board of Trade Miscellanies, 11, pp. 34-38.

[116] The following annual report [January 22, 1708, Board of Trade *Journal*, 20, p. 23] of the office force shows the salaries and personnel of the entire establishment:

"For himself as Secretary . . . . . . £ 500
" Adrian Drift Deputy Secr'y or Chief Clerk . . 100
" Wm. Barker   Clerk 80
" Bryan Wheelock   - " 70
" Maurice Carroll   " 60
" Justinian Loggan   " 50
" Nathaniel Estwick   " 50
" Samuel Gellibrand   " 40
" Matthew Bertin   " 40
" Daniel Child, Doorkeeper 40
" Samuel Clark, Doorkeeper and Assistant Messenger . 45
" John Gray, Messenger and Assistant Doorkeeper . . 45
" Mary Wright, Necessary Woman . . . 30

In all amounting to the aforesaid sum of . . . £1150"

were often in arrears, and the Board was repeatedly petitioned to assist the clerks in getting their pay.[117] In one of these petitions the clerks stated that the treasury had offered them a quarter's pay in "tin tallies," but they could sell these only at a discount. The doorkeeper, who received only forty-five pounds a year, added that he had paid out thirty-four pounds for coal and unless he could get his money "he would be a great loser." [118]

In spite of the low salaries and the slow payments, the clerks were probably not so badly off as their statements indicate.   They state in their petition that "they had no perquisite or other advantages in this office or other way of supporting themselves, but from their salary."   This statement is not quite true, for the general tipping system prevailed in England then as it does now; and the man who wished any work done, even in a public office, had to pay for it.   There was no direct charge, nor any fixed scale of fees, but there were other ways of making it plain that the clerks expected gratuities for every service rendered. There was no secret about this, for in 1714 the Board found it necessary to make a rule that no clerk should "presume to demand any money from any person for any business done in the office." [119]   Evidently, how-ever, the clerks received their customary fees without demanding them, for the fee system continued to flourish.   This source of revenue for the clerks was

---

[117] See Board of Trade *Journal*, 12, pp. 99, 105, 123, 308; 13, pp. 320, 424.

[118] Petition of the clerks, November 17, 1710, in Board of Trade *Miscellanies*, 11, pp. 465-467.

[119] Order of the Board respecting clerks, salaries, and hours of work, December 20, 1714, in Board of Trade *Journal*, 24, pp. 242-243.

so firmly established that they protested in 1722
against Mr. West's clerk giving out copies of colonial
statutes which had been referred to him by the Board
and were awaiting his report in point of law.[120] Had
the clerks not received extra pay for copies of laws,
they would have been the last persons to object to a
clerk in another office doing the work. The Board
recognized the legitimacy of their monopoly over such
papers and directed that in future Mr. West should
not permit his clerk to give out any copy of acts or
other matters referred to him by the Board.[121]

From many sources it is evident that money was
necessary for the successful transaction of business at
the Board, and that the clerks systematically increased
their small annual allowances by whatever opportunities fell in their way. There is no direct proof that the
members of the Board themselves required these
money favors, but it is plain that they knew of the practices of the clerks. They did, however, try to keep
conditions in their office such as not to excite serious
criticism or seriously to hamper the official work.
This is seen in the rule preventing a clerk acting as
agent for any American plantation;[122] and the rules

---

[120] Board of Trade *Journal*, 33, p. 25.

[121] Ordered by the Board, February 8, 1722. See: Board of Trade
Journal, 33, p. 25.

[122] April 30, 1724, the *Journal* has this entry: "Their Lordships considering the inconvenience of any clerk in their office acting as agent for any
American plantation do hereby direct, that if any such be employed as agents,
the secretary do acquaint them with this resolution, and dismiss them if they
continue to act as such." — Board of Trade *Journal*, 34, p. 110.

The next day one of the clerks, a Mr. Sanderson, petitioned that he be
permitted to act as agent for the Massachusetts assembly until the dispute
between it and the governor had been settled; but the Board refused to
grant him the indulgence he desired. As he continued as clerk, it is presumed he resigned as agent. See: *Ibid.*, p. 111.

as to hours of service and returning all papers to the secretary before leaving the office.[123]

The line between accepting a gratuity for doing a service which should be done without one, and the accepting of one for a service which should not be rendered at all, is a shadowy one; but that is the line which separates tipping and bribery in a public office. That money would secure any desired information as to the position of business in the plantation office is evident from the letters of Richard Partridge and Ferdinando John Paris to their American employers.[124] We would call their methods bribery today; the clerks called it accepting gratuities. In 1730 the Board considered conditions so serious that they forbade the clerks demanding or accepting any gratuities for ordinary services, but did not restrain

[123] September 15, 1724. "The Board observing that several books of entry in this office were very much in arrears by neglect of clerks, their Lordships have thought fit to order, that for the future the clerks should attend here every day from 9 a.m.-2 p.m., and as much longer as the Board shall at any time sit."

They were also required to attend evenings, when directed to do so by the secretary, were to deliver to him or to the under secretary, before leaving the office, all books and papers in their custody, and the secretary was ordered to give an account of the attendance of the clerks for each week. Board of Trade *Journal*, 34, pp. 250-251.

[124] Complaint had been made to the Board that a copy of a letter of Governor Thomas to the Board had been secured surreptitiously by Richard Partridge and transmitted to Philadelphia, to the great injury of the governor. The Board called Partridge before it, but he refused to answer any questions. He was considered guilty of the charge and an order was entered excluding him from transacting any business before the Board as agent for any colony until he had cleared his record. It was further ordered that no clerk should give out any copies of papers in the office unless directed to do so by the secretary, on pain of immediate dismissal; and also that no one should be permitted to inspect books or papers in the office or to enter the clerk's room without an order from the Board. March 17, 1741, Board of Trade *Journal*, 50, pp. 30-31.

them from receiving such reasonable gratuities as "any person shall think fit to bestow for extraordinary service" or for copies of papers "made at the request of parties therein concerned." [125] This rule sounds well, but it accomplished little more than to bring about the establishing of fixed fees for the work of the clerks. This was done at the request of Secretary Popple, who states in his petition that the annexed schedule "is much less than the voluntary gratuities" formerly received. The matter was settled in the usual way by an Order in Council [126] which required the table of fees to be posted in the Plantation Office, and all other fees prohibited.[127]

[125] August 6, 1730. The Board was informed that several persons had paid money to their secretaries or clerks for their trouble in matters transacted in the office, "more particularly, on the passing of commissions and instructions for governors, on reports for appointing of councillors, and upon hearings before their Lordships in matters of controversy. As these gratuities have been received without their Lordship's privity or consent, who do neither know nor allow of any fees or gratuities due, or to be taken for business in their office." The Board expressed its utter disapproval of the practice and strictly forbade its secretaries, clerks, or other officers demanding, taking, or receiving any fee, gratuity, or reward, under any pretense whatever, for business done in the office. But they were not restrained from receiving "such reasonable gratuities as any person should think fit to bestow for extraordinary attendance, out of the office, or for copies of papers made at the request of parties therein concerned." See: Board of Trade *Journal*, 40, p. 203.

[126] Order dated August 12, 1731, Privy Council *Register*, "George II," vol. ii, 447.

[127] Table of fees annexed to the representation of the Board, June 1, 1731 [Board of Trade *Miscellanies*, 12, p. 328]:

Draught of commission for governor . . .	£ 6- 6-0
Draught of general instructions for governor . .	12-12-0
Draught of instructions for trade	6- 6-0
Representation for recommending councillors for plantations	4- 4-0
Representation on private business at request of persons concerned	2- 2-0
Caveat entered by private persons with relation to any business depending in the office	10-0

In 1730 a new officer, known as the "solicitor and clerk of reports," was appointed.[128] His duties were to solicit business for the Board at other offices, and to secure reports upon matters which had been referred to the attorney-general and other law officers – a duty which had formerly been cared for by a solicitor from the treasury department.[129] In addition the new officer had the task of getting out the special reports to Parliament and other papers which required a search of the records of the office.

The creation of this office was caused by the growth of business. Parliament was demanding many reports upon the conditions in the colonies and upon various matters connected with the trade of the plantations and foreign countries. In addition to this,

---

Examining the proprietary governor's security and the draught of a bond for his observance of the acts of trade .	£4- 4-0
References to the Attorney, or Solicitor General or to any of the king's counsel upon private business at the request of the parties	10-0
Entering patents for employment in the plantations . .	2- 2-0
Certificates of the dates of commissions or of any matter granted at the request of private persons . .	10-0
Issuing summons at the particular request of any party .	10-0
For copies of papers	10-0

These are the fees which the clerks demanded in their petition, and the ones finally established.

[128] The request was made August 11, 1730. The new officer was to receive a salary of £200 per year, to be paid out of the incidental fund of the office. The request was promptly granted and Mr. Onslow Burrish was appointed by the Board, August 18, 1730. See: Board of Trade *Miscellanies*, 12, pp. 314-315; Board of Trade *Journal*, 40, p. 212.

[129] Mr. Borrett of the treasury department was frequently used. See the requests for him to secure reports on laws which had been in the hands of the attorney-general more than a year, February 18, 1712, Board of Trade *Journal*, 23, p. 100. In other cases the laws of Pennsylvania were sent to him with directions to secure the solicitor-general's report as promptly as possible. See: Letter to Mr. Borrett, August 3, 1713, in C.O. 5, 1292, p. 393.

commissioners had been appointed to settle matters left unsettled by the Treaty of Seville with Spain. The Board had been directed to correspond with these commissioners and to supply them with whatever information they needed in their negotiations.[130] These demands were more than the regular office force could meet, especially as some required much time and special talents for research; consequently an additional clerk was appointed to do the work.

Mr. Onslow Burrish [131] was the first of these officers. He was succeeded by Alured Popple,[132] a former secretary of the Board, and he in turn by John Pownall,[133] who later became secretary. The careful and detailed reports upon conditions in New York, New Jersey, and other provinces during the presidency of Halifax are most probably the work of Pownall. As it became more and more necessary to go over back records in order to understand how conditions had developed and thus be in a position to suggest proper remedies, the efficiency of the Board was more and more dependent upon an able clerk of this kind.[134]

The special attorney for the Board was also a very important official. Until 1718 the Lords of Trade had referred all questions of law to the attorney- or

[130] Board of Trade *Journal*, 40, p. 205; Board of Trade *Miscellanies*, 12, pp. 310-315.

[131] The Board itself appointed him the same as it did all other clerks, August 18, 1730.

[132] June 3, 1737.   See: Board of Trade *Journal*, 47, p. 107.

[133] May 1, 1745, *Ibid.*, 53, p. 63.

[134] Pownall continued to act as clerk of reports until he was appointed joint secretary of the Board, June 6, 1753.   Mr. Edward Sedgwick succeeded him as clerk of reports and, as will be noted later, was appointed secretary when Pownall accompanied Halifax to Ireland. See: Board of Trade *Journal*, 61.

solicitor-general, but in time the business became so great that these officials could not attend to it. To relieve them of some of their least important work, a crown counsel was assigned to the Board. He was not intended to replace the attorneys- and solicitors-general so far as the work of the Board was concerned; but only to take over such "Law business relating to trade and plantations as the Board do not conceive important enough" to require the opinions of the higher officers.[135] The latter could still be appealed to upon any knotty questions of law, but the board had to pay their fees out of its incidental fund, instead of having the treasury defray all such charges,[136] for apparently the attorneys- and solicitors-general gave no opinions, even to official boards, without charging the usual fees.

Three men, Richard West,[137] Francis Fane,[138] and Matthew Lamb,[139] successively filled the office of consulting counsel. Wherever the policy of the Board turned upon a point of law, these men did much to shape it; hence they played an especially important part in the treatment of colonial legislation. Practically all the laws passed in the colonies were referred

[135] Letter of Stanhope to the Board announcing the appointment of Richard West as attorney, April 21, 1718, in Board of Trade *Journal*, 27, p. 206.

[136] Order of the Treasury Board, August 17, 1720. See: *Ibid.*, 30, p. 326.

[137] He resigned in 1725 to become Chancellor of Ireland. See: Chalmers, George. *Opinions*, 26.

[138] The patent under the great seal for his appointment was received by the Board, September 9, 1725. Board of Trade *Journal*, 35, p. 227. He served until 1746 when he resigned to become a member of the Board. Matthew Lamb was appointed as attorney at this time. See: Board of Trade *Journal*, 54, p. 91; Chalmers, George. *Opinions*, 26.

[139] Apparently he died in office in 1768. See: Chalmers, George. *Opinions*, 37.

to them for consideration; if they found any objections to such acts, they were pretty sure to be disallowed. Generally they confined their opinions to "objections in point of law," but at times they took into consideration the effect of an act upon the whole constitutional development of a colony, and sometimes they even offered advice as to administrative policy.[140] These men, although they were behind the scenes and are seldom heard of in the historical accounts, must be taken into serious consideration in any adequate treatment of the relations of the American colonies to the mother country in the eighteenth century.

The secretary, however, was the one official in the office who exercised the greatest power in shaping the administrative policy of the Board. He opened and read the letters, arranged the business for the consideration of the Board, drafted its letters, prepared the commissions and instructions for the governors, and in many cases drafted the representations of the Board. Many of the letters to the governors and to other officials are signed by him alone.[141] He was the man who knew what was going on, who was familiar with the precedents of the office and who could advise as to the proper action in a particular case. In fact, it was he who conducted the whole work of the office under the direction of the Board.[142] In addition to that, those

[140] See Chalmers, George. *Opinions, passim*, especially Francis Fane's opinion on the Virginia acts of 1726 for the relief of William and Mary College, page 403.

[141] See: New York *Colonial Documents*, vols. iv, v, vi, *passim*.

[142] How important he was in the eyes of the Board may be seen from the following incident. Mr. Charles and Mr. Franklin desired copies of some observations of the proprietors of Pennsylvania on the complaints of Sir Wm. Johnson of land purchases in the Indian country. These had been

transacting business with the Board had to deal with him. His influence and information were always valuable, and he received the lion's share of the fees of the office,[143] and no doubt a similarly large proportion of the gratuities.

John Pownall is probably the most noted of all these secretaries.[144] He was a brother to the governor of Massachusetts and far more than a mere permanent secretary. Coming to the Board in 1745 as clerk of reports,[145] he became the trusted confidential adviser of Halifax,[146] was made joint secretary in 1753,[147] full secretary in 1758,[148] and continued to serve in that capacity until he was given leave of absence to accom-

refused and Charles complained of the action of the secretary in refusing his request. The Board resolved that his action was "arrogant and indecent," and "that the calling in question the propriety of the rules and orders made by this Board with respect to the delivery of copies of papers, and to the conduct of their officers in relation thereto, is highly insolent and indecent, and that Mr. Charles' complaint against the secretary concerning a motion which Mr. Charles desired might be made to the Board for leave to have copies of certain papers is groundless and injurious, inasmuch as it is the secretary's duty to arrange the business for the Board and to bring the several matters before them for their consideration in such method, time and place as he shall judge best for the convenience and dispatch of business, or as their Lordships shall think proper to direct." — December 21, 1757, Board of Trade *Journal*, 65.

[143] The secretary received, by order of the Board, two-fifths of all the fees. See: Board of Trade *Journal*, 42, pp. 97-98.

[144] The secretaries in their order of service were:
William Popple, 1696-1707 — Board of Trade *Journal*, 19, p. 165.
William Popple, Jr., 1707-1722 — *Ibid.*, 32, p. 64.
Alured Popple, 1722-1737 — *Ibid.*, 47, p. 107.
Thomas Hill, 1737-1758 — *Ibid.*, p. 186.
John Pownall, 1758-1761 — *Ibid.*, 66, Oct. 25, 1758.
Edward Sedgwick, acting secretary, 1761. — *Ibid.*, 69, p. 305.

[145] — *Ibid.*, 53, p. 63.

[146] *Dictionary of National Biography*, article "Halifax."

[147] Board of Trade *Journal*, 61, June 6, 1753.

[148] — *Ibid.*, 66, October 25, 1758.

pany Halifax to Ireland.[149] Even after the retirement
of his patron from the Board, he continued to exercise
much personal influence.   His support of any measure was especially valuable, because he knew so well
how influence in its favor could best be exerted.   It is
evident from the letters of Cadwallader Colden that
the chief "back stair" access to the whole Halifax influence was by way of Pownall.[150]   Because of this fact,
Colden offered him the position of agent for New
York; he refused, but suggested the name of Edmund
Burke as a proper person for such duties.   It was
through this suggestion that Burke was afterward selected by the assembly for its representative.

All of the clerks got their positions through the personal support of either a member of the Board or a
chief minister; the general practice being to allow
members of the Board to name the subordinate clerks
and helpers, while the secretary and attorney were
appointed by a secretary of state.[151]   Once appointed,
however, their positions were permanent.   Only continued persistent neglect of duty or disregard of rules
was sufficient cause for removal.[152]   There was no "ro-

---

[149] June 23, 1761. At the request of Halifax, Pownall was permitted to
accompany him to Ireland. Mr. Sedgwick, the clerk of reports, was appointed clerk during Pownall's absence. See: Board of Trade *Journal*,
69, p. 305.

[150] "Cadwallader Colden Papers" in New York Historical Society *Collections*, vol. ix, 37, 38, 80-81.

[151] For appointments of clerks by the Board see Board of Trade *Journal*,
16, p. 111; 24, pp. 342-343; 26, p. 223; 31, p. 336; 32, p. 100. Many others
could be cited. For appointments of clerks of report by the Board, see Board
of Trade *Journal*, 40, p. 212; 47, p. 107; 53, p. 63. For appointments of
secretaries, see *ibid*.

[152] May 8, 1745, George Armitage, chamber-keeper, was dismissed for
neglecting his duty "for some months past." See: Board of Trade *Journal*,
53, p. 66. Other cases of similar indulgence may be found.

tation in office," nor were men dismissed when they became more or less incapacitated by age; they were retained on full or on part pay until they resigned or died.[153] In some cases sons succeeded fathers and, in the case of the secretary, the office was filled successively by father, son, and grandson.[154] Changes in ministry and monarchs did not in the least affect the clerks, as they were regularly advanced according to seniority of service.[155] When a man got an appointment as clerk, he could feel that he was entering upon a career; and for efficient service promotion was almost certain. Practically all the higher officers, as the clerk of reports and the secretary, began work in the office as subordinate clerks.[156] One, Alured Popple, rose from a minor clerkship to secretary, clerk of reports, and finally was appointed governor of Bermuda.[157] Thus, while the Board was subject to sweeping changes in its personnel, the efficiency of the plantation office was not seriously affected so far as its working force was concerned. This may be one reason why British colonial policy shows as much consistency as it does during the eighteenth century.

[153] December 20, 1714, Maurice Carroll was allowed to retire because of age on an allowance of £30 a year; he was receiving £80. Another case is that of Mr. Gedney, who was allowed to retire in 1738 and a half pay clerk employed to fill his place. The case of Thos. Hill has already been referred to. Numerous entries in the *Journal* may be cited of clerks dying in office. See: Board of Trade *Journal*, 24, p. 343; 48, part i, p. 63; 31, p. 336; 45, pp. 50, 74.

[154] William Popple, William Popple, Jr., and Alured Popple. The relationship is stated in the *Journal* at the time of the changes. See references in *footnote* 153.

[155] This was the regular rule, as indicated by many *Journal* entries.

[156] This was true of William Popple Jr., Alured Popple, Thomas Hill, and Edward Sedgwick.

[157] Board of Trade *Journal*, 53, p. 63.

II. RELATIONS OF THE BOARD OF TRADE TO OTHER DEPARTMENTS OF ADMINISTRATION

The Privy Council and its Committees

By its commission the Board was not empowered to issue important executive orders on its own authority, but was directed to make representations to the king or to the king in council; and the final action appeared as an Order in Council. That fact raises the important question of the relation of the Board to the Privy Council. As first organized, the former was considered a committee of the latter body and is still so considered by the officials of the Privy Council office. All of the chief officers of state were members of the Council and ex officiis members of the Board.[158] In addition to this two or more of the active working members of the Board were sworn to the Privy Council and frequently attended its meetings.[159] During the reigns of William and Anne the ordinary representations of the Board were disposed of by the Council very much as were reports from its other committees, and orders issued on the strength of such representations do not show the action of any intermediate committee.

---

[158] See the copy of the commission of the Board of Trade in New York *Colonial Documents*, vol. iv. Cf. Board of Trade *Miscellanies*, 12, pp. 439-453.

[159] See the Privy Council *Register* for these reigns.

The regular form of order was like the one of March 14, 1700, approving the boundary agreement between New York and Connecticut. The day preceding, the Board had made a representation to the king, stating the dispute as to the jurisdiction over the towns of Rye and Bedford, and recommending that the question be settled according to the agreement arrived at by commissioners appointed by the two colonies. At the meeting of the king in council, this representation was read and approved in the following words:

> Upon reading this day at the Board a representation from the Lords Commissioners of Trade and Plantations dated the 13th of this month relating to the boundaries between the Province of New Yorke and the Colony of Connecticut in America. . . His Majesty in Council, approving the said representation is pleased to order, as it is hereby ordered, that the Lords Commissioners of Trade and Plantations do prepare the draughts of letters to be sent to the Earle of Bellomont, and to the governor and company of Connecticut from His Majesty, signifying to them His Majesty's approbation and confirmation of the said agreement in 1683; With such other directions, as are proposed by the said representation; and that the said draughts be presented at this Board, for His Majesty's further directions thereupon.[160]

In this order there is no mention of any previous action by a committee; it is also evident that the action of the Board was approved without serious question and without limitation. This order is typical of scores of others printed in the documents relating to New York, North Carolina, Massachusetts, New Jersey, and Pennsylvania, as late as 1720. In that year an Order in Council regarding bills of credit in New

---

[160] New York *Colonial Documents*, vol. iv, 626.

York recites that the order had been recommended by
the "Lords of the Committee for Hearing Appeals
from the Plantations." [161] Two years later a reference
to such a committee appears for the first time in the
New Jersey *Archives*. This was an order issued on a
report from the "Lords of the Committee of his Majesty's most Honorable Privy Council;" [162] and from
that time on, a committee of the Privy Council is
usually mentioned. This change in the wording of
the orders indicates that it was becoming more and
more the practice to transact all important council
business in the committees and consider only formal
reports in the king's presence. This practice relieved
the king of much wearisome service and at the same
time diminished his actual participation in determining the policy of the government. The committees
reported only their conclusions. There is no record
of any dissenting opinions, and whatever action the
committees recommended appears to have been carried into execution by the council without question.

At the time the Board of Trade was established,
executive and judicial business from the Channel Islands and appeals from the plantations were regularly
referred to committees. So far as the Privy Council

---

[161] New York *Colonial Documents*, vol. v, 539.

[162] New Jersey *Archives*, vol. v, 28. The first reference in the Pennsylvania *Archives* to the action of such a committee occurs in 1726 in an order
for repealing an act of the assembly of that colony. There is a slight reference to such a committee in the scheme of government submitted to the
Board by Stanhope in 1714. In this case, its recommendation was adverse
to an instruction given by the Board to the governors as regards appeals.
The Board got the matter recommitted to its consideration and finally carried
its point. See: Pennsylvania *Archives*, vol. i, 190; North Carolina *Colonial
Records*, vol. ii, 162. The Massachusetts *Acts and Resolves* [vol. ii, 272]
record the first action of a committee on the laws of that province in 1723.

Register shows, questions of this character from the non-contiguous territories, which had their relations with the British government chiefly through the crown, were treated alike. The form of procedure developed for judicial appeals from Jersey and Guernsey was used for the same class of business from the various British colonies. Each petition for an appeal was referred to a committee which investigated the merits of the case, determined what should be done, and reported its findings to the council with recommendations.[163]

When committees of the Privy Council are mentioned they must not be thought of as standing or special committees, such as are common in modern legislative bodies; they correspond more to committees of the whole, as in fact they were. Names for these committees describe the business done instead of designating a certain group of men, consequently there is considerable variety in the names used in the *Register*. Thus out of nineteen such committee meetings between May, 1700, and December, 1701, there are no less than seven different names used to describe them; the most common being, "At the Committee for Hearing of Appeals from the Plantations and for the Affaires of Jersey and Guernsey." [164] Evidently

---

[163] The Privy Council *Register* shows this to have been the constant practice, and no distinction is to be noticed between the manner of determining appeals from the plantations and those from Jersey and Guernsey. The action of July 9, 1701, was typical of many others. On that day appeals were considered by the same committee from Barbadoes, from Jersey, and from Guernsey. See: Privy Council *Register*, "William III," vol. vi, 231.

[164] The names were: "At the Committee of the Councill for Hearing of Appeals from the Plantations." — May 3, 1700, Privy Council *Register*, "William III," vol. vi, 21.

"At the Committee of the Councill for Hearing of Appeals from the Plantations, Jersey, Guernsey, etc." — May 22, 1700, *Ibid.*, 31.

it is one committee and not a series of committees which is referred to by these seven different names. This is indicated by the looseness with which the names are used,[165] by the character of the business transacted at the various meetings, by the general presence of the same group of men, and by the lack of consistency in changes in personnel with changes in the name of the committee. Not only is it a single committee, but it also appears to be the one great committee of the British government, the cabinet council; for one or both of the chief secretaries of state were nearly always present,[166] usually accompanied by the lord president and one of the chief justices,[167] and sometimes by the chancellor of the exchequer. As the attendance in the above cases was

---

"At the Committee of the Councill of the Affaires of Jersey and Guernsey and for Appeals from the Plantations." — June 28, 1700, Privy Council *Register*, "William III," vol. vi, 69.

"At the Committee for Hearing of Appeals from the Plantations, etc." — July 8, 1700, *Ibid.*, 70.

"At the Committee for Hearing of Appeals from the Plantations and for the Affaires of Jersey and Guernsey." — November 2, 1700, *Ibid.*, 93.

"At the Committee for the Affaires of Jersey and Guernsey." — December 19, 1700, *Ibid.*, 121.

"At the Committee for the Affairs of Jersey and Guernsey and the Plantations." — April 9, 1701, *Ibid.*, 183.

A still more descriptive title was used on September 2, 1698: "At the Committee for hearing Appeales from the Plantations, For the Affaires of Jersey and Guernsey and for the Redemption of Captives." — *Ibid.*, vol. v, 223-224.

[165] The Committee is called one on appeals when no appellate business was done [Privy Council *Register*, "William III," vol. vi, 123]; on appeals from the plantations when only those from Jersey were heard [*Ibid.*, 263]; and a committee with the common heading given above considered the question of a light house at Dublin [*Ibid.*, 123]

[166] Secretary Vernon was present fourteen out of the seventeen meetings, while Hedges attended eight of them. Both Hedges and Vernon were present on six occasions. See: Privy Council *Register*, "William III," vol. vi, 21-316.

[167] Chief Justice Holt was absent three times, and the lord president seven.

never more than six nor less than three, and was most commonly four, the resemblance to a cabinet council is still further emphasized.[168]

During Queen Anne's reign this committee of the Privy Council was very much the same as during the reign of William.   It was still a committee for disposing of various business from Jersey, Guernsey, and the plantations.   The attendance, in general, was somewhat larger; and there was a little more regularity in the title, although there was still the general variation to make the titles descriptive of the work which was done at each meeting; [169] and in one case where a variety of business was transacted, no attempt was made to name the committee.[170]

The tendency to refer all matters requiring investigation or deliberation to committees continued; and these references are to committees of the whole coun-

[168] September 17, 1701, when only appellate business was considered, the committee consisted of Secretary Vernon, Secretary Hedges, Chancellor of the Exchequer, and Chief Justice Holt.   See: Privy Council *Register*, "William III," vol. vi, 263.

[169] The titles which were most commonly used were:

A Committee for the King's funeral and the Queen's coronation; Committee for the Affairs of Jersey and Guernsey; Committee of the Whole Council and to Consider of Barbadoes Lawes, and for ye Affaires of Jersey and Guernsey; At a Committee for hearing of Appeals from the Plantations and for Jersey and Guernsey; Committee for Jersey and Guernsey; Committee for hearing Appeals from the Plantations and for the Affaires of Jersey and Guernsey; At the Councill Chamber at Whitehall; the Committee for hearing Appeals from the Plantations; and At the Committee of the Whole Councill for the Affairs of Jersey and Guernsey and for hearing of Appeals from the Plantations.   See: Privy Council *Register*, "Anne," vols. i, iii, iv, v, *passim*.

[170] This entry is "At the Councill Chamber at Whitehall."   A variety of business was transacted, among other things an order was entered for hearing an appeal from Barbadoes.   This is preceded with the statement that the petition for an appeal "had been referred to the Right Honourable the Lords of this Committee," but the reference was to the Committee on Appeals from the Plantations.   See: *Ibid.*, vol. iv, 248, 259.

cil, instead of to specially named groups.[171] The one exception was bills from Ireland which were regularly referred to a special committee.[172] That and the two special committees for the king's funeral and the queen's coronation are the only committees which were specially appointed; all others are simply committees of the whole council.

The principal secretaries of state, members of the Board, the lord president, and other officers attended these committees very much as they did in the preceding reign.   It was still a compact group of the most influential men in the administration.   There is additional proof that it was but one committee, which was still masquerading under various names; for business which was referred to the Committee for Hearing Appeals from the Plantations was considered by a committee which also calls itself one on the Affairs of Jersey and Guernsey, and vice versa.[173]

[171] July 15, 1710: "It is this day ordered by Her Majesty in Council that a committee of the whole Council do meet on Wednesday next being the 19th of this instant, July, at ten of the clock in the morning, to consider of proper expedients for furnishing the city of London with coals, and regulating the coal trade, and to report their opinion what Her Majesty may fitly doe therein." — Privy Council *Register*, "Anne," vol. iv, 24.   When this committee met to consider the matter, it consisted of the Lord Treasurer, Lord President, Earl of Radnor, Dartmouth, and Vernon, or in other words the Cabinet.   See: *Ibid.*, 27.

Another entry which is still more descriptive of the tendency to refer business to committees is that of November 2, 1710: "It is this day ordered by Her Majesty in Council that the cause of the Canary merchants against Mr. Pauldon, Her Majesty's consul of the Canary Islands, which was to be heard this day before Her Majesty be, and it is hereby referred to a committee of the whole council, who are to meet at the Council Chamber at Whitehall on Saturday evening 11th instant, whereof the several parties concerned are to take notice and come prepared to be heard accordingly." — *Ibid.*, 138.

[172] — *Ibid.*, vol. i, 512; vol. iv, 347.

[173] May 20, 1708, two appeals from Barbadoes were referred to the Committee on Appeals from the Plantations.   They were considered eight

The relations of the Board of Trade to the Privy Council during Queen Anne's reign were essentially those of a committee of that body; and its representations, in general, were confirmed without reference to any other committee.   There are a few exceptions, however, which seem to indicate that any objection to a representation, or a petition against it, would lead to the reference of both to the Committee on Appeals from the Plantations.[174] If there was no objection to a representation of the Board, it was not so referred. Another fact stands out prominently.   The committee of the Privy Council, so far as plantation business was concerned, confined itself almost wholly to the consideration of appeals, petitions, and complaints. It was not a committee for general plantation business, nor did any such committee exist.

It is well known that George I, because of his inability to understand English, left the general management of affairs much more in the hands of his ministers than had preceding kings; but it is possible

days later by a "Committee for hearing of Appeals from the Plantations and for the Affairs of Jersey and Guernsey." The entry in the latter case, however, states that they had been referred "to this Committee." The same thing occurred on October 27, of the same year. August 9, 1710, an appeal of Rawlin Robbins from Jersey was referred to the "Committee on Jersey and Guernsey." October 24, following, this appeal was considered by the "Committee of the Whole Council for the Affairs of Jersey and Guernsey and for hearing Appeals from the Plantations," with the entry that it had been referred "to the Committee." See: Privy Council *Register*, "Anne," vol. iv, 95-96, 101, 176, 79, 135.

[174] July 2, 1702, a representation of the Board of Trade on some laws of Barbadoes was referred to the "Committee of the Whole Council." See: Privy Council *Register*, "Anne," vol. i, 166. October 25, 1714, a representation of the Board for the disallowance of a Jamaica law was referred to the Committee on Appeals from the Plantations. The petition against the representation in this case was contested. See: *Ibid.*, "George I," vol. i, 102, 122.

that this change, so far as colonial affairs were concerned, has been exaggerated.[175] It has already been shown that the Privy Council was rapidly becoming a registering body instead of a deliberative one. The action of George I only tended to complete this movement. All colonial business, except that of registering actions already decided upon, was transferred to committees, or rather to a committee. October 1, 1714, it was ordered:

> That the whole Privy Council or any three or more of them be, and hereby are appointed a Committee for the Affairs of Jersey and Guernsey, Hearing of Appeals from ye Plantations, and other Matters that shall be referred to them, and that they proceed to hear and examine such causes as have been referred to committees of ye council by her late Majesty and report the same with their opinions thereupon to this Board.[176]

This was followed up in February, 1715, by another order referring all petitions already before the council to this committee of the whole.[177]

It should be noted that these two orders transferred business from the Privy Council to one committee and not to a series of committees. Nevertheless the Privy Council *Register* for the next few years shows a be-

---

[175] The Privy Council *Register* shows that during the reign of Anne extraordinary matters which came before the sovereign in council were referred to a committee to investigate and recommend whatever action seemed desirable.

[176] Privy Council *Register*, "George I," vol. 1, 89. This order supplied a general rule for cases which had received a similar disposition under Anne, the difference being that during her reign each case was disposed of separately.

[177] February 23, 1715. "It is this day ordered by His Majesty in Council, That all petitions presented and depending before the Board be, and they are hereby referr'd to the Right Honoble the Lords of the Committee of the whole Council to examine the same and give such directions thereupon as their Lordships shall judge proper." — Privy Council *Register*, "George I," vol. 1, 189-190.

wildering array of variously named committees. There are committees on "Appeals from the Plantations;" of the "whole Council;" "for Appeals from the Plantations and for the Affairs of Jersey and Guernsey;" for "the Irish bills and other Affairs;" for "Jersey and Guernsey;" [178] for "Appeals from the Plantations and from Jersey and Guernsey;" for hearing "Appeals, Complaints, etc.;" for hearing "Appeals, Complaints, etc., from the Plantations and for the Affairs of Jersey and Guernsey;" [179] for the "Affairs of the Planta- from the Plantations, Jersey and Guernsey;" [181] and the Plantations;" for the "Affairs of the Planta- tions;" [180] for the "Irish Bills and to hear Appeals from the Plantations, Jersey and Guernsey;" [181] and simply "Committees" with no further title. [182] Here are a dozen different names used to describe commit- tees and the list is not exhaustive. [183] It looks as if the clerks in the Privy Council office exercised their wits to get every possible variation in the names.

Aside from the different names used to designate these committees, there is nothing to indicate that there was more than the one committee of the whole at work.   General plantation business was considered by the committee on appeals from the plantations as were also appeals from Guernsey. [184] The Committee

---

[178] Privy Council *Register*, "George I," vol. i, 102, 304, 222, 402, 248.

[179] — *Ibid.*, vol. ii, 81, 112, 124.

[180] — *Ibid.*, vol. iii, 441, 76, 340.

[181] — *Ibid.*, vol. v, 124.

[182] — *Ibid.*, vol. iv, 93, 129, 162.

[183] Several variations of the above titles occur and each name appears more than once, some of them very frequently, although for the sake of brevity one reference only is cited.

[184] January 29, 1717, the "Committee for hearing Appeals from the Plan-

for the Affairs of Jersey, Guernsey and the Plantations heard appeals from Jersey and from the plantations.[185] Questions concerning the internal administration of England, such as waterworks for Chelsea, and a charter of incorporation for the musicians and dancing-masters of London, and colonial business were considered at the same committee meeting.[186] Most significant of all, however, is the very common reference of business to a committee of the whole council and the later consideration of this same business by some committee calling itself by a different name, though the entry states that it had been referred "to this committee." [187]

tations" considered appeals from New York and from Guernsey [Privy Council *Register*, "George I," vol. ii, 84]. July 25, 1722, a committee with this title prepared heads of a scheme for a civil court in Gibraltar [*Ibid.*, vol. iv, 66]. December 17, 1720, a committee "for hearing Appeals, etc., from the Plantations" considered an appeal from Guernsey [*Ibid.*, vol. iii, 88]. November 8, 1714, a committee "for hearing of Appeals from the Plantations" reported upon a representation of the Board of Trade on an act passed in Jamaica, which later became the most common business for the "Committee on Plantation Affairs" [*Ibid.*, vol. i, 102].

185 — *Ibid.*, vol. v, 80.

186 December 14, 1722, "a Committee" disposed of the following: acts and appeals from Barbadoes; business from Jersey, Guernsey, Gibraltar, and the Isle of Man; and waterworks for Chelsea, England. May 29, 1725, a similar committee investigated a murder case at Newgate prison, London, and the dispute between Governor Shute of Massachusetts and the House of Representatives of that colony. May 10, 1717, a committee "for hearing Appeales, Complaints, etc." examined a petition against a charter incorporating the musicians and dancing-masters of London, considered Mumford's appeal from New York, and disposed of some miscellaneous business from Jersey and Guernsey. See: Privy Council *Register*, "George I," vol. iv, 162, vol. v, 60, vol. ii, 112.

187 July 6, 1716, Peter Somnas' petition for lands in New Jersey was referred "to a Committee of the Whole Council." January 14, 1717, this petition was reported upon by a committee on "Appeals from the Plantations from Jersey and Guernsey." Numerous other entries similar to this occur. See: Privy Council *Register*, "George I," vol. i, 425, vol. ii, 81.

The personnel of this variously named committee during the reign of George I is very much the same as it was under Anne. One or more of the chief secretaries of state were frequently present, the lord president and one or both of the chief justices nearly always so, and usually the president or some other member of the board.[188] The attendance is frequently larger than under Anne or William, being as high as fourteen, although four, six, and eight are common.

This committee considered a much wider range of plantation business than it did during the preceding reigns. Practically all of the representations from the Board were referred to it by the council, the only exceptions, apparently, being those for the appointment of colonial councillors.[189] Petitions, complaints, memorials, etc. were regularly referred to the same committee. In most cases these were further referred to the Board of Trade for examination, and the committee usually confined itself to a consideration of the facts as reported by that body.[190] The most important member of the committee was the secretary of state for the Southern Department, who was responsible

---

[188] The attendance at the "Committee on Plantation Affairs" on October 25, 1721 [Privy Council *Register*, "George I," vol. iii, 340], is fairly representative of the regular attendance at these various committees. Those present were: Lord President, L. Lechmere, E. of Sutherland, Mr. Comptroller, L. Vis. Townsend, Mr. Chancellor of the Exchequer, L. Carteret, Master of the Rolls.

[189] Privy Council *Register*, "George I," vol. iv, 60. See also the other volumes for this reign.

[190] December 17, 1720, the committee had before it a representation of the Board of Trade upon a petition of William West for some waste lands in Maine. Counsel for Mr. West, that against his claims, and the committee examined the maps submitted in proof of the various claims. It is apparent that this is the work of a court of appeals and not of a court of first instance. See: Privy Council *Register*, "George I," vol. iii, 88.

for the colonies.[191] This would seem to indicate that the relation of the Board of Trade to the Privy Council was gradually resolving itself into its relation to the secretary of state. It has already been shown that the latter official was gradually taking over the functions of the Board after 1715. This change synchronizes with the growth in the activity and the increase in the general range of colonial business considered by the Committee of Council.

September 20, 1727, the Privy Council was again dissolved and a new one appointed.[192] In almost the same words as those used in 1714, the whole of the Privy Council or any three or more of them were appointed "a Committee" for the affairs of Jersey and Guernsey, for hearing appeals from the plantations, and other matters which might be referred to them. They were also to take over such questions as were still pending before "committees" of the Privy Council.[193] This again is a record of the appointment of one committee and not a series of committees; but, nevertheless, the record shows the same general confusion of titles as before.

The three names which appear regularly in the

---

[191] He was not always present at the meetings, but frequently was. Newcastle was much more regular in his attendance during the first few years of his administration than he was in the later years.

[192] Privy Council *Register*, "George II," vol. 1, 118.

[193] "It is this day ordered by His Majesty in Council that the whole Privy Council or any three or more of them be and they are hereby appointed a committee for the affairs of Jersey and Guernsey, Hearing of Appeals from the Plantations and other matters that shall be referred to them, and that they proceed to hear and examine such causes as have been already referred to committees of the Council and report the same with their opinion thereupon to His Majesty at this Board." — Privy Council *Register*, "George II," vol. 1, 121.

printed colonial records are: "A Committee of the
Lords of His Majesty's Most Honourable Privy
Council," "The Right Honourable the Lords of the
Committee of Council for Hearing Appeals from the
Plantations," and the "Committee of Council for
Plantation Affairs." [194] These are used so constantly,
especially after 1722, as to give the impression that
they were permanent organs of the Privy Council, and
writers on colonial history have assumed that there
were at least two distinct committees; one on general plantation affairs and one on appeals. This
impression is almost inevitable if only the printed
records or even the Board of Trade papers are examined; but an investigation of the Privy Council
Register soon convinces one that no such distinct committees existed in function, in organization, or in
personnel.

The "Committee on Plantation Affairs" appears in
the colonial records to have limited its activity to miscellaneous administrative questions from the colonies;
but it did not, for on January 15, 1735, a committee
bearing this title issued orders for hearing appeals
from Massachusetts, Virginia, Rhode Island, and
Jamaica, and also considered a complaint from
Guernsey.[195] Another such committee reported on a
scheme for supporting sea officers' poor widows.[196]
Others considered appeals from Jersey,[197] issued or-

194 See the printed records for New York, New Jersey, North Carolina,
and Pennsylvania.

195 This same committee approved an additional instruction for the
Governor of South Carolina. See: Privy Council *Register*, "George II,"
vol. iv, 82-85.

196 July 12, 1732, *Ibid.*, vol. iii, 1.

197 July 21, 1729, *Ibid.*, vol. ii, 30.

ders for sending supplies to Alderney,[198] ordered the
Northumberland militia to be put in readiness,[199] reported on building a hospital in Jersey,[200] and issued
orders on appeals from the plantations and from the
Isle of Man.[201]

Appeals were usually heard by a committee specifically called one for "Hearing Appeals from the
Plantations," but such committees by no means limited their activity to judicial business, as the work
done on two different dates will show.   July 1, 1740,
such a committee considered appeals and in addition
reported on the commission for settling the boundary
dispute between Massachusetts and Rhode Island,
confirmed the appointment of councilors for Nevis,
recommended that stores be sent to Jersey and referred
back to the Board a proposed instruction about bills
of credit.[202] Another committee of the same name disposed of some appeals from Jamaica, and then reported on the laws of Massachusetts and of Pennsylvania, recommended that ordnance stores should be
sent to North Carolina, and reported upon a petition
for some islands in the Delaware River.[203] Almost any
number of similar illustrations could be given of the
action of committees on appeals, as they appear to
have disposed of whatever miscellaneous business
awaited the action of a committee.[204]

[198] November 19, 1745, Privy Council *Register*, "George II," vol. x, 250-
255.

[199] December 3, 1745, *Ibid.*

[200] May 3, 1750, *Ibid.*, vol. xiii, 4.

[201] October 6, 1763, Privy Council *Register*, "George III," vol. iii, 112.

[202] — *Ibid.*, vol. vii, 132.

[203] June 24, 1756, *Ibid.*, vol. xvi, 210-228.

[204] July 8, 1745, a "Committee on Appeals" after disposing of some ap-

The work of the "Committee of the Privy Council" shows about the same variety as the two committees considered above. At one session it considered an appeal from Guernsey, heard a complaint about the election of a vintner for Cambridge University, and examined and revised the instructions for the governor of Barbadoes.[205] At another meeting it had under consideration the dispute between Governor Burnet and the assembly of Massachusetts; complaints against Governor Everard of North Carolina and of the obstruction to admiralty jurisdiction in the same colony;[206] disputes about the office of town clerk in Falmouth, England;[207] referred numerous petitions to the Board of Trade; considered representations from that body on the laws of various colonies; and transacted a variety of other business. Thus this committee heard appeals and took charge of general plantation matters.

Appeals from the plantations were considered, not only by the above committees, but also by those called "Committees for the Affairs of Jersey and Guernsey,"[208] and even by those "to consider the Irish

pellate business considered the draft of a charter for Maidstone in the county of Kent, a subject rather far removed from appeals from the plantations. December 8, 1736, another committee with the same name heard appeals from Jamaica; made orders on appeals from Barbadoes, Jersey, Guernsey, Rhode Island, and Gibraltar; considered a representation of the Board of Trade on a petition from Messrs. Crimble and Huey of North Carolina; and referred to the Board a report of the exports of the East India Company and a complaint of South Carolina against the government of Georgia. See: Privy Council *Register*, "George II," vol. v, 27-33, vol. x, 148.

[205] July 16, 1728, *Ibid.*, vol. i, 336.

[206] All of the above matters were disposed of, October 23, 1729. See: Privy Council *Register*, "George II," vol. ii, 63.

[207] November 1, 1734, *Ibid.*, vol. iv, 22.

[208] November 21, 1745, *Ibid.*, vol. x, 255.

A PRIVY COUNCIL COMMITTEE MEETING

Note the presence of the principal cabinet officers. After disposing of this question from Virginia it considered business from Jersey, Guernsey, and the West Indies

[*Privy Council Register, "George II," vol. II, 58*]

Bills;" [209] consequently, even on judicial business, there were no absolutely distinct committees other than the "Committee of the whole Council." The same is true for all general plantation business. This is further emphasized by the continual consideration of affairs at a committee bearing one name when the record shows it was referred to, or was appointed to be heard before, one of a different name.

So far as mere names are concerned, however, usage in the council office was gradually evolving a somewhat settled phraseology. For the first twenty years after the Board was organized the most common reference of colonial business was to the Committee for Hearing Appeals from the Plantations.[210] That became a settled form of reference for petitions, for appeals, and, in general, for specific complaints. General plantation business was regularly referred to "a Committee" of the Privy Council until about 1732, when the more familiar reference to the "Committee for Plantation Affairs" becomes the accepted form of entry. The other forms of reference, however, were still used more or less. The change in the form of entry by the clerks accounts for most of the changes in the name of the committee of the Privy Council which occur in the printed colonial records.

The personnel of none of these differently named committees distinguishes it from the others. The secretaries of state were occasionally present, but somewhat more frequently when the committee is

[209] November 25, 1745, the "Committee to consider the Irish Bills" after finishing that business heard appeals from Jersey and Rhode Island. Privy Council *Register*, "George II," vol. x, 258.

[210] See the Privy Council *Register* for the period.

called one for plantation affairs.[211] The attendance of others, such as the president of the Board, the president of the council, and one or both of the chief justices is not materially different from what it was during the earlier reigns. Halifax seems to have been a little less constant in his attendance after the increase in the authority of the Board than he was before. He and the others mentioned above, however, attended committees bearing different names without apparent discrimination.

A great deal of the work of council committees was of a purely formal character, such as referring papers to the proper officials or boards. It was, apparently, only more important business which brought out the chief officers of state, routine matters being largely left to the president of the council and its minor members.

As this committee had no special title, the clerks evidently tried to make the name descriptive of the chief business transacted at the meeting, which was the simplest method of making the entries. As time went on usage settled upon three or four descriptive titles for the various meetings, and these appear in the Board of Trade papers, and in the colonial records. Such names, however, are descriptive and not specific, and do not represent distinct organs of the Privy Council, as there was but one committee of that body, namely, the Committee of the whole Council, which had power to hear and dispose of any business that awaited the action of a committee.

The relation of the Board of Trade to the Privy

---

211 Newcastle rarely attended these committee meetings from 1735 to 1748. Bedford attended frequently while he was in office.

Council was a combination of its relation to the council and to this committee of many names. Colonial laws, especially those from the charter colonies, were transmitted to the council and by it referred to the Board. The same was true of petitions, complaints, etc.[212] All formal actions of the Board, such as appointment of members of colonial councils, instructions, recommendations, and representations had to be transmitted to the council for registration and approval before they were binding. For many years these were disposed of directly by the council, but afterward they were regularly referred to the committee and were approved and registered only on its favorable report.

This committee was not hostile to the Board as the latter's president was usually one of the most regular attendants at its meetings. It was the body, however, which coördinated all the various divisions of colonial administration. Here was represented in the persons of the secretaries of state and the chief justices the highest administrative and legal authority in the nation. So long as the Board of Trade was not itself responsible for colonial affairs, it was necessary that the men who were responsible to the nation should direct and control the final action in important cases. This responsibility was in part secured by having all the important work of the Board reviewed by the committee. If the Board desired to explain any of its actions to the committee, the president was so instructed; and the committee occasionally directed the president of the Board to see that certain things were

[212] After 1722 they were regularly referred, first to the committee, and by it to the Board of Trade.

stated in his letters to colonial officials.[213] The committee sometimes ignored and sometimes disapproved the recommendations of the Board; but, considering the importance of this body and its responsibility to the nation, such action was to be expected, although it might lead to delays in colonial administration at critical times.

The relations of the Board and the council are best seen in a case that actually came up for determination. The intestate law of Connecticut is a good illustration. This had been annulled by the decision in the famous case of Winthrop *vs.* Lechmere, and the effect of the decision was of such importance that Governor Talcott and the legislature of Connecticut determined to use every agency possible and to spare no expense in getting the decision reversed. A petition to the king was drawn up by the agents of the colony, who asked that a bill might be brought into Parliament for quieting the people in their estates and enabling them to bequeath their property in future in the manner they had been accustomed to under their former law.[214] This petition was read before the council and referred to the "Committee for hearing Appeales, Complaints, etc.,"[215] which in turn referred it to the Board of Trade to investigate the facts and report with recommenda-

---

[213] March 15, 1742, a Committee of Council considered a representation of the Board of Trade on a law of Massachusetts creating £3600 in bills of credit. The representation was read and "the Committee desired Lord Monson, first Commissioner for Trade and Plantations, to recommend it to that Board, to write to Governor Shirley, acquainting him with the objections against the bill." — Privy Council *Register*, "George II," vol. vii, 112.

[214] "Talcott Papers" in Connecticut Historical Society *Collections*, vol. iv, 187.

[215] Order in Council dated June 10, 1730. *Ibid.*, 200.

tions.[216] The Board summoned the agents, heard their testimony, accepted such documentary material as they offered, and after much deliberation reported its conclusions in the form of a representation. This proposed a bill which granted the desired legislation, but at the same time abrogated the charter. Any proceedings which could call the charter in question were most undesirable from the point of view of the Connecticut officers; consequently the agents, through their attorneys, opposed the representation of the Board before the Committee of Council.[217]

That case brings out the essential difference in the nature of the proceedings before the Board and before the committee. The Board called witnesses, heard testimony, asked questions, examined written proofs, and so arrived at the facts in the case. These facts were then submitted in writing, together with recommendations, to the committee. If no one interfered, this body took final action on the data before it. If the interested parties objected, they could contest the representation before the Council Committee. If it were a question in which one party was working for a certain representation and another against it, both parties could be and usually were heard,[218] but the hearing in this case was purely of the nature of an appeal. No witnesses were called; the agent could not present his case in person, but had to present it

[216] Reference to the Board of Trade by the Committee of Council, June 15 of the same year. "Talcott Papers" in Connecticut Historical Society *Collections*, vol. iv, 201.

[217] Letter of Francis Wilks, the London agent for Connecticut, to Governor Talcott. *Ibid.*, 216-219.

[218] See the complaint of the Mohegan Indians against the colony of Connecticut. *Ibid.*, vols. iv, v, *passim*.

through his counsel, and the hearing took the form of a legal argument of opposing lawyers. With the facts as found by the Board and the case of each party, as presented by the lawyers, before it, the committee either made a definite recommendation to the Privy Council or remanded the whole matter to the Board of Trade for further investigation. Thus the committee was not only a body for keeping colonial affairs, as administered by the Board, closely coördinated with the policy of the cabinet, but it was also a court of review for all actions of the Board.

The whole machinery of the British government for colonial administration included a Board of Trade to investigate, gather facts, and make recommendations; a Committee of the Privy Council to act as a board of review and a court of appeals, both administrative and legal; and the Privy Council, meeting with the king, before which all final actions of importance were registered. This machinery was often slow in action, but the provision for appeals before registration, and even the necessity of registration, afforded all interests an opportunity to be heard, and in the long run it was better to sacrifice speed for fairness.

Frequently the opposing interests abused the privilege of appeal by dilatory motions before the Board and the Committee, such as requests for time to secure proofs from America, delays to enable an agent to secure instructions in regard to some matter that was being considered, and even repetitions of these requests. Another method of delaying final action was to present a counter proposal in some form. The delays and evasive tactics became so apparent in the case of the boundary dispute between Massachusetts and Rhode Island, that the Committee of Council attempted a reform.

This boundary controversy had existed since 1664. In 1734 Rhode Island petitioned the king to determine the question, inasmuch as the colonies had failed to do so through their own commissioners. This petition passed through the regular form of reference, by Order of Council to the Committee of the Privy Council for Plantation Affairs, and by that body to the Board of Trade. There each party was heard by agents and counsel and proofs were submitted on both sides. Finally, in 1738, the Board reported that commissioners should be appointed by the crown to mark out and settle the disputed boundary. This representation went to the committee; and while it was pending there, Francis Wilks, the agent for Massachusetts Bay, petitioned to be heard against the said representation.[219] This petition was referred by Order in Council to the committee,[220] which heard what Wilks had to offer against the representation of the Board, and reported to the king in council that the petition should be denied, and that the proposed commission should be appointed.

In addition, however, the committee sought to check such dilatory motions for the future, by the following recommendation:

> And the said petition appearing to the Lords of the committee to be frivolous and vexatious and to have been preferred only with intent to delay and prevent the settling of the boun-

---

[219] Privy Council *Register*, "George II," vol. vi, 12.

[220] This committee is designated as the one on "Plantation Affairs." The meeting was held November 1, 1738. Those present were the Lord President, Earl of Abercorne, Lord Harrington, Lord Monson, Mr. Speaker, Lord Chief Justice Willes.

daries of the said provinces, their Lordships humbly conceive it may be necessary in order to prevent such frivolous and vexatious applications for the future which tend not only to delay and interrupt the course of proceedings but also to bring unnecessary expense upon those who are obliged to defend themselves against such application that Your Majesty may be pleased to order that the Lords of Your Majesty's most honorable Privy Council for Plantation Affairs do not proceed upon any applications by petition or otherwise praying to be heard against any determinations of the Lords Commissioners for Trade and Plantations upon any matters which have or shall be referred to them by Your Majesty in Council or by the Lords of the Committee for Plantation Affairs, upon which it shall appear that the said Lords Commissioners have heard the persons concerned, either by themselves their counsel or agents unless such petitioner or petitioners or some person in his or their behalf do first enter into some sufficient security to pay such costs as shall be awarded by Your Majesty in Council thereupon. And their Lordships do further humbly pray that Your Majesty may be pleased to order the same rule to be observed in all cases, which shall come before the said committee of Council in consequence of any commissions that may have been or shall hereafter be issued by order of Your Majesty in council for settling or adjusting any boundaries or other special matters in dispute in any of Your Majesty's Colonies on Plantations in America.

This recommendation was embodied in an Order in Council and remained as a rule of procedure before the committee.[221]

By this order the Committee of Council was made even more strictly a court of appeals than before, and from its date, November 30, 1738, it was necessary to give bond before any person would be heard before the committee against any representation, order, in-

[221] Privy Council *Register,* "George II," vol. vi, 12-36.

struction, or recommendation of the Board.[222] This added to the expense of the prosecution of affairs at the Board of Trade and before the council, yet the colonies could not safely spare any expense when their interests were at stake.

The pleading of causes before the committee was a phase of legal practice which became so important that some lawyers made a specialty of that class of business. The best legal talent in England was frequently employed by contestants, and even the attorney- and solicitor-generals at times appeared as counsel.[223] Ferdinando John Paris was perhaps the most efficient of the lawyers who were frequently employed by the colonies, and his letters reveal both the customary methods of procedure and the tricks which were sometimes employed to win a case.[224]

The Secretary of State and Executive Boards

The relation of the Board of Trade to the secretary of state for the Southern Department is difficult to state, as it varied from time to time. The secretary was responsible for all colonial business and the Board was in a great measure only a division of his department. Some colonial business was transacted directly by the secretary, although much of it was in the hands of the Board. The amount of work done in the secretary's office was not the same under different

---

[222] References to this regulation are frequently met with. See especially the letters of Ferdinando John Paris in the New Jersey *Archives, passim.*

[223] Attorney-general York and Solicitor-general Talbot were attorneys for Winthrop in his case against Lechmere. Connecticut Historical Society *Collections,* vol. v, 77.

[224] See the tricks of Winthrop's attorneys in the hearing before the council in the case of Winthrop *vs.* Lechmere, cited in *Ibid.,* vol. v, 78.

administrations, and seems to have been determined by the personal wishes of the official in charge. At times he left the whole management of colonial affairs to the Board; at other times he transferred almost all of its work to his own office.

Until after the accession of George I the general rule was to give the Board a free hand, and to hold it responsible for all colonial correspondence, instructions, and even the main features of administrative policy. The secretary of state, however, was the head of the colonial department and kept a close grasp of all that went on. William Penn appears to have depended upon his influence with the chief ministers to ward off any hostile attacks from the Board; but his letters indicate that it was not an easy task at times, especially when the Board was attacking his proprietary rights.[224a] None of the secretaries permitted any action which had even the appearance of ignoring their office. Sunderland at one time required that all representations of the Board to the queen should be sent to him, as he had a right to know the contents of any document relating to his department before it was submitted to the sovereign.[225] Carteret enforced the same rule during his administration, and there are many entries in the Board of Trade Journal of re-

---

[224a] See the Penn-Logan *Correspondence*, vol. i, *passim*.

[225] "Amongst the papers which were carried yesterday to the Council to be laid before the queen there was one from your Board in behalf of Colonel Lambert to be Lieutenant-governor of Nevis; which I was surprised to find, having never seen it, or heard anything of that matter from you before. I thought it had been usual to acquaint the secretary of state with all business that relates immediately to his province before it be brought to the Council; I am sure it is so reasonable that I may very well expect it; therefore I must desire that it may be so for the future." — Sunderland to the Board, January 3, 1707, C.O. 324, 9, p. 133.

quests that he lay the enclosed representation before the king.[226] The more common practice, however, was to send the original representation to the council and a copy of it to the secretary of state for his information.[227] In addition to this the Board regularly sent a letter to the secretary of state summarizing the changes in such long documents as the instructions to a governor,[228] which could be done in one or two pages, while the document itself covered nearly a hundred.

Certain kinds of business were regularly referred directly to the secretary of state by the Board. In general these were questions which involved the relations of the colonies to foreign countries, such as disputes over the boundary between the French and the English in the Ohio country or in the region of the Great Lakes;[229] events which concerned the regulation or disposal of the armed forces in America; relations with the Indians, especially if they threatened trouble;[230] violations of the trade and navigation laws;[231] and domestic disorders, such as the riots in New Jersey over land titles or the resistance to the

[226] New York *Colonial Documents*, vol. v, 584, 650, and *passim* give copies of many of these letters.

[227] Sunderland made this the rule, June 1, 1708, for the rest of his administration.

[228] Sometimes these were also addressed to the Privy Council or its Committee. See the *Journal* for the years 1725-1749.

[229] New York *Colonial Documents*, vol. v, 815, 845, vols. vi, vii, *passim*.

[230] — *Ibid.*, vol. v, 468, 815, and *passim*, vol. vi, 772-773 and *passim*, vol. vii, *passim*; North Carolina *Colonial Records*, vol. iii, 334.

[231] January 5, 1708, the Board notified Sunderland of illegal trading it had discovered between Carolina and Portugal by way of Rhode Island. It advised that the only successful method of breaking it up would be to empower the British consul in Portugal to examine all ships from the plantations and seize all that carried prohibited goods. See: Board to Sunderland, C.O. 5, 1292, p. 73. Many similar instances are given in the records. See, also: Beer, Geo. *British Colonial Policy*, 1754-1765, 229-244, for a full discussion

Stamp Act.[232] Sometimes information on the above was received in the letters of the colonial officials and sometimes by direct testimony before the Board.[233] In either case it was promptly transmitted to the secretary of state for his information.

The secretaries of state were members of the Board of Trade but were excused from regular attendance. When questions of more than ordinary importance came up, they were summoned to attend, and were occasionally present without special invitation.[234] The secretary of state for the Southern Department attended more frequently than did other members of the ministry, but on several occasions practically the whole cabinet was present at the Board meetings.[235] The subjects under consideration which led to these conferences with the ministers were Indian Wars in America, bounties on naval stores,[236] provisions for the settlement of the Germans from the Palatinate,[237] and the disorders in New Jersey. The Board was request-

of illegal trade and the general reference of such information to the secretary of state.

[232] Any serious situation in the government of any colony was regularly brought to the attention of the secretary of state. See: New York *Colonial Documents*, vol. vi, 597; New Jersey *Archives*, vol. vii, 299.

[233] For an investigation of illegal trade to Curaçoa, in which witnesses appeared before the Board, see: Board of Trade *Journal*, 21, pp. 270-336.

[234] See: Board of Trade *Journal*, 21, p. 98; 23, p. 100; 28, January 8, 13, 27, 28; 36, pp. 84, 87, 115.

[235] April 14, 1726, Newcastle and Townshend were in attendance as members of the Board. Trade to Africa was under consideration and they attended regularly for several days. Newcastle, Bedford, Sandwich, and Pelham attended the Board, July 12, 1749, to consider the disorders in New Jersey. See: Board of Trade *Journal*, 36, pp. 57, 84-225; also Board of Trade *Commercial Series I*, 13, M. 88 and *Commercial Series II*, 646, pp. 256, 284.

[236] January 8 and 13, 1719, Board of Trade *Journal*, 28.

[237] — *Ibid.*, 21, p. 98.

ed to attend cabinet meetings and the Committee of the Privy Council, even more frequently than it summoned the chief officers of state to attend its own meetings.[238] In this way the work of the secretary of state's office was closely connected with that of the Board of Trade.

The Board was kept informed of whatever was done in the secretary of state's office relating to the colonies until the accession of George I. April 14, 1715, the Board requested Secretary Stanhope to give it notice of any nominations of lieutenant-governors in the colonies before their commissions were issued, so that it could object to unsatisfactory or unsuitable officers. This request was disregarded, and George Vaughn was appointed lieutenant-governor of New Hampshire without consulting the Board. This action brought forth an unusually crisp note from the latter on the unfitness of Vaughn for his office, because he was a trader and an owner of saw-mills and hence was not interested in protecting the woods.[239]

---

[238] October 14, 1729, the Board was summoned to attend the Committee of Council on a hearing of two of its representations. In January, 1731, it was asked to appear before the same Committee to assist in the consideration of the bill advocated by the sugar islands. See: Board of Trade *Journal*, 39, p. 262; 41, p. 16.

[239] In stating the unfitness of Vaughn, the Board quoted from a letter of Bellomont's in regard to the appointment of Partridge to the same position as more to the point than anything it could say.

"Mr. Partridge is a millwright by trade, which is a sort of carpenter, and to set a carpenter to preserve woods, is like setting a wolf to keep sheep; I say, to preserve woods, for I take it to be the chiefest part of the trust and business of a lieutenant-governor of that province, to preserve the woods for the king's use.

"Besides he is of the country, and the interest of England is neither in his head or heart. If it be not presumption in me to give advice, I wish some few things were observ'd in the management of the plantations for the time to come. First, that there be great care taken in the choice of the per-

Apparently Stanhope ignored this protest; and as colonial business was gradually transferred to the secretary of state's office, the Board became a mere bureau of information for other parts of the government.

Correspondence with the royal governors had regularly been conducted by the Board of Trade, although governors also frequently sent almost identical letters to the secretary of state. Any matter of grave importance in a colony was reported directly to the latter by the governor, and a statement of the matter also sent to the Board. During the administration of Newcastle all this was changed, as he took over practically the entire correspondence with the colonial governors. Their important letters were then addressed to him; and more or less frequently a summary of their contents was sent to the Board. As Newcastle had also taken over practically all of the executive and administrative work of the Board, there was very little for the latter body to do, except when it had matters directly referred to it for consideration. For that reason the letters of the Board to the colonial governors became short and infrequent. The average of one letter to each governor every two years during this time was not due to any difficulty of communication or of getting work done in the plantation office. It was simply because the Board had nothing to say. If

sons employ'd by the king, from the governor to the meanest officer; I mean that they be men of undoubted probity and well born; secondly, that they be not men of the country, but Englishmen. Thirdly, that they be men of some fortune in England, to be a tye upon them to behave themselves honourably in their respective trusts."

The Board expressed its hearty agreement with this opinion and added that, as Vaughn was interested in several saw mills, he was not one who would care for the woods. See: Board of Trade to Stanhope, August 3, 1715, C.O. 5, 914, pp. 85-87. Cf. Chalmers, Geo. *Introduction to the Revolt.*

letters from America required replies, they were supposed to emanate from Newcastle's office, and not from
the Board.[240] The latter was inefficient, of course, but
it was solely because the secretary of state had made it
so. This period of inefficiency is in marked contrast
with the energy shown in the earlier years of the Board
and can be explained only by the pernicious influence
of Newcastle.[241]

He practically ignored the Board on all questions
of colonial administration and did not even take the
trouble to inform it of the various orders which were
issued by his office, the instructions given to colonial
officials, or the permits for them to absent themselves
from their posts of duty. This condition is disclosed
by the regular and repeated requests of the Board for
Newcastle to furnish information as to what was done,

[240] Governor Belcher in his letters to his brother-in-law and agent in
London, Mr. Richard Partridge, frequently speaks of appealing over the
heads of the Board to the secretary of state, indicating a clear knowledge
of where the real authority resided. See: Massachusetts Historical Society
Collections, sixth series, vol. vi, *passim*.

[241] Channing [*History of the United States*, vol. ii, 235-236] indicates
that the delay in answering letters at times was chargeable to the clerks.
He has evidently overlooked the periods of varying efficiency due to varying
authority.

Apparent slowness in reading communications after they were received
may easily lead to wrong inferences, as the term "read" was used by the
Board in a technical sense. It meant read officially to a quorum of the Board.
No doubt all letters were opened by the secretary of that body and their
contents known to some of the members long before they were read in a
technical sense.

In 1700 letters from Maryland, written on February 2, March 12, and
May 28 were read respectively on May 14, July 26, and July 30, following.
This shows an average of only a little more than two months between the
writing of a letter and its reading by the Board. See: Board of Trade
Journal, 13. The New York *Colonial Documents* show the same promptness
for letters from that colony. They also show similar efficiency after Halifax
became president of the Board.

and further requests that it be notified from time to time of the business transacted in his office. But the later repetition of similar requests indicates that they were ignored by Newcastle and that the Plantation Office remained in ignorance of what was or was not done.[242] This condition, added to the absorption by the secretary of state of the chief work of the Board, made membership on the latter a mere sinecure; but it was only because Newcastle had made it so. The whole responsibility for conditions, good or bad, rests upon him.

Conditions changed soon after the appointment of Halifax as head of the Board, because the relations with the secretary of state were changed.[243] Business was transferred back to the Plantation Office; and, because of the insistent demands of Halifax, more and more authority was given to the Board, until it had practically the full power of a secretary of state. It retained this power for a number of years, was reduced

[242] March 12, 1725, the Board requested Newcastle to apprise it of whatever passed in his office relating to the plantations. See: Board of Trade *Journal*, 35, p. 63. August 23, 1727, it wrote him again that: "Upon looking into our books, we find our predecessors have sometimes found themselves under difficulties for want of being informed of such commissions, orders or instructions as may have passed in the secretaries' offices for persons and matters relating to the plantations. And therefore we desire your Grace would be pleased to give directions that for the future proper notice may be given to this Board of all such commissions, orders and instructions which we apprehend will be for His Majesty's service." — C.O. 324, 11, p. 50.

July 31, 1735, the Board addressed a similar letter to him and called his attention to its letter of 1727, and asked for particular information about leaves of absence. See: *Ibid.*, 12, p. 123.

[243] The friendly relations between Bedford and Halifax have already been indicated. The letters of F. J. Paris to James Alexander also indicate that whatever information reached the secretary of state was soon known to the president of the Board. This was particularly true in 1749. See: New Jersey *Archives*, vol. vii, 238.

in authority for a short time in 1761,[244] and again in 1766; but in 1768 the president was made a full secretary of state for the colonies, thus rendering him entirely independent of the secretary for the Southern Department, and remained so until the Board was abolished in 1782.

The Administrative Boards

The Board of Trade and the commissioners of customs were mutually helpful to each other. The enforcement of the acts of trade rested largely with the customs officials; but it was necessary that they should have the countenance and support of the governors,[245] all instructions to whom were drawn up in the plantation office. A part of these instructions dealt specifically with the enforcement of the acts of trade and navigation, and before they were submitted to the king in council, they were sent to the commissioners of customs for their ratification.[246] This gave the latter an opportunity to add any new clauses or omit any old ones in order to make the instructions correspond with changes which were made in the laws from time to time. Thus, while the Board drafted the governors'

---

[244] Board of Trade *Journal*, 69, p. 265.

[245] "A complaint made by the commissioners of her Majesty's customs in Barbadoes to the Lords commissioners of her Majesty's treasury having been referred to our consideration," it was found that he and other officers had become unpopular because of their enforcement of the laws of trade. "We found it absolutely necessary that not only the officers of the customs, but also of the admiralty should be very particularly recommended to the respective governors of all His Majesty's plantations." — Report of Matthew Prior to the House of Commons, April 24, 1702, in Commons *Journal*, vol. xiii, 502.

[246] Note the modification of Governor Lovelace's instructions at the request of the commissioners of customs. See: New York *Colonial Documents*, vol. v, 41.

instructions, their content, so far as trade laws were concerned, was determined by the commissioners of customs.[247]

Sometimes the latter officials conferred directly with the Board, as they did in January, 1709, when they discussed the desirability of a Virginia law establishing ports in that province, the administration of the law recently passed by Parliament granting bounties on naval stores imported from the plantations, and the question of proper convoys for the merchant fleets from America.[248] Other similar conferences were held from time to time as business seemed to require it. All laws passed in the colonies, which in any way affected the customs or the enforcement of the trade laws, were sent to the commissioners of customs for their criticism. If they found any serious objections to any such laws, the Board recommended them for the royal veto.[249]

The Board of Trade and the customs officials were also mutually helpful to each other as information bureaus. Governors were called upon to furnish reports of the violation of the acts of trade and the best means of enforcing them. This information was

[247] Every copy of an instruction was not necessarily sent to the commissioners of customs, but this was done when changes were made in them. Note the revision in 1752 and the reference to the opinion of the customs officials on the instructions in 1737. See: C.O. 324, 15, p. 324.

[248] Board of Trade Journal, 19, pp. 31-33.

[249] In December, 1730, the Board sent a law of Virginia regulating the shipping of tobacco, to the commissioners of customs for their opinion. They returned the law with a polite refusal to express an opinion unless particularly directed to do so by the king. When it was explained to them that it was only an opinion so far as their own board was concerned, the report was given. See: Board of Trade Journal, 12, pp. 313, 326. Other reports were regularly made and will be discussed more fully under the head of disallowed colonial legislation.

transmitted to the secretary for the commissioners of customs to be laid before that board.[250] On the other hand, the Board of Trade had frequent recourse to the customs officials for information. Some of this was for statistical data of the exportation of various articles from America to England and the colonial imports of British goods, the trade of various ports, and the actual workings of various trade laws affecting the colonies.[251] These accounts are among the most important extant for a study of the trade conditions in America. They also show the actual operation of such laws as those paying bounties for naval stores produced in America,[252] and the famous Molasses Act of 1733, including the eloquent story of its evasion for a long period of years.[253]

The customs officials in America were also used by the Board to gather information, and Randolph and Quary became its most active secret agents. They were untiring in their search for evidence which could be used against the proprietary and charter

[250] See the Bellomont correspondence, in New York *Colonial Documents*, vol. iv, *passim*. Not infrequently information of this character was also sent to the secretary of state. See: Board of Trade *Journal*, 52, p. 31; Board of Trade *Proprieties*, 30, p. 73.

[251] These are bound up mainly in the Board of Trade papers known as *Commercial Series I*, although many are to be found in the set known as Plantations General, and a few are bound up in the most unexpected places. Beer in his *British Colonial Policy, 1754-1765*, has made extensive use of this information and it is copiously cited in his footnotes.

[252] Board of Trade *Commercial Series I*, 13, M 12; C.O. 323, 11, K. 64.

[253] This report is characteristic of all and was as follows:

"An account of the amount of the duties paid in the northern colonies upon the importation of rum or spirits, molasses or syrups, sugar and panels of the growth and produce of any foreign settlements from the year 1733 to the present time, in pursuance of the acts passed in the 6th of his present Majesty's reign for the better encouraging the trade of his Majesty's sugar

colonies;[254] and, as the encouragement given to pirates
and the failure to observe the acts of trade were the
main charges against those governments, the policy
of the Board readily dovetailed into the plans of the
customs officials.

The Board had no control over these men, although
it did at one time use them as agents.[255] Their appointment belonged to the commissioners of customs or
their political superiors. If members of the Board
played any part in their selection, it was because of
their personal influence with those who held the ap-

colonies in America, distinguishing each year, also, how much of the said
duties was received on merchandise and how much on prizes.

		DUTIES					
		Merchandise			Prize		
From Xmas	To Xmas	£	s.	d.	£	s.	d.
1733	1734	330	11	1½			
1734	1735	151	4	¼			
1735	1736	292	13	9½			
1736	1737	220	1	6			
1737	1738	68	16	0			
1738	1739	108	11	4			
1739	1740	25	0	0			
1740	1741	100	15	6			
1741	1742	722	7	6	140	1	6
1742	1743	461	19	1½	41	5	9
1743	1744	234	17	9	66	14	2¾
1744	1745	98	8	9	3081	10	6¼
1745	1746	354	17	7½	124	17	3
1746	1747	460	15	5½	1259	5	3¼
1747	1748	693	4	6	2762	13	4¾
1748	1749	1279	0	4½	139	16	3
		5603	4	4¼	7616	4	2

Customs House London, 3 Dec., 1750."   C.O. 5, 38, Appendix 4.

[254] See the numerous letters of Quary to the Board, in New York *Colonial
Documents*, vols. iv, v, *passim*; Chalmers, Geo. *Introduction to the Revolt*,
vol. 1, 380; Penn-Logan *Correspondence, passim*; Shepherd, Wm. *Proprietary Government in Pennsylvania*, 355, 502-503, 508, 542.

[255] See the correspondence with Robert Quary and Edward Randolph, in
New York *Colonial Documents*, vol. iv, *passim*.

pointing power, and not because of their official connection with the Board of Trade. The surveyors of customs were members of the councils in each of the royal provinces in their departments, which enabled them to perform their duties to better advantage and afforded them additional opportunities of securing information for the Board.

As in the case of the customs and the admiralty the Board of Trade and the treasury assisted each other. Claims from America for money were referred to the Board for its opinion as to whether they should be paid. Colonial officers also appealed to it for aid in securing a settlement of their claims upon the treasury. Perhaps the most prominent case of this is that of Bridger who, for many years, was surveyor of the woods in America.[256] According to his own accounts he was a most efficient officer, but for some reason he was finally dismissed by the treasury without a settlement of his salary and expenses. As he had considered himself chiefly responsible to the Board of Trade and had reported most regularly to that body, he appealed to it for support in pressing his claims upon the treasury. The Board also asked for the support of the treasury in securing such a revision of the laws of trade as would encourage non-competitive American industries, such as the production of potash[257] and pig iron.

In time of war the treasury as well as the secretary

---

[256] Board of Trade to the commissioners of the treasury, October 22, 1719, C.O. 5, 915, pp. 306-307.

[257] March 15, 1751, the Board advised the treasury officials that the removal of the tariff of 1672 upon American potash would encourage its production in the colonies. See: C.O. 324, 15, pp. 172-174.

of state had recourse to the Board. The latter needed information as to the condition of the colonies for defense, how many troops each could furnish, what kind and what quantity of arms they had, and the time necessary for them to supply their forces for any undertaking.[258]

In the last two wars against the French, the crown adopted the policy of repaying to the colonies the principal part of the expenditures which they had incurred in aid of the British arms. It was no small task to apportion the parliamentary grant in just proportion to the actual expenditures of the different colonial governments. The treasury did not attempt the task, but asked the Board to investigate the accounts and claims of various kinds and to determine the amount of money justly due each claimant.[259] Some of these accounts were very complicated, as each colony had its own paper money the value of which was not the same in any two; and, as colonial accounts were in terms of paper money, it was difficult to reduce them to equivalent sterling values. Prices of clothing and supplies also varied in the different colonies, and some commissaries had paid higher prices for their supplies than had been paid by other colonies for similar goods. It was manifestly unfair to pay for the bad bargaining of colonial agents, as it might become a means of fleecing the British

[258] See the report of the Board of Trade, May 11, 1756, for the detailed information it supplied for the use of other departments of the government in time of war, in New Jersey *Archives*, vol. viii, part ii, 217.

[259] In the latter part of 1749 the Board had under its consideration the claims of the northern colonies because of the expedition to Canada. See: Board of Trade *Journal*, 57.

treasury.   New Jersey had a number of claims for unusual charges and after careful investigation the Board rejected them.[260]

During the French and Indian War the Chancellor of the Exchequer asked the Board for advance estimates of the colonial expenditures, which were furnished and show the probable expenses of each colony.[261]   Thus the Board was made the agency for determining the amount of aid the colonies should receive and for distributing these large sums of money among them in accordance with their deserts.   Even in time of peace, any unusual expenditure in behalf of the colonies was entrusted to the Board, such, for example, as the distribution of the £103,300 for the relief of the settlers in Nevis and St. Christopher Islands.[262]   In this case the act of Parliament which appropriated the money specified that the Board should take charge of the disbursements.

The relations of the Board of Trade to the admiralty were very similar to those with the customs officers. All governors were given instructions as to admiralty jurisdiction; but these, like the instructions in regard to trade, were prepared by the law officers of the crown and the Admiralty Board.   The governor's commission for holding admiralty courts came directly from the admiralty, and the Board of Trade only

---

260 See the detailed report of the Board, February 28, 1750, on the above, especially its discussion of the claims of New Jersey, in New Jersey *Archives*, vol. vii, 383-400.

261 See the request of Secretary Hardinge of February 5, 1756, and the answer of the Board a week later, in New Jersey *Archives*, vol. viii, part ii, 205 and *note*.

262 The above provision is a part of the act for licensing hackney coaches. See: Commons *Journal*, vol. xvii, 224.

acted as a forwarding agent.   The latter was also able
to furnish the Admiralty Board with information
which came to it from its correspondence with the
royal governors, the surveyors of the customs, and
from direct testimony in regard to illegal trade.   In
some cases of this kind the admiralty was asked to
furnish protection for witnesses who had promised
to testify before the Board.[263]   It was also informed by
the latter body of the need of revenue cutters in America to enforce the trade laws, and the places where
they could render the most efficient service.   The
Board also rendered efficient aid to the admiralty in
stamping out piracy in America by instructing all
its officers to assist in destroying the nefarious practice, and the first governor sent to New York under
the Board rendered the greatest possible service in this
cause.[264]

The admiralty had the general disposition of the
fleet, and at times the Board of Trade asked that war
vessels be sent to America to protect colonial interests; sometimes the admiralty opposed these requests.
Halifax was not content to take no for an answer in
1750 when he desired ships of force for the protection
of Nova Scotia and appealed to Newcastle and the
rest of the cabinet to overrule the admiralty in the
matter.[265]   Such cases are not common, but this inci-

---

[263] January 16, 1760, the Board of Trade asked the admiralty to furnish
protection for one, Radcliffe Cross, a mariner who had promised to testify
about illegal trade, but was afraid he would be pressed if he attended the
Board as often as the latter wished. See: Board of Trade *Commercial
Series II*, 645, p. 19.

[264] See the correspondence of Bellomont with the various executive boards,
in New York *Colonial Documents*, vol. iv, *passim*.

[265] "The Board of Admiralty being of opinion that it will not be necessary to send any ships of force to Nova Scotia, I take it for granted Lord

dent shows how insistent an able and energetic man at the head of the Board could be in securing what he conceived necessary from the admiralty.

The Bishop of London

The Bishop of London exercised ecclesiastical jurisdiction in the colonies, and was an ex officio member of the Board of Trade.[266] His relations to that body were very similar to those of the Admiralty Board and the commissioners of customs. He used it as a clearing house for many of his dealings with the colonies and through it controlled the governors' instructions in regard to ecclesiastical affairs. He usually attended the Board when commissions or instructions were under consideration, and in case he could not be present, copies were sent to him for his approval before they were submitted to the council.[267]

Information in the governors' letters which concerned his ecclesiastical jurisdiction was transcribed and sent to him for his information.[268] In this way

Sandwich will not think himself obliged to lay the affair before the Cabinet Council.

"As I conceive it to be a measure absolutely necessary and one, which if neglected, is likely to be attended with the worst consequences, I have in the inclosed paper thrown together my reasons in support of it in as short and clear a manner as I have been able to do and beg leave to submit them to your Grace's consideration. If they have weight with you, My Lord, I hope you will support the measure proposed, and recommend it to such other ministers as compose his Majesty's Cabinet Council. The pursuance of it, My Lord, will be attended by neither hazard nor expense; the neglect of it will probably be attended by both." — Halifax to Newcastle, March 6, 1750, in British Museum *Additional Manuscripts*, 32724, f. 165.

[266] His name is given among the other great officers of state in the commission of the Board, in Board of Trade *Miscellanies*, 12, pp. 439-453. The *Journal* shows he was present on many occasions.

[267] This was done only in case of changes in that portion of the instructions relating to ecclesiastical affairs.

[268] This was done in the case of Bellomont's statements as to the needs

he was supplied with a great deal of first-hand knowledge of religious needs and conditions in America. He frequently gave suggestions as to how conditions could be improved, and at his instance the Board added a new clause to the governors' instructions which directed them to see that suitable laws were enacted for the punishment of blasphemy, profanity, adultery, polygamy, profanation of the Sabbath, and other crimes against common morality. The instructions also specified that these laws should be enforced by the civil courts upon testimony furnished by the church wardens.[269]

When new members of the provincial councils were to be approved, their names were submitted to the bishop for any objections he might have to the religious principles of any of the men.[270] Colonial laws touching religion or religious questions were referred to him for his consideration as regarded his ecclesiastical jurisdiction,[271] just as they were sent to the crown attorneys for any objection "in point of law." Sometimes the bishop was requested to be

of religious instruction among the Indians. See: Board of Trade *Journal*, 12, p. 429. Extracts from Hunter's letters were also sent to him. See: C.O. 5, 995, p. 301.

[269] The bishop had petitioned the king to have new instructions given on this point and also in regard to schools. This petition was referred to the Committee of Council, which on May 3, 1727, ordered the Board to prepare instructions in accordance with the petition. See: New Jersey *Archives*, vol. v, 160-161. When the Board took up the matter the bishop was summoned to assist in the work. See: Board of Trade *Journal*, 37, p. 128. See also the bishop's request that protestant ministers alone should celebrate marriages, Bishop to the Board, November 12, 1764, New Jersey *Archives*, vol. ix, 504.

[270] — *Ibid.*, vol. iv, 168-169.

[271] Note what was done with the North Carolina laws in 1761, C.O. 5, 325, p. 170.

present and assist the Board in the consideration of such laws, as was done in 1705 in the case of a Maryland law relating to popery;[272] at other times the bishop insisted that he should be heard before laws were confirmed.[273] Any serious objection by him was fatal to an act and was certain to lead to the royal veto.[274]

The Board did not always show entire sympathy with the way the bishop exercised his ecclesiastical control, especially with the class of ministers which were sent to the colonies. Complaints of the character of several of these had come to the Board, and in 1715 that body informed the bishop that he should see that "persons of piety, principles and exemplary life" should be sent to America. It also informed him that it had received accounts of some ministers "which rather administers to the occasion of scandal than contributes to the propagation of Christianity."[275]

Two years later it took occasion to administer an-

[272] The following entry appears in the *Journal*, November 28, 1705: "Ordered that a letter be writ to the Lord Bishop of London to acquaint him that the Board are desirous of his Lordship's assistance tomorrow morning in the consideration of two laws lately received from Maryland relating to popery." He was present the next day and was listed with the regular members. Such entries are common in similar cases. See: Board of Trade *Journal*, 18, p. 117; 37, pp. 250-251.

[273] See his caveat against the laws of Massachusetts for the support of ministers, May 24, 1704, *Ibid.*, 17, p. 48.

[274] The repeal of the Virginia law for the payment of ministers' salaries in tobacco was due in part to an objection of the bishop, C.O. 5, 1329, X, 64. It was this repeal which finally led to the famous "Parsons' Cause" in which Patrick Henry figured as an attorney. See also the reference to the bishop of the North Carolina Act of 1755 establishing parishes and providing for the clergy, C.O. 5, 324, p. 278.

[275] C.O. 5, 995, p. 48.

other slight rebuff and also some excellent advice to his lordship. A complaint had been made against the operation of the bishop's ecclesiastical court recently set up in Barbadoes. This complaint had gone to the Board for investigation and was finally reported upon as follows:

> We thought it our duty to examine upon what foot the bishops' authority is established in the plantations; but by the best enquiry we have been able to make, we can find no other foundation for the same, but an article in the general instructions to all your Majesty's governors in America; nor could the bishop inform us of any other; tho' in all probability the plantations may have been formerly recommended to the inspection of the bishops of London by some Order in Council, from whence this instruction might take its rise.
>
> Considering therefore that the Lord Bishop of London's ecclesiastical jurisdiction in America depends entirely upon Your Majesty's pleasure, that his Lordship's present commissary in Barbadoes is reported to be a very indiscreet person and that Your Majesty's good subjects in the said island are extremely uneasy under his authority, we would humbly submit to Your Majesty's great wisdom, whether it may not be proper my Lord Bishop should be directed to supersede the said Gordon, and for the present to employ his care and inspection more immediately upon the clergy there; since the lives and conversation of the laity will in all humane probability much sooner be reformed by the pious examples of their spiritual pastors than by any ecclesiastical censure, or coercion from the secular arm.[276]

This seems a fair illustration of the policy of the Board. It was willing to take every reasonable precaution in checking legislation which encroached upon the rights of the clergy or upon the bishop's rightful authority, but it did not readily lend itself to any

---

[276] Board of Trade *Commercial Series I*, 23, pp. 319-328.

schemes for pernicious and irritating ecclesiastical activity in America.

Parliament

The relations of the Board to Parliament were more intimate than has generally been supposed. The members occupied seats either in the House of Lords or in the House of Commons. Whenever questions of special interest to the plantations were under consideration, the members of the Board in each house were most frequently charged with the duties connected with such consideration, whatever they happened to be. The Board prepared all bills which affected the colonies alone, and sometimes it asked for and received permission to offer bills embodying its favorite policies. Such, for example, were the various bills for resuming to the crown the powers of government in the charter and proprietary colonies, which were almost constantly before Parliament during the years 1700-1706.[277] Other favorite measures of the Board were the bills for establishing a fixed civil list in New York,[278] those for protecting such white pine trees as were suitable for masts for the

---

[277] North Carolina *Colonial Records*, vol. i, 538-539; Commons *Journal*, vol. xv, 151, 168, 183. Sometimes this was varied somewhat by the secretary of state sending a bill to the Board with a request to examine it and to make any alterations it saw fit. See the letter of Secretary Hedges to the Board, February 18, 1706, in C.O. 5, 1263, O, 30.

[278] One of these bills was drafted by the Board in accordance with an Order in Council of March 1, 1711. It was then sent to the attorney- and solicitor-general for their examination before it was offered in Parliament. Another was drafted two years later and Sir John Hynd Cotton, one of the members of the Board, was ordered to present it to the House of Commons. See: Board of Trade *Journal*, 22, p. 257; 23, p. 349; New York *Colonial Documents*, vol. v, 389 and *passim*.

royal navy, bills to encourage the production of naval
stores in America,[279] and the bills against legal tender
acts in the colonies.

The Privy Council and both houses of Parliament
frequently called upon the Board to draft bills for
special purposes.   The request of 1708 for a draft of
a bill to enforce the proclamation regulating the value
of foreign coins in the plantations,[280] and that for a
bill for punishing murders committed in the admiralty jurisdiction of the plantations are good illustrations.   Besides these bills that were officially drafted
by the Board, numerous others were practically so
drawn.   The House of Commons would direct that
certain men, of whom the most important were members of the Board, should prepare and bring in bills;
and when these were afterwards reported to the house,
they were presented by one of the members of the
Board.   To all intents and purposes such bills were
drawn by the Board and may have been actually prepared in its offices.   The names of Molesworth,
Blathwayt, Chetwind, Docminique, Bladen, Dupplin,

279 See the letter of Secretary Hedges, December 18, 1704 [C.O. 324, 9,
p. 45], notifying the Board that the House of Commons had given leave for
the introduction of such a bill and requesting that it be prepared and sent
to him for presentation to the House. The Board was empowered to include
in the bill whatever it saw fit. Another similar measure sought to encourage
the colonial production of raw iron. January 26, 1711, Dartmouth gave the
Board permission to prepare a clause for insertion in some bill which would
prevent the payment of drawbacks on foreign iron, re-exported to the colonies [Ibid., p. 450]. The clause was drawn and Sir Charles Turner, a member of the Board, was directed "to follow it in the House of Commons." See:
Board of Trade Journal, 22, p. 220; also the recommendations of the Board
to the House of Lords for removing the duty on colonial pig iron and for permitting the sale of colonial rice to southern Europe, January 14, 1735, C.O.
324, 12, p. 117.
280 Chalmers, Geo. Introduction to the Revolt, vol. i, 320-321.

Fane, Grenville, Pitt, Bacon, and Oswald constantly appear in the lists of the committees on bills affecting the colonies.[281]

In addition to preparing legislation for the consideration of Parliament, the Board was the source of information upon all questions of trade or colonial affairs. In the House of Commons addresses were constantly being presented which called for reports on such questions as the following: the production of naval stores, indigo, silk, rice, and other staples; commercial questions, such as piracy, violations of the trade laws, and the increase in bills of credit; and such questions as the administration of justice, relations with the Indians, and the condition of the colonial defenses. The reports in answer to these addresses were usually prepared by the Board and presented to the two houses by prominent Lords of Trade, and the names which occur so frequently in the lists of committees are met with again in this connection.[282] At other times some of the members of the Board were summoned before one or the other of the houses of Parliament to give information[283] on some

---

[281] See the Commons *Journal* for the period, especially vol. xv, 157, vol. xxiv, 658, vol. xxv, 746.

[282] Commons *Journal*, vol. xiii, 502, vol. xv, 436, vol. xvii, 224, vol. xviii, 698, vol. xix, 352, vol. xxiii, 609, vol. xxv, 568, vols. xxvi-xxx, *passim*.

[283] The Board of Trade *Journal* has many entries like the following: "Another order of the House of Lords, dated yesterday, requiring some of the commissioners of trade and plantations with their secretary to attend that house tomorrow at 12 o'clock, was read." — *Journal*, 24, p. 262. The secretary of the Board was also frequently called upon to attend committee meetings of the houses with such books and papers as bore upon the matter under consideration. This was done when the bill to regulate the charter and proprietary colonies was under consideration. See: August 17-18, 1715, C.O. 5, 1292, pp. 464-465.

measure.   Nothing shows the really ministerial character of the Board more than the fact that its members were evidently accustomed to speak for it in the House of Commons.[284]

The ministerial character of the Board is still more apparent after the settlement of Nova Scotia, the surrender of Georgia to the crown, and the acquisition of Florida.   In all of these colonies the charges of government were paid by the crown from annual grants made by Parliament, and the control of these expenditures was vested in the Board.   When estimates for the coming year were laid before the House of Commons, those for these three colonies did not come from the chancellor of the exchequer but from the Board of Trade.   They were presented by one of its members as the representative of the Board,[285] and if they should be attacked, he and his colleagues had to defend them.

In view of the close relations between the Board of Trade and Parliament, the reasons advanced for its establishment by Order in Council appear insignificant.   Created originally in such a way as to prevent its control falling into the hands of the House of Commons, it had come to be chosen almost exclusively from that house.   Its authority depended upon the influence it could muster in the Commons, it was constantly called upon to furnish information to that body, and in its representation of estimates for cer-

---

[284] See Commons *Journal.*

[285] — *Ibid.,* vol. xxvi, 629, 935, vol. xxvii, 363, 653, vol. xxviii, 103, 396, 693, 1019, vol. xxix, 99, 468, 877.   The names of Oswald, Hamilton, Bacon, and Jenyns, all of whom were members of the Board, are constantly connected with these estimates.

tain colonial expenditures, it might have subjected the entire ministry to an attack by the opposition.   It is thus seen that the very thing had happened which William III feared, namely, the control of this Board by Parliament instead of by the sovereign.

III. DIFFICULTIES OF COLONIAL ADMINISTRATION

Communications

One of the serious difficulties of colonial administration was the lack of communication between England and the plantations. There was no regular mail
service of any kind until 1755,[286] and all letters and
other communications were entrusted to the ordinary
merchant vessels. This method furnished reasonably
prompt service between Boston, New York, Virginia [287] (and later Charleston), and the home country; but other colonies were not so fortunate, for they
had to depend upon more precarious means for sending letters. Connecticut and North Carolina were
probably the worst situated in this respect, for very
few ocean-going vessels touched at the coast of either,
and what ships did enter their ports were usually
small coasting vessels, which were worthless for purposes of communication. The records show that the
governor of Connecticut received his letters by way
of Boston and sent them by the same route.[288] In
North Carolina some of the governor's letters could

[286] See the letter of the Board of Trade to Secretary Robinson, September
18, 1755, in New Jersey *Archives*, vol. viii, part ii, 138.

[287] Letters from Virginia and Maryland reached the Board in from two
to three months in 1700. See: Board of Trade *Journal*, 13.

[288] Talcott Papers, in Connecticut Historical Society *Collections*, vols. iv,
v, *passim*.

have been sent directly to England and some reached
him by that route, but many more of them had to go
by way of Virginia,[289] and letters for the latter colony
frequently went by way of New York.[290] Even the
colonies which had direct communications with England were not so much better situated, so far as the
governor's correspondence was concerned.   Trading
vessels seldom made ports at regular intervals.   They
came in unannounced and sailed again as soon as cargoes could be discharged and new ones taken on; consequently the governors often had to prepare their
dispatches in haste while ships were in port, and such
is frequently stated to be the case in their letters.[291]

The ports having the best means of communication
could not expect vessels to enter at all times of year.
Apparently Boston had almost no transoceanic commerce in the winter months.   Governor Talcott's letters to the Board of Trade were frequently written in
the late fall months, but usually they were not delivered to that body until the latter part of April or the
first of May.   In preparing reports for the houses of
Parliament, the Board was frequently disappointed
by receiving the information too late to be of use that
year.   It was thus practically impossible for the
Board to furnish Parliament with information from
Connecticut, even though it had been instructed to

---

[289] Letters frequently took even a more circuitous route.   See the North
Carolina *Colonial Records*, vol. ii, 185, vol. v, 586, and *passim*; also vols.
iii, iv, *passim*.

[290] This was true of a number of letters of the Board written in 1712 and
1713.   See: Spotswood to the Board, December 29, 1713, C.O. 5, 1364.

[291] See the New York *Colonial Documents*, vol. iv, *passim*; vol. v, 241
and *passim*.   Letters from or to New York frequently went by way of Boston.   See: Bellomont's letters, *Ibid.*, vol. iv, *passim*.

secure it before the adjournment of the previous session; consequently reports from that colony were regularly about a year behind what they should have
been.[292]

The most striking example of bad communications,
however, is furnished by North Carolina. In June,
1745, the Board wrote Governor Johnson that it had
received no letter from him for three years, that it
had complained of his negligence in its letter of the
previous year, and that it had great reason to renew its
complaint on that head.[293] Johnson answered a year
later that he had been a regular correspondent and
that he was very much surprised at the complaint of
the Board, which apparently had just reached him.[294]
The case was so serious that the Board informed Newcastle in 1746 that it had received no letters from the
governor since April, 1742.[295] The discrepancy between the existing correspondence and Johnson's
statements could easily be explained by assuming
that his letters were lost, or possibly by assuming
that he never wrote and that he simply lied when he
insisted that he had. That the former may have
been true is evident from his letter of January 20,

[292] See the letter of the Board of Trade to Talcott, October 22, 1736.
The latter's letter of October 28, 1735, in answer to a request for information,
had not reached the Board until April 12, too late to be of any value in
making the report to Parliament. See: Talcott Papers, in Connecticut Historical Society *Collections*, vol. iv, 378; also vol. v, *passim*, for other illustrations.

[293] North Carolina *Colonial Records*, vol. iv, 756.

[294] "It is with very great surprize and concern that I read in your Lord-
ship's [letter] of the 27th of June last, which I have received but lately." —
Letter of Johnson to the Board, June 6, 1746. North Carolina *Colonial
Records*, vol. iv, 792.

[295] This letter was written in December, 1741, and was the last received
until the one of June, 1746. See: *Ibid.*, 797, 844.

1747, in which he stated that the Board of Trade's letter of July 19, 1744, had just reached him and that he had been a regular correspondent since 1741. Two years and a half for a letter to cross the ocean was certainly not very rapid transit.

The last illustration was, of course, exceptional,[296] but it is enough to condemn conditions which made such an occurrence possible. Letters, packets, and other communications were entrusted to the master of any convenient sailing vessel, who might be bound to another port and have to transfer them to some other master who could deliver them in England. After reaching there, it was by no means certain that they would be delivered promptly to the Board, as packages of papers addressed to it were sometimes allowed to lie in the customs house for a year or more before they were delivered.[297] In a letter of May 17, 1748, Johnson makes the following statement concerning some legislative records he had sent over:

> I am informed these pacquets got safe home in the month of May 1747. And yet I am now told by a gentleman lately arrived from London that they were never sent to your Lordship but lay at Mr. Samuel Wragg's house last Christmas.[298]

---

[296] The communication with Boston was almost as bad, at times, as with the southern colonies. June 18, 1748, the Board wrote Governor Shirley that it had received his letters dated December 1, 1747, and January 6, 1748, and no others since his letter of November 16, 1745, although Shirley says he wrote five letters in addition to the two which were received. See: C.O. 5, 918, p. 210.

[297] February 20, 1728, the Board sent a messenger to the customs office to get a package of papers which had been lying in the customs warehouse since January 17, 1727. At the same time the Board requested that any future packages of that kind should be delivered, or that notice of their receipt should be given. Evidently this was not always done, for similar requests are found in after years. See: Board of Trade *Journal*, 39, p. 62; 45, p. 176.

[298] North Carolina *Colonial Records*, vol. iv, 868.

Possibly his letters suffered a similar fate,[299] for dispatches to the governors sometimes had to undergo just as strange adventures.   It is evident that those addressed to the governors of North Carolina were frequently passed on from hand to hand across Virginia and Carolina until they reached the governor. Occasionally a special messenger was employed, but only in cases of unusual urgency, and even in those cases the governors had to bear the charges.[300]

Postal conditions in England also contributed to the rather haphazard method of handling mail addressed to the Board.   None of its communications were permitted a free passage through the mails until 1746.[301] Before that time the postage had to be paid by the Board, both on its own letters and those addressed to it.   As this charge had to be defrayed out of the incidental fund of the office, the Board endeavored to economize by having the large packages of papers delivered to it through other channels than the post-office.[302]

---

[299] It is evident from the letter of Governor Everard to Carteret in 1729 that such things did happen.   One Mr. Durley had been entrusted with many letters, public papers, and similar packets to deliver to Carteret, but he was "lately informed by some gentlemen here that he either gave the said writings to Lovicks Brother in London or destroyed them." — North Carolina *Colonial Records*, vol. iii, 27.

[300] See the correspondence between the governors of Virginia and of North Carolina, in North Carolina *Colonial Records*, vols. iv, v, *passim*.

[301] August 19, 1746, an Order in Council directed the postmaster-general to pass through the mail, free of charge, all letters and packages addressed to the Board of Trade.   Prior to that time the records of the plantation office show numerous expenditures for postage.   The Board of Trade had asked for free postage, but it was informed that all the revenues of the post-office were appropriated, and that it should pay its own postage.   Postage from April, 1699, to September, 1700, amounted to £63 1s.   See: Board of Trade *Journal*, 13, p. 244; 54, p. 85; Order in Council of July 6, 1697, Board of Trade *Miscellanies*, 11, pp. 40-41.

[302] September 5, 1739, the Board informed Governor Gooch that the last

The slowness of the service was not its worst fault from an administrative point of view. Letters which were passed from person to person, and entrusted to parties who were not responsible and who were probably curious, enjoyed no protection against being opened before they were delivered. Under such circumstances it was difficult to secure that secrecy which is often necessary in directing the policy of a governor in difficult situations. The following extract from one of Governor Talcott's letters illustrates a not uncommon occurrence: The packet from London,

> Together with a duplicate from our agent, of his of Feb. 12th, came to Boston, so along to Fairfield, then back to me; both of which I have great cause to suspect, had been opened and closed again, before they came to my hand, and I doubt by our adversaries, but can't learn by whom.[303]

Under such conditions it was possible for the plans of the Board to be nullified by being known in advance by the opposition.

The existence of war during more than a third of the period from 1696 to 1765 greatly increased the danger of dispatches being lost. Duplicates, triplicates, and even five copies of letters were sent by the

---

box of papers from him had been sent by post from one of the out ports and the charges amounted to £11 16s. 1d. As such charges fell heavily upon the incidental fund, he was directed to have the masters of vessels not to deliver such packages, in future, until they reached the Thames; then they were to be turned over to some individual to deliver to the Board. In that way only a messenger fee was paid. See: C.O. 5, 1366, p. 325.

[303] Letter to Governor Belcher of Massachusetts, July 6, 1731, in Talcott Papers, Connecticut Historical Society *Collections*, vol. iv, 238. Similar statements are met with in the New York and the North Carolina Correspondence. Letters opened by mistake are also not infrequently mentioned. March 1, 1705, Governor Nicholson of Virginia informed the Board that he had reason to think that some of his letters had been intercepted. See: C.O. 5, 1361, p. 239.

governors,[304] and usually the Board resorted to the same precaution.[305] As these different copies were sent by different routes, one of them ordinarily got through safely, although frequently all were lost. As the letters and papers from America often contained information of great value to the enemy, the governors were given strict orders to direct the captains of all vessels carrying dispatches to sink them if there was danger of their capture.[306] Probably this accounts for the great number of papers lost during the war, although many were captured. The danger of loss was not only increased, but since fewer ships ventured out, the opportunity for sending letters was greatly diminished during the periods of hostility. Thus communications were seriously crippled at the very

[304] The letters of Governor Ellis of Georgia to the Board, dated March 11 and 20, 1757, were not received, except a fifth copy which finally arrived by way of New York. Board to Ellis, April 21, 1758. C.O. 5, 673, p. 4. See also the letters of the governors to the Board of Trade in the New York *Colonial Documents*, vol. iv, *passim*.

[305] November 24, 1758, the Board, in answering letters of Governor Ellis, said that it was much concerned that its letter of April 21 had not reached him, as it contained much information as to conditions in Georgia. Two copies of this letter had been sent, one by a direct conveyance and the other by the New York packet, a third was included in this letter. See: C.O. 5, 673, p. 182; also the letters of the Board of Trade to the governors, in the New York *Colonial Documents*, vol. iv, *passim*.

[306] "The directions given you relating to the sinking of letters, are the same as were sent to the governors of all his Majesty's other plantations, and was done in order to prevent the enemies getting intelligence of the state of the plantations by letters taken on board of ships coming from thence.

"We understand the assembly are of another opinion, but we continue nevertheless to enjoin you to direct that all your letters, and such as in any manner relate to her Majesty's service, be thrown overboard in such case of imminent danger, and you nevertheless recommend to the people, the causing their letters to be thrown overboard as aforesaid, as being for the benefit and safety of the colony and the trade thereof." — Board of Trade to Governor Nott of Virginia, February 4, 1706, C.O. 5, 1361, p. 438.

time the governors needed the most encouragement
and support from the home authorities to prevent the
assemblies from assuming full control of all branches
of the government.

The Board of Trade was not indifferent to the lack
of proper facilities for transmitting dispatches, and
looked with favor upon the proposal of 1703 to establish regular packet boats to ply between New York
and the Isle of Wight. As the owners of the vessels
wished unlimited privileges of carrying freight, however, the scheme was abandoned,[307] and there was no
improvement in methods of communication until the
presidency of Halifax. As the quarrel with the
French in America developed into open war, the
Board [308] realized the necessity for better postal service. September 18, 1755, it made a representation
to the king in which the conditions of the existing
systems were described.

> The great delays, miscarriages and other accidents, which
> have always, but more especially of late, attended the corres-
> pondence between this kingdom and Your Majesty's colonies
> and plantations in America from the very precarious and un-
> certain method, in which it is usually carried on by merchant
> ships, have been attended with great inconvenience and preju-
> dice to Your Majesty's service and to the trade and commerce
> of Your Majesty's subjects.[309]

As a remedy, it was proposed to establish regular
packet boats to ply between Falmouth and New York

---

[307] Letters of the Board of Trade to the Earl of Nottingham in regard to
the proposals of Sir J. Jeffrys, in New York *Colonial Documents*, vol. iv,
1030, 1031.

[308] During the period from 1748 to 1761 Halifax was the Board of Trade,
and practically all questions of policy put forward by that body were his
personal ideas.

[309] Board of Trade *Journal*, 63 ; New Jersey *Archives*, vol. viii, part ii, 138.

or some other important colonial port. The recommendation was acted upon, and October 25, following, the postmaster-general informed the Board that he had put on boats to make monthly voyages to both the West Indies and New York, "with which it shall be our endeavor that nothing except unavoidable accidents shall interfere, and Your Lordships shall constantly have the earliest notice of every intended dispatch." As this was the first step that had been taken "in the establishment of a regular correspondence with the main of His Majesty's American dominions," the boats were to be allowed to stay at New York for twenty days on the first trip and could be held for a short time while dispatches were being prepared.[310]

The ships were of two hundred tons and fitted for war.[311] By this measure correspondence with America was rendered much more certain and regular; and the Board had scored at least one important administrative triumph. The governors were promptly informed of the establishment of the new service and instructed to transmit reports and dispatches every month.[312] From this time on the whole colonial correspondence shows that the Board had the details of colonial administration much more completely at its command than at any time before.

Lack of responsibility

The commission which created the Board of Trade gave it the power to nominate but no power to ap-

---

[310] Board of Trade *Journal*, p. 144. Cf. Board of Trade *Journal*, 63, October 29, 1755.

[311] New Jersey *Archives*, vol. viii, part ii, 145.

[312] Circular letter signed by John Pownall and dated November 4, 1755, in New Jersey *Archives*, vol. viii, part ii, 146.

point colonial officers.[313] This was one of the fundamental weaknesses of the Board as an administrative
body, as officials readily obey only when they know
they must. The Board was not the agency through
which most of the governors and other officials secured their positions, nor was it able to secure their
removal for failure to obey its orders. Quite frequently both governor and Board were appointed by
the same influence. Governors knew this and at times
presumed to treat the Board with indifference. The
plan of placing administrative affairs in the hands of
the Board and expecting that body to carry out an
effective policy through officials who were not responsible to it could not have been expected to work
successfully, as there was too much division of responsibility at a time when effective administration
was most essential.

The colonial patronage belonged to and was exercised by the secretary of state for the Southern Department, who appointed the governors and other
chief officers. If the members of the Board were consulted before such appointments were made, there is
little evidence to show that such was the custom.
Frequently their protests against an appointment
which seemed especially ill advised were useless.

The remonstrance of the Board in 1714 against the
appointment of Vaughn as lieutenant-governor of
New Hampshire has already been cited. When his
successor, Wentworth, was appointed the Board filed
a similar objection, on the ground that it was not for
the best interest of Britain to appoint men of the coun-

---

[313] See the commission in the New York *Colonial Documents*, vol. iv,
145-147.

try to hold such important positions.[314] Neither of these protests, however, was effective. Each secretary of state retained full control over the selection of governors and lieutenant-governors, and the Board was communicated with only after the appointments were made.[315] The records, down to 1752, show the brief official notice of such appointments, with an occasional period when even this notice was not sent until the information was asked for by the Board.[316] The only successful interposition of the latter in the selection of a lieutenant-governor appears to have been in 1731, when there was a vacancy in New Hampshire caused by the death of Lieutenant-governor Wentworth. The Board recommended Dunbar, who was then surveyor of the woods, and urged his appointment on the ground that it would greatly strengthen his authority as a protector of the forests; and added that, as there was no salary nor other perquisites attached to the office in question, Newcastle would probably have few applicants for it. After some hesitation on the part of Newcastle, the nomi-

---

[314] Chalmers, Geo. *Introduction to the Revolt*, vol. ii, 34.

[315] See the notice of the appointment of Robert Dudley as governor of Massachusetts Bay, in C.O. 5, 911, p. 424. The note from Craggs, April 19, 1720, notifying the Board that Burnet had been selected for the governorship of New York is in the same form. All of these notices were essentially like the following: "His Majesty having been pleased to appoint John Montgomery, Esq., to be Governor of New York and New Jersey in the room of William Burnet, Esq., it is His Majesty's pleasure that the draughts of his commission and instructions may be prepared in order to be laid before His Majesty, for his approbation." — Townshend to the Board, April 12, 1727. See also: New York *Colonial Documents*, vol. v, 536, 823.

[316] April 14, 1715, the Board asked Stanhope for a list of the governors and lieutenant-governors that had been appointed, in order that it might know with whom to correspond. This was answered, May 2, and a list of nine such appointments enclosed. C.O. 324, 10, pp. 60-69. Similar requests were addressed to Newcastle from time to time.

nation was confirmed.[317] With this exception, that politician kept the control of the patronage in his own hands and seldom consulted the Board when appointments were to be made.

Office seekers naturally ignored the Board and applied directly to Newcastle, as is seen in the attempts of William Keith to secure the governorship of New Jersey.[318] Merit and proper qualifications were not always carefully looked after by Newcastle, and some of his officers were far from efficient. Two of these were commented upon by Governor Burrington of North Carolina, in a letter to Newcastle in 1732, as follows:

> The chief justice and attorney general of this province ought to be men of understanding and lawyers; neither of the persons your Grace bestow'd these places upon in this government ever knew law enough to be clarke to a justice of the peace.[319]

In the same letter there is an intimation that Martin Bladen, who was so long an energetic member of the Board, had a certain amount of influence over colonial appointments and that he was opposed to Burrington.[320] Governor Belcher of Massachusetts

---

317 Governor Belcher had tried to prevent the appointment of Dunbar, and Newcastle asked the Board to consider the charges he had made against him. In spite of these, the Board again recommended the latter for the office and finally secured his appointment. See Letter of the Board to Newcastle, February 10, 1731, in C.O. 5, 916, pp. 400, 403, 420.

318 New Jersey *Archives*, vol. v, 446-447 and *note*.

319 North Carolina *Colonial Records*, vol. iii, 438. Burrington was himself one of Newcastle's appointees and apparently was little more competent than the men he condemns. Some allowance must be made for Burrington's choleric disposition, in accepting his opinion of the qualifications of the two officers.

320 "Your Grace I hope has not forgot, that I made bold to mention a suspicion I had of Col. Bladens ill intentions to me, nor the generous

makes similar statements as to Bladen's hostility to himself.[321] Lieutenant-governor Dunbar of New Hampshire apparently owed his appointment to Martin Bladen's influence, and Belcher seems to think that all his efforts to displace him failed because of Bladen's opposition.[322] These incidents show that some members of the Board had at least sufficient power to make themselves feared. Probably it was the power of the Board to present and encourage complaints, which caused the governors somewhat to dread its anger or opposition. But it was a serious administrative situation when the leading members of the Board of Trade and the governors were intriguing against each other. The real difficulty lay in the apparent inability of Newcastle to use men, to assign them responsible duties, and to trust them to perform them faithfully. Jealous of his own authority, he insisted upon keeping all the essential threads of administration in his own hands, apparently heedless of his inability to attend to everything personally or too vain of his authority to entrust any portion of it to others.

---

answer you were pleased to give (*viz.*) that if I faithfully performed my duty I need not fear any man; I presume to mention this because it was reported in London, I should very suddenly be turned out, the same has been constantly said here and declared particularly by Montgomery the attorney-general the first day he came." — North Carolina *Colonial Records*, vol. iii, 437.

[321] "I find Col. B—n is my enemy, yet he always writes me fair and plausible. It must be on Dunbar's account and for no other reason, and no doubt he influences the Board of Trade to my prejudice; we must therefore constantly apply to their superiours that I may be always treated with justice and reason." — Letter to Richard Partridge, April 27, 1732, in Belcher Papers, Massachusetts Historical Society *Collections*, sixth series, vol. vi, 120-121.

[322] — *Ibid.*, vol. vi, 83 and *passim.*

The Board of Trade had control of a certain class of appointments. The members of the provincial councils were usually appointed on the suggestion of the governor and the subsequent nomination by the Board. This was true in the time of Bellomont, Cosby, Hunter, Belcher, Burrington,[323] and by 1730 had become an established custom with which Newcastle apparently did not interfere.[324] It was intended that the governor should have control of his council as far as possible, and the Board regularly honored his recommendations and usually supported his removals. There was an exception, however, in the case of Belcher during the later years of his administration of New Jersey. The disorders in that province and the complaints against him had resulted in his losing caste with Halifax who refused to honor his nominations. April 21, 1749, Belcher protested in vain against the appointment of Richard Saltar as a member of the council,[325] and in November of the next year he wrote to Partridge, his agent in London, to

[323] See the numerous illustrations of this in the correspondence of the different governors, in New York *Colonial Documents*; New Jersey *Archives*; Belcher Papers; North Carolina *Colonial Records*.

[324] Among the papers in the Public Record Office known as *Plantations General* there is a bundle containing four note-books, which were used to keep lists of colonial councillors. These show, in most cases, when an appointment was made, vacancies from time to time, and upon whose recommendation the appointment was made. Usually the governor's recommendation was accepted, although there are several cases of nominations by Bladen, Fane, Halifax, and Bridger. Bladen's and Bridger's activities were confined largely to New Hampshire. In New Jersey the proprietors frequently recommended, and the same was true for Maryland while it was a royal province.

[325] Letter of Belcher to the Board of Trade. One of the objections he made to this appointment was that it violated his instructions to keep the council composed of an equal number of men from each division of the province. See: New Jersey *Archives*, vol. vii, 247.

endeavor by every possible means to secure the appointment of William Morris.   His letter indicates that Bedford's influence was important as was also that of Halifax.[326] The favor of the latter was not secured, however, and in a letter to Halifax complaining of the lack of credit given his nominations, Belcher says:

> When I was formerly for eleven years governor of His Majesty's province of New Hampshire I never had one nomination of a counsellor for that province set aside at your Lordship's honourable board and if it must be otherways now it cannot tend to support the honour and dignity of the king's government intrusted to me.[327]

He was right in saying that the lack of credit given his nominations weakened his position and influence as governor, but the Board continued to disregard them.[328] Thus the Board exercised at all times pretty complete control over the appointment of councillors.

The Board also selected the colonial secretaries, apparently without interference on the part of the

[326] New Jersey *Archives*, vol. vii, 578.

[327] New Jersey *Archives*, vol. vii, 595.   August 10, 1751, he wrote a letter to Lord Hardwicke in regard to this matter: "I am sorry to acquaint your Lordship that the Lords commissioners for trade and plantations have lately rejected my nomination for filling vacancies of councillors . . . and in their stead recommended others I suppose named to them by young Mr Morris. . . I would earnestly intreat your Lordship to interpose, etc. that I may be treated as one of His Majesty's governors." — *Ibid.*, 611.

[328] Some reason for this action of the Board is found in its letter to Belcher of March 27, 1751: "We have enquired into the character of Mr. Samuel Smith, whom you recommend to us as a proper person to supply the vacancy in the council occasion'd by the death of Richard Smith Esq., and we find that he is a wellwisher to the rioters, and his family active in that faction. When we recollect that Mr. Morris, the last person you recommended to the same office, was found upon enquiry to bear the same character, we cannot but express our surprise, that . . . you should thus attempt to fill the Council Board with persons disaffected to His Majesty's government." — New Jersey *Archives*, vol. vii, 586.

secretary of state; [329] but as these were merely clerical offices with exceeedingly small salaries attached to them, the power of filling them did not amount to much. Law officers, such as the colonial chief justices and attorneys-general, were usually appointed by the Board on the recommendation of the chief justice and the attorney-general in England.[330] As long as this was the practice, it would seem that men should have been appointed because of merit. Apparently Newcastle seized upon this portion of the colonial patronage, however, with the result indicated by the blustering Burrington. If the latter is correct in saying that Newcastle appointed the officers in question, it indicates a wide departure from the earlier practice in colonial affairs and is but another evidence of that politician's pernicious activity. The appointment of these minor officers, however, was of little importance. The one officer in each colony with whom the Board had to deal and who should have acted in harmony with its plans was the chief executive, and so long as the latter held his position independent of the former, the Board could not be an effective administrative body.

[329] Applications for these offices were frequently made to the secretary of state, but were by him referred to the Board. The latter investigated each application, heard what the candidates had to say, and secured from them assurances that they intended to reside in the colony to which they were accredited before they were recommended for appointment. See the appointment of Edmund Jennings, secretary of Virginia, and Sir Thomas Lawrence of Maryland in 1701-1702, in Board of Trade *Journal*, 14, pp. 20, 28, 53, 56, 68, 247, 296; also the letter to Sunderland, December 17, 1708, recommending Mr. Rhodes for a similar position, *Ibid.*, 20, p. 381.

[330] See the appointment of an attorney-general for Virginia in 1703, in Board of Trade *Journal*, 16, pp. 168-197, also that of a similar officer for New York in 1705, *Ibid.*, 17, p. 398.

The governors of the proprietary colonies were appointed by the proprietaries, but had to receive the royal approbation.   In practice the Board of Trade exercised the power of accepting a proposed governor.   Thus Markham was not approved as governor of Pennsylvania in 1699,[331] and, on the death of Governor Hamilton in 1700, William Penn named a new governor and asked that he might be approved.   His request was referred to the Board, which promptly returned a favorable report.[332] In 1711 the Board reported that it had no objections to the approval by the queen of the appointment of Edward Hyde as governor of North Carolina, provided he gave bond and qualified according to law.[333] Not only did the Board exercise a sort of royal veto on the nominations of the proprietaries on general grounds; but it was responsible for seeing that the governors, when accepted, gave sufficient security for their observance of the laws of trade and navigation.   This is clearly shown by the *Journal* of the Board for July 28, 1702.   Sir Matthew Johnson had been appointed governor of North Carolina; Archibald Hutcheson attended with him and asked that Mr. Johnson, a son of the governor, and Thomas Carey might be accepted as security. The Board consented and directed them to lodge the bond with the treasurer.   Similar action was taken

---

[331] Board of Trade *Journal*, 12, p. 157.   See also the difficulty over the approval of Captain Haskett as governor of the Bahama Islands, *Ibid.*, 13, pp. 4-66.   Also *Proprieties*, 26, pp. 203-245.

[332] Penn-Logan *Correspondence*, vol. i, p. 206.

[333] The usual bond was two thousand pounds, but as the trade of North Carolina was insignificant, the Board suggested that a bond of half that amount should be accepted.   See: North Carolina *Colonial Records*, vol. i, 773.

when Charles Eden was appointed governor of the same province in 1713.[334] This power over the selection of the proprietary governors, such as it was, afforded the Board one of its most effective weapons for extending the royal control over those governments.[335]

The absence of the appointing power in the hands of the men who were entrusted with colonial affairs, causing division of responsibility and lack of control, was doubtless one of the most fundamental weaknesses of the Board of Trade; but it was no longer a defect after 1752.   It has already been stated that one part of the bargain by which Halifax assisted in forming the ministry in 1751 was that control of colonial affairs, including the patronage, should be entrusted to him.[336] The arrangement was made legal March 11, 1752, by an Order in Council which empowered the Board of Trade to appoint all colonial officers from governor down to the lowest appointee.[337]

---

[334] North Carolina *Colonial Records*, vol. i, 557; vol. ii, 51.

[335] See the Penn-Logan *Correspondence* [vol. i, 136 and *passim*] for the difficulties Penn encountered because the Board of Trade condemned Governor Hamilton as not properly qualified.

[336] See page 49.

[337] "It is therefore hereby further ordered, that the said Lords commissioners for trade and plantations do, from time to time, as vacancies shall happen by death or removals, present unto His Majesty in Council, for his approbation, the name or names of such person or persons, as the said commissioners from the best of their judgment and information, shall think duly qualified to be governors or deputy governors, or to be of His Majesty's council or his council at law, or secretaries in the respective plantations, and likewise to present to His Majesty for his approbation, the names of all other officers, which have been, or may be found necessary for the administration of justice, and the execution of government there, excepting only such as are or may be appointed for the direction and regulation of His Majesty's customs and revenues, and such as are or may be under the directions and authority of the Lords Commissioners of the admiralty." — New Jersey *Archives*, vol. viii, part i, 24-25.

The Board of Trade in this case meant Halifax, but
he soon found that he had to insist upon his legal
rights to prevent Newcastle from continuing his policy of conferring colonial governorships upon men un-
fitted for the offices, and who had no intention of doing
anything more strenuous than drawing their salaries.
Nothing shows more plainly the pernicious side of
Newcastle's control of colonial affairs than the blunt
demand from Halifax for him to keep his hands off
of the Virginia governorship and to permit the selection of an able man for that place.[338]

Halifax not only insisted upon his rights, but exercised them vigorously himself.   Officials in America soon learned that they must look to him for pre-

---

[338] The sudden death of the Earl of Albemarle in 1754 left a vacancy
in the governorship of Virginia and called forth the following personal
letter from Halifax to Newcastle: "You are sensible, my dear Lord, that in
consequence of the late order in council, which your Grace has so frequently
assured me, you would strictly observe, the right of recommending to this
employment belongs to the Board of Trade. . . It is unnecessary for me
to trouble you with the several reasons that occur to me, evincing the inex-
pediency of any longer suffering the government of Virginia to remain a
sinecure, yet it is my duty to observe that at this time it would be attended
with the worst consequences." The people of Virginia had long complained
that though they have given a considerable salary to a governor they have
been ruled by a substitute. "And I think they have the greater reason to
complain, as being the only province in North America who have granted
a permanent revenue to the crown for the support of government, and indeed
this complaint so justly founded has been constantly used by the other
provinces as an argument in support of their disobedience to the king's
commands, and their refusal to pass revenue laws of the same sort, but if
at this critical conjuncture when both from ye danger that threatens them,
and the efforts they are exerting by his Majesty's orders in their defense
they have more than a common right to be well governed and by the person
they pay, late precedents should be suffered to prevail, and that employment which ought to be so busy and is so important an one should be continued a sinecure — I leave your Grace to judge what uneasiness it would
create and how little serious the world would think us in the present measure

ferment,[339] and the records all indicate that apppoint-
ments emanated from the Board. This not only
strengthened the control of that body over colonial
administration, but enabled it to carry out a general
merit system as regards promotions. Some governorships were looked upon as more important than others,
and the remuneration varied greatly. Under Halifax, when a vacancy occurred in a desirable position,
there was a general shifting of governors, which
amounted to a promotion for each one. Thus in 1759
the death of Governor Haldane of Jamaica resulted
in the following changes: Governor Littleton of
South Carolina became governor of Jamaica; Thomas Pownall, governor of Massachusetts Bay, went to
South Carolina; Francis Bernard, governor of New
Jersey, went to Massachusetts Bay; and Thomas
Boone was appointed governor of New Jersey to fill
the vacancy thus created.[340]

The most striking example of the new spirit back
of the Board was its treatment of Governor Hardy of
New Jersey, who had succeeded Thomas Boone in
1761, and in less than a year had violated his instructions by appointing the justices of the supreme
court during good behavior instead of during pleas-

of embarking troops for the defense of Virginia, should she be denied what
she has a title to expect in time of ye profoundest peace, the use of her own
governor.

"A man of quality, a military man, and a sensible and honest one should
be sent and such an one I hope may be found." — British Museum *Additional Manuscripts*, 32737, f. 505.

[339] See the letter of Governor Sharpe to William Sharpe, July 6, 1756,
in "Sharpe's Correspondence," Maryland *Archives*, vol. ix, 47; also that of
Thomas Cant to Reverend Doctor Johnson, November 4, 1760, in New York
Colonial Documents, vol. vii, 449.

[340] Board of Trade *Journal*, 67, p. 245. At the meeting of the Board

ure. January 20, 1762, he wrote the Board of his action.[341] Two months later that body sent a strong representation to Secretary Egremont stating the offense of Governor Hardy and concluding:

> But aggravated as his guilt is by the mode of the appointment and by the influence which it will necessary have in the neighboring Provinces of Pennsylvania and New York, and particularly in the latter, where the utmost zeal and efforts of the lieutenant-governor has been hardly sufficient to restrain the intemperate zeal and indecent opposition of the assembly to your Majesty's authority and royal determination upon this point: It becomes under these circumstances our indispensable duty to propose that this gentleman may be forthwith recalled from his government as a necessary example to deter others in the same situation from acts of disobedience to Your Majesty's orders, and as a measure necessary to support your Majesty's just rights and authority in the colonies and to enable us to do our duty in the station your Majesty has been graciously pleased to place us in, and effectually to execute the trust committed to us.[342]

This representation was promptly confirmed and William Franklin appointed in the place of Hardy.[343] Councillors were removed in the same summary way for partisan opposition to the governor, and the long, tedious investigations and delays which were former-

which prepared the formal recommendations, Halifax informed the members that the royal assent had already been secured to the changes. This indicates clearly that Halifax personally controlled appointments during his administration. See: Board of Trade *Journal*, 67, p. 247.

[341] "I must observe to Your Lordships likewise that I found the general assembly had come to a resolution not to make any provision for the judges in the bill for support of government if they accepted commissions during pleasure." — New Jersey *Archives*, vol. ix, 346-347.

[342] Representation of the Board of Trade, March 27, 1762, in C.O. 5, 999, pp. 137-138.

[343] Franklin was probably appointed directly by Egremont. See: New Jersey *Archives*, vol. ix, 368.

ly so common were no longer allowed.[344] In a word, the control of the Board of Trade over appointments after 1752 was as direct and unlimited as any executive board could desire, division of responsibility had ceased, and direct, responsible authority on the part of the Board was on trial.

Weakness of the governor's position

There was another serious difficulty in colonial administration very closely connected with the division of responsibility so characteristic of the period down to the time of the appointment of Halifax.   This was the weakness of the position of the governor, due to the method of his appointment and the conditions under which he had to work.   At home he was constantly subject to intrigues connected with the vicissitudes of English politics.   His position was coveted by other men who were anxious for an opportunity to try their fortunes in official life in America, and who exerted more or less constant pressure upon the leading ministers to secure an appointment.   Each governor was thus under the necessity of keeping the good will of the secretary of state through whom he had secured his appointment or by whom he could be removed.

More important, however, and farther reaching in its influence was the effect of these attacks upon his position in his government.   British administrative control of the American colonies centered in the exec-

---

[344] See the case of the suspension of Jonathan Rutherford from the council of North Carolina.   In this case the Board confirmed the action of Governor Dobbs in removing him, without even awaiting his defense, and maintained that its action was justified.   See: Board of Trade to the Com-

utive, and anything which weakened the position of
the executive was certain to weaken the control by
the home government.

Sent over with instructions requiring him to keep
administrative affairs closely under his own supervision, and which if followed would have prevented any
growth of independence on the part of the colonies,
he found he could not even secure his own salary, except on such conditions as the assemblies chose to
make with him.   His commission made him commander of the military forces, but he found none to
command, none even to protect him from insult. Such
military stores as existed were the property of the
assembly and were controlled by it.   If the militia
was needed in any emergency, the money for its support had to be voted by the local legislature,
and too often the entire control of it was assumed by that all powerful body.   Instead of being
independent, he found that the few powers he still
had were slowly but surely slipping from him, and
there was a constant temptation to bargain them away
for what he could get.   Under such conditions it was
of the greatest importance for imperial purposes that
the governor should have the most constant and un-
qualified support by the home officials.   It was at
this point that the system of divided responsibility
showed its greatest weakness.

Each governor had to contend with more or less
intractable elements.   If he observed his instructions,
he had to face strong opposition, which sometimes

mittee of the Privy Council, July 28, 1758, in North Carolina *Colonial
Records*, vol. v, 959-960.

centered in his own council,[345] sometimes in the assembly, and at times in both.   It was always an easy matter for the opposition to find grounds for complaints against him.   These complaints were referred to the Board of Trade for investigation, which always gave the governor an opportunity to deny the charges and justify his conduct.   But it took his time, and it cost money.   As he could not go to England to defend himself, he was nearly always required to maintain an agent in London to look after his interests and protect him from attacks.[346] Sometimes this agent was paid by the assembly but more frequently by the governor himself, and at times he even had to face complaints which were prosecuted by the assembly through its own paid agent in London.   Under such conditions, any rumors of lack of support by the home government rendered the position of the governor doubly difficult and increased the opposition to him. Governor Bellomont found it necessary to convince the factions in New York that he had the full support of the Board of Trade and the king.[347] Hunter was subject to constant attacks and intrigues for his

[345] Such was the situation when Bellomont entered upon his administration in New York. See his correspondence, in New York *Colonial Documents*, vol. iv, *passim*.

[346] Not only did the interests of the governor require the presence of an agent in London, but the Board of Trade insisted that he maintain one. In a letter to Governor Hunter in 1713 concerning the taking out of the orders for the appointment of members of the council it said: "If you had an agent here, we could send to him to do it, but as you have none, we do not know how long the orders may lie before they are dispatch'd to you. This shows you the necessity of having an agent for each of your governments, and we desire therefore that you use your utmost endeavours to get such a one established." — New Jersey *Archives*, vol. iv, 183.   See other letters on pages 375, 388, and *passim*.

[347] New York *Colonial Documents*, vol. iv, 395.

removal, but his actions were finally fully approved in England, the news of which apparently greatly decreased the activity of his opponents.[348]

The most striking illustration of the effect upon the position of the governor of lack of support by the home officials is that of Belcher in New Jersey. It was confidently expected that he would lose his position, and people were awaiting news of the appointment of his successor; consequently he was helpless, as he could get no effective support from either council or assembly. In the meantime rioters held control of a considerable portion of the colony and prevented the courts from sitting.[349] That was the situation of affairs when Halifax secured an extraordinary meeting of the Board for the consideration of conditions in that colony.[350]

Governor Burrington of North Carolina also found his difficulties greatly increased on account of the real or fancied opposition of Martin Bladen. He says in one of his letters to Newcastle that his enemies are confidently asserting that his recall is imminent.[351] Governor Sharpe of Maryland, in his long struggle with his assembly over financial affairs, could not convince that body that the authorities in London really supported him, and it took a letter from the secretary of state himself to convince the assembly that it would

---

[348] New York *Colonial Documents*, vol. v, 173, 405-411, and *passim*. See also the efforts to secure an act of Parliament in his behalf.

[349] New Jersey *Archives*, vol. vi, *passim*, especially the letters of Morris, Partridge, Alexander, and Paris.

[350] See the report of the Board of Trade, June 1, 1750, in New Jersey *Archives*, vol. vii, 466-528.

[351] North Carolina *Colonial Records*, vol. iii, 437.

not receive enough support from that source to force Sharpe and his council to give way.[352]

Illustrations could be multiplied, for almost every governor had to face the problem. After the appointing and investigating powers were consolidated in the hands of the Board, the difficulty does not appear to have been so great, but the mischief was already done. A half century of such conditions had resulted in a serious situation for the empire. The hands of the executive had been weakened by lack of support and even by opposition in England at the very time that the assembly was usurping the whole field of government within each colony.

The Rise of the Assembly

The greatest problem before the Board of Trade, however, was not one of poor communications, of divided responsibility, nor of lack of power to issue orders unchecked. Its greatest task was to operate a constitution which contemplated what was really an impossible form of government. The constitution of the royal province was embraced in the commissions and instructions of the governors, which corresponded to the charters in the proprietary and charter colonies, and regularly supplanted them as the proprietary colonies were transformed into royal provinces.

The commissions and instructions contemplated a government by a governor and a two-chambered leg-

---

[352] Egremont to Sharpe, July 10, 1762. "His Majesty has judged it proper to direct me to express His sentiments on the conduct of the assembly of your province, which you will make known to them in the manner you shall judge most expedient for the King's service, in order that they may not deceive themselves by supposing that their behavior is not seen here in its true light." — Sharpe's *Correspondence*, vol. iii, 63.

islature, one chamber of which was to be elected by the people and the other appointed by the crown. The upper house acted as an executive and advisory council for the governor, and was also supposed to have as much voice in legislation as the lower house. All executive power was vested in the governor and his council, and the governor had a veto on all legislation.[353]

Aside from the somewhat insignificant sums realized from quit rents, all public money had to be raised by taxation on votes of the assembly. The money so raised should have been lodged with the receiver-general appointed by the crown, and should have been paid out on warrants drawn by the governor in council.[354] Thus while the assembly voted the taxes, it had nothing to do with their expenditure.

Such was the constitution of New York in 1696 and such continued to be the constitution *de jure* of that and the other royal provinces. History has proved that such a constitution is unworkable for any great length of time, for the power that grants the taxes is bound sooner or later to control their expenditure. The constitutional history of the American colonies

[353] Commission of Governor Bellomont, in New York *Colonial Documents*, vol. iv, 266-273, 284-292; instructions to George Burrington, 1730, in North Carolina *Colonial Records*, vol. iii, 90-118; instructions to Arthur Dobbs, 1754, *Ibid.*, vol. v, 1107-1144; instructions to Francis Bernard as governor of Massachusetts, 1758, in Greene's *Provincial Governor*, 234-260.

[354] Bellomont's instructions: "You shall not suffer any publick money whatsoever to be issued or disposed of otherwise than by warrant under your hand, by and with the advice and consent of the council." — New York *Colonial Documents*, vol. iv, 286. This clause was later changed so as to allow the assembly to examine the records of receipts and expenditures. Instructions to George Burrington and to Arthur Dobbs, in North Carolina *Colonial Records*, vol. iii, 100, vol. v, 1115.

during the first half of the eighteenth century is a history of the subversion of the constitution by the growing ascendency of the colonial assemblies.

The financial power of the assembly was the device by which the council was excluded from all effective control over legislation, and by which the executive powers of the governor and council were successfully usurped. The process in all the colonies was essentially the same, but the stages in the development of the assumptions by the assembly are best seen in the case of New York, where the movement began in the administration of Cornbury. His mismanagement and corrupt use of the public money led the assembly, in 1704, to demand that money raised by taxation should be lodged with its own treasurer who was accountable only to the assembly itself.[355] This proposal involved a clear infraction of Cornbury's instructions.[356] The council sought to amend the revenue bill so as to remove this objection, but it was met by the point blank assertion that the assembly would permit no amendment of a money bill.[357] As a consequence of this difference of opinion, the money bill failed; but the dangers to the colony made some provision necessary, and two years later the governor and the council were forced to give way. The money was raised, Abraham de Peyster was made treasurer, commissioners were appointed to supervise the ex-

[355] Letter of Cornbury to the Board of Trade, New York *Colonial Documents*, vol. iv, 1145-1149.

[356] His instructions directed him "not to permit any clause whatsoever to be inserted in any law for levying money or the value of money, whereby the same shall not be made liable to be accounted for unto us here in England, and to our high treasurer or our commissioners for our treasury for the time being." — *Ibid.*

[357] Cornbury says this is a "new Doctrine in this part of the world."

penditures, and the treasurer was directed to pay out money, on their warrants and "by no other order mandate or warrants whatsoever." [358]

Cornbury reported the attempted encroachments to the Board of Trade in 1705, but the members of that bureau did not fully grasp the significance of the movement.   They answered him as follows:

> The assembly was very much to blame in disputing the council's amendments in that bill, for that the council has undoubtedly as much to do in the forming of bills for the granting and raising of money as the assembly, and consequently have a right to alter or mend any such money bills as well as the assembly.   In other Her Majesty's plantations, the assemblies do not pretend to the sole right of framing money bills, but admit of the council's amendments to such bills, as there may be occasion.   No assembly in the plantations ought to pretend to all the privileges of the House of Commons in England, which will no more be allowed them, then it would be to the council, if they should pretend to all the privileges of the House of Lords here.[359]

The letter went on to say that the assembly might be permitted to have its own treasurer when it raised extraordinary taxes, and that in such cases receipts could be used instead of warrants from the governor in council.[360]

The point once gained by the assembly was never surrendered.   Money continued to be raised and lodged with the treasurer instead of with the receiver-general, and the receipt of the party to whom the

[358] Act for raising three thousand pounds for the defense of the city of New York, passed October 21, 1706, cited in New York *Colonial Laws*, vol. i, 596.

[359] New York *Colonial Documents*, vol. iv, 1171-1172.

[360] In such cases the instructions required the treasurer to be accountable to the officers of the treasury in England.   See clause 30 of the instructions to Dobbs, in North Carolina *Colonial Records*, vol. v, 1116.

money was paid was the only warrant which was required or allowed.[361] In some cases the troops were paid on the presentation of their muster rolls, and in 1711 even the governor was paid his salary on his own receipt.[362] The act of 1713, levying import duties to pay the ordinary charges of government, lodged the proceeds of such duties with the receiver-general but made that officer accountable to the treasurer.[363] In the final settlement two years later, the assembly allowed the ordinary expenses of government to be paid out on warrants of the governor in council, but Hunter had to consent to the issue of bills of credit and to the treasurer becoming the sole custodian of the public taxes.[364] The arrangements of that year were reënacted from time to time until the administration of Lieutenant-governor Clarke. When the last five-year revenue act expired in 1737,[365] that gentleman was engaged in a quarrel with his assembly over the question of accounts, consequently no appropriation bill was passed for two years.[366] Finally in 1739, the

[361] See the acts of 1708, 1709, 1711, 1712, in New York *Colonial Laws*, vol. i, 607, 628, 654, 669, 693, 746, 812.

[362] — *Ibid.*, 730, 753.

[363] New York *Colonial Laws*, vol. i, 779-780. It seems a curious anomaly that the receiver-general of the province should be made accountable to an officer who was himself not accountable to the crown.

[364] — *Ibid.*, 847-858. This involved two violations of his instructions, one in the issuing of bills of credit, the other in lodging public money with an officer not accountable to the auditor-general in England. The power of the governor and council to lay out the money was also limited by the oath imposed on the treasurer not to issue any money except as provided for by specific appropriation acts.

[365] The last five year act was passed in 1732. See: New York *Colonial Laws*, vol. ii, 768-806.

[366] A tax bill was passed in 1737, but the last clause forbade the treasurer to disburse the money until an appropriation bill had been passed. *Ibid.*, 1071.

governor and council had to give way and accept a bill on the terms offered by the assembly. This bill constitutes a landmark in the growing power of the assembly. Salaries of officers were ordered paid by name and amount; [367] and as the bill was an annual one, the governor was practically forced to select officers who were acceptable to the assembly or that body would grant them no salaries.

The power to issue public money had been taken from the governor and council in 1706; and while it was partly restored in 1715, it could only be exercised according to the specifications of the appropriation acts.   In 1739 all control over expenditures was taken away and the treasurer ordered to accept receipts as vouchers.[368] In addition the assembly had used the money bill as a means of controlling appointments.   This result had been achieved by the exclusion of the council from all power to amend a revenue measure; for had the power of amendment been preserved, the most objectionable features of these bills might have been eliminated.

The Board of Trade was not allowed to remain ignorant of the change which was taking place, as Hunter besieged it with complaints and appeals for assistance.[369] It assured him again and again of its hearty support and that the council was a coördinate branch of the legislature with full power to amend any bill laid before it, that the assembly had no rights other than those given by the commission and instruc-

---

[367] New York *Colonial Laws*, vol. iii, 38-50.

[368] Except the salaries of the governor and the other chief officers of the colony, for which warrants were to be issued by the governor in council.

[369] See his numerous letters to the Board, in New York *Colonial Documents*, vol. v, *passim*.

tions of the governor, and that "the assuming a right no ways inherent in them, is a violation of the constitution of the government of that province and is derogatory to her Majesty's royal prerogative." [370] Such opinions, however, were futile unless they were backed by actions. Hunter had seen this and had asked for a settlement by act of Parliament, and added "that if the remedy for these evils be long delay'd it may cost more than the province is worth." A bill to establish by act of Parliament a permanent civil list for the colony was prepared, but for some reason it was never introduced; * consequently Hunter was left to make the best terms he could with his all-powerful assembly.

That body having once acquired a privilege never surrendered it. The appropriation bill continued to be drawn in the form of that of 1739. The governor

[370] Letter of the Board of Trade to Governor Hunter, June 12, 1712, in New York *Colonial Documents*, vol. v, 333, 359. The effect of the example of New York upon the action of the other colonies was also considered. "Most of them have already shewn too much inclination to assume pretended rights tending to an independency on the crown of Great Britain."

* Two attempts were made to secure a settlement by act of Parliament, one in 1711, another in 1713. See the letters of the Board to Governor Hunter and Dartmouth. There is a manuscript copy of this bill among the Newcastle papers. It states that, whereas the general assembly of New York had enacted a general revenue act for two years, beginning May, 1693, which was afterward extended to May, 1709; and whereas, upon frequent application to the assembly it had refused to grant other subsidies sufficient to run the government, in spite of the fact that four companies of soldiers and many ships of war were maintained at the expense of the crown for their defense; the Commons of Great Britain, being desirous that a revenue should be settled in that province upon her Majesty, sufficient to defray the expenses of that government and equal to what had formerly been granted, grant that the following rates should hereafter be maintained. Then follows a detailed customs act in apparently the same form as the former revenue act. See: British Museum *Additional Manuscripts*, 33028, ff. 23-31; New York *Colonial Documents*, vol. v, 285, 359.

was permitted, however, to issue warrants for the payment of those officers who were appointed directly by the crown, although their names and salaries continued to be inserted in the appropriation bill. A small contingent fund of one hundred pounds was also placed at the disposal of the governor.[371]

The war from 1744 to 1748 only tended to expand the functions of the assembly. Large sums were needed for military purposes, but their expenditure was always kept closely in the hands of the assembly or its commissioners.[372] Even the control of the troops was practically assumed. Governor Clinton could not resist as long as the war lasted, but at its conclusion he entered into a struggle to regain the executive functions which had been assumed by the assembly. He, too, made continuous appeals to the Board of Trade, and to the secretary of state for the Southern Department.[373] These resulted in an investigation by the Board, which was begun in 1750 and continued for more than a year. The report of this investigation is a most complete statement of the gradual subversion of the whole constitution by the assembly, and its exclusion of the governor and council from all control over the administration.[374]

The movement by which the council was steadily excluded from the field of financial legislation was not confined to New York, but extended practically to all the colonies. Mr. Lewis Morris, in a letter to

---

[371] New York *Colonial Laws*, vol. iii, 996.

[372] See the various acts providing for the defense of the colony, in New York *Colonial Laws*, vol. iii, 442, 450, 452, 528, 577, 634, 660, 700, 733.

[373] See his letters, in New York *Colonial Documents*, vol. vi, 305, 307, 352.

[374] See the report with the abstract of the evidence, in New York *Colonial Documents*, vol. vi, 614-703.

Sir Charles Wager in 1739, says that the assembly of New Jersey

> When they rais'd any money by act have pretended a right not to admit the council to amend a money bill and the council on the other side have insisted on a right to amend any bill if they thought fit; tho' they often declin'd doing of it rather than hazard the support of ye government.[375]

In the case of the bill disposing of the interest on the money accruing from the loan scheme, the council determined to amend it and asked for a conference. The assembly "declar'd it to be inconsistent both with the interest of the province and the priveleges of their house to admit of any alterations to be made in it." Morris concludes, "the excluding one of the branches of the legislature I conceiv'd to be a matter of too dangerous tendency and too open an attempt on the constitution for me to let pass unnoticed." The next year a bill granting two thousand pounds for transporting troops to the West Indies provided that the sum should be disbursed by commissioners. The council obtained a conference, but the assembly would permit no alteration in what they called a money bill.[376] The assembly's control over the treasurers in that colony was just as absolute as it was in New York. Their accounts were audited by a joint committee of

---

[375] New Jersey *Archives*, vol. vi, 63.

[376] The quarrel over land titles, resulting in the disorders and riots of Belcher's administration, furnishes several other illustrations. In 1749 the council sought to amend a bill for the support of government. The assembly resolved that "the Council had no right to amend any money bill whatever, and therefore rejected the said amendments and sent the Council a message that they look'd upon the mending of said bill to be a manifest infringement upon the rights and privileges of the House of Assembly and those they represented." — Report of the Board on the state of New Jersey, June 1, 1750, in New Jersey *Archives*, vol. vii, 466-528.

the two houses, but the majority of that committee was always made up of the assembly members.[377] The assembly also used its powers to grant money as a weapon for making itself dominant in executive affairs, especially in all military operations.

Massachusetts exhibits a similar practice. Conditions there can best be described by quoting from Governor Shute's memorial to the Board in 1723. He says that on his arrival in the province in 1716 he found the house of representatives possessed of all the powers of the House of Commons of Great Britain and much greater, as it had the power to select, once a year, the members of the council. It also had the power to fix the salaries of the governor and lieutenant-governor, which it did every half year.

> By appointing the salary of the treasurer every year they have full control over that office, which they often use to intimidate the treasurer from obeying the proper orders for issuing money, if such are not agreeable to their views. . . Not content with the privileges they enjoy by virtue of their charter, they have for some years been making attempts upon the few prerogatives remaining to the crown.

The following are instances: The house of representatives tried to refuse his power of a negative in the choice of its speaker. It voted a public fast, "a thing never attempted by their predecessors," as "that power was vested in the governors of that and all other provinces in America." It adjourned itself and refused to meet on the day to which the governor prorogued it.

---

[377] On this joint committee, the assembly appointed five members, three of whom constituted a quorum; the council appointed three, two being necessary to act. See: New Jersey *Archives*, vol. xvii, 248.

Tho the charter as well as Governor's commission gives to the governor the command of all forts in the province, and the power of building and demolishing such forts, the House voted a committee to go down to Castle William and take an account of all the stores there, and receipts from the officers for the same, without any application to me; and in the same manner, without my consent, ordered the treasurer to pay no more subsistence to the officers and soldiers of Fort Mary at Winter Harbor, and ordered that all the stores of war be removed from thence to Boston. As this is the only fort that can secure the fishing vessels in the eastern parts, the inhabitants to the number of one hundred and thirty-two petitioned them to desist from the dismantling; which they did, and ordered the fort to be supported. The people are thus taught to address themselves to the Assembly, whereas they should appeal to the Commander. . . The House voted to suspend Mr. Moody, a major in the forces there, and that without being paid, and sent their vote to the council for concurrence; the council not concurring they ordered his pay to be discontinued; when I expostulated, they sent me a message justifying their proceedings in terms not usually used in addressing the Governor.

The House of Representatives order'd a committee to command the officers at the eastern and western parts of the province, to draw out their forces and muster there; only under colour of an order sign'd by their speaker . . . [and the house] has been so far from returning to a just sense of their duty – that they have, since my departure from the province – repeated this unprecedented attempt, by pretending to the power of drawing off the forces from the place where they were. . . [And in the last session Governor Shute had received no salary at all because of his attempts] to prevent encroachments upon the Royal Prerogative.[378]

Although the Massachusetts council was much more dependent upon the assembly, because of the manner of its selection, than that of the other royal

---

[378] C.O. 5, 915, p. 366 *et seq.*

provinces, the popular house showed the same jealousy of its control over finance. While the council not infrequently managed to secure changes in a revenue or appropriation bill, the control of accounts was in the hands of the house of representatives. Governor Belcher in 1732 shows his appreciation of the danger involved in the practice.

> If every account of the province must be subjected to a House of Representatives, the king's governor will be of very little signification. They that have the controul of the money will certainly have the power; and I take the single question on this head to be, whether the king shall appoint his own governor, or whether the House of Representatives shall be governor of the Province.[379]

His warning bore no fruit and the lower house continued its encroachments. No branch of executive authority escaped, and in time of war the control and payment of the forces was directed by the agents of the House of Representatives instead of by the governor.[380]

In Maryland there was a permanent revenue sufficient for the ordinary charges of government, but wholly inadequate in time of war. There, as elsewhere, the council could refuse but was unable to amend a money bill. The colony was unable to play any important part in the French and Indian War because of the disputes between the council and the assembly.[381] The former could not accept the bill as offered, and the latter would permit no change.[382]

---

[379] *Belcher Papers*, vol. i, 227.

[380] Massachusetts *Acts and Resolves*, vol. iv, 95-96; Hutchinson, Thomas. *History of the Province of Massachusetts Bay*, vol. iii, 66; Greene, Evarts B. *Provincial Governor*, 189-190.

[381] See Sharpe's *Correspondence*, vols. i, ii, iii, *passim*.

[382] In a letter of April 25, 1762, to Secretary Egremont, Sharpe, in speak-

Governor Sharpe in a letter to Calvert in 1756 says: "It would be thought a little irregular for the Upper House to offer amendments to a money bill." [383] This remark shows it was a well recognized custom of the constitution to leave financial affairs to the exclusive control of the assembly.

The Pennsylvania council had very doubtful legislative powers; and although it acted in a very similar capacity to the councils of the other colonies, the assembly never recognized it as a coördinate branch of the legislature.[384] It is not surprising that it was excluded from all control over financial affairs; yet F. J. Paris says, "The assembly taking upon themselves, solely, to grant, apply issue, and pay the money, is very irregular." [385]

In 1755 the assembly did something still more irregular, for on a resolve, without the knowledge or consent of the governor, it authorized a committee of its own members to borrow any sum up to five thousand pounds on the credit of the house.[386] Two months later when Governor Morris vetoed a bill creating

ing of the failure of the money bill eight times before refused by the upper house, says it was "because in their opinion it was calculated to introduce such innovations in our constitution as would create the greatest confusion and disorder, sacrifice a part of the inhabitants to the humour of the rest and invest the lower house of Assembly with executive powers which have been hitherto exercised by other branches of our legislature." — Sharpe's *Correspondence*, vol. iii, 47.

[383] — *Ibid.*, vol. i, 419.

[384] See: Shepherd, Wm. *Proprietary Government in Pennsylvania*, part ii, chaps. iv, v.

[385] Letter to R. Peters, in Pennsylvania *Archives*, first series, vol. i, 628.

[386] Letter of Governor Morris to Secretary Robinson, January 30, 1755. He concludes, "if a house of assembly by their own authority, without the consent or approbation of a governor, can borrow and dispose of money as they think proper, they may hereafter use that power in a manner inconsistent

twenty-five thousand pounds in bills of credit, the house, on its own responsibility, and again without consulting the governor, issued notes of credit to the extent of ten thousand pounds.[387] In the face of such action any attempt to thwart the power of the assembly was vain.   Yet it was but the logical step in such a case, and the other assemblies might just as appropriately have taken similar action.   It only remained for the Pennsylvania assembly deliberately to corrupt the governor, which it did most successfully, and in that way secured whatever laws it desired.[388]

In North Carolina the power of the lower house over revenue had developed under the proprietary government, and the crown acquired that difficulty by purchase, along with the other proprietary rights. The treasurer was an appointee of the assembly and was responsible to that body.[389] The council was represented on a joint committee, similar to that in New Jersey, but the members from that house had no real

with the publick good, and the just dependence of this province upon the crown." — Pennsylvania *Archives*, first series, vol. ii, 250.

[387] Morris to Robinson, April 9, 1755, in Pennsylvania *Archives*, first series, vol. ii, 284.

[388] Governor Denny like all governors was under bond to observe his instructions. He signed the law taxing the proprietary estates on condition that the assembly indemnify him for his bond, which would thereby become forfeited. See: Shepherd, Wm. *Proprietary Government in Pennsylvania*, 456-461; Sharpe's *Correspondence*, vol. ii, 178, 344, 351.

[389] Edward Mosley, who was for so long a time treasurer and speaker of the assembly, says in a letter to Governor Burrington, April 13, 1733: "To the best of my remembrance for upwards of twenty-eight years I have been concerned in the publick affairs of this province. The constant practice has been for the assembly to appoint the treasurers and gatherers of money raised by the assembly. And this was always the practice before as far as I can learn by those journals and acts of assembly which I have seen nor do I remember to have met with any precedents to the contrary." — North Carolina *Colonial Records*, vol. iii, 490.

voice in auditing the accounts.[390] The council was also denied the right to amend money bills, and money was issued on the letter of the speaker, even after the governor had refused his warrant.

South Carolina offers little that is new, as the assembly there was practically supreme. By a law of 1721, which was apparently never disallowed, practically all officers were to be appointed by the lower house,[391] which made the constitution very little different from that of Massachusetts. South Carolina developed the committee system to the fullest extent; if there were forts to be built, troops to be raised, provisions to be bought, Indians to be treated with, or any other ordinary executive act to be performed, commissioners were appointed for the purpose. This left comparatively little for the council and the governor to do.

So wide spread in fact was the tendency of the assemblies to assume new powers and to usurp the executive functions of government, that the Board of Trade, in 1730, sought to check it by instructions to the governors. In those issued to Governor Burrington of North Carolina the fourteenth clause was as follows:

---

[390] The assembly "receive the accounts from the treasurers and pretend to keep all the vouchers which the assembly pass or reject at their pleasure, I may say exclusive of the council which they do by the majority of the voices of a joint committee from the two houses which generally consists of two members of the council and six or eight of the lower house in two separate committees of claims and accounts and tho the members of the council should dissent they are outvoted and the report is made by the majority and agreed to by the Assembly." — Letter of Governor Dobbs to the Board of Trade, December, 1761, in North Carolina *Colonial Records*, vol. vi, 619.

[391] South Carolina *Statutes at Large*.

And whereas the members of several assemblies in the plantations have frequently assumed to themselves privileges no way
belonging to them especially of being protected from suits at
law during the term they remain of the assembly . . .
and some have presumed to adjourn themselves at pleasure
without leave from our governor first obtained and others have
taken upon them the sole framing of money bills refusing to
let the Council alter or amend the same all which are very
detrimental to our prerogative. If upon your calling an
assembly in North Carolina you find them insist upon any of
the abovesaid privileges you are to signify to them that it is
our will and pleasure you do not allow [them any unusual
immunity from arrest, nor permit them to adjourn, except
from day to day, unless by consent of the governor, and that]
the council have the like power of framing money bills as the
assembly.[392]

This clause continued to be inserted in the instructions to the governors of North Carolina, but as has
been shown, was powerless to accomplish its purpose.

It is not the purpose of this monograph to describe
in detail the extent to which the assembly had acquired control of affairs. It is only intended to point
out the actual change in the colonial constitutions in
half a century, by which the center of gravity of colonial administration had been shifted from England
to America. The Board of Trade had exercised what
authority it could by directions given to the governors
and by controlling them, their councils, and the chief
law officers. The assemblies had usurped the chief
functions of the first two, and had made the last dependent upon the popular house for their salaries.[393]

---

[392] North Carolina *Colonial Records*, vol. iii, 93-94.

[393] The attempt was made to use the power over salaries to regulate the
form of the judges' commissions. See: Cadwallader Colden papers, in New
York Historical Society, *Collections*, vol. ix, 159 and *passim*; New Jersey

The change had lifted into power a body of men who were able to put forth the entire power of the province and over whom the Board could exercise no efficient control.

The far reaching effect of the actual change which had taken place can hardly be exaggerated. Government rests ultimately upon force, and that no longer remained in the hands of British officials. As long as the governor and council had control of expenditures, it was possible to exert force when necessary, but the absence of money paralyzed all efforts which were not supported by the lower house. The trade laws could not be enforced because there was no fund to employ attorneys to prosecute offenders. Officers refused or neglected to make reports to the governor, because they were not responsible to him.[394] Riots and insults to the executive could not be suppressed or prevented for lack of money to pay a military force.[395] There could be no secret service, no central police, no standing military force. The militia was practically useless on account of lack of munitions and supplies or funds to purchase them,[396] consequently the frontiers could not be protected in an emergency.

Archives, vol. ix, 346-347, 348-349, 350, 360, 364; North Carolina *Colonial Records*, vol. vi, 900; New York *Colonial Documents*, vol. vii, 470, 483, 503, 505, 527.

[394] See the letters of the governors in answer to requests from the Board of Trade for information, in the colonial records of New York, New Jersey, and North Carolina.

[395] See the riots in New Jersey, cited in New Jersey *Archives*, vol. vii, *passim*.

[396] See the letters of Governor Clinton of New York for a description of the method of keeping the supplies of munitions in its own hands and its practice of selling any surplus of gunpowder, in New York *Colonial Documents*, vol. vi, *passim*.

The governors were also powerless to carry out the Indian policy of the Board of Trade, which would have required some kind of police to protect the Indians against illegal traders and unscrupulous adventurers. A force was necessary to protect the whites against violence and compel the Indians to observe their treaties. Attorneys and courts would also have been required to prevent the whites from encroaching upon the Indian lands, and for breaking illegally acquired titles.[397] Almost every policy which the Board attempted to carry out under the efficient administration of Halifax – and the Board was efficient at that time – failed, because the officers in America had surrendered their control of financial affairs. The fact was the colonies had secured the power to govern themselves so far as internal matters were concerned.

It has been said that Grenville lost the American colonies because he read the dispatches,[398] which implies that before his administration the dispatches were not read. That is far from the truth, as Halifax knew the real situation in America in 1750, and was thoroughly in earnest about checking the movement.[399] Although it cannot be shown that the extensions of authority given to the Board were due to the needs of a more vigorous administrative policy in the plantations, nevertheless that change marks the beginning of what may well be termed a fighting ministry, so

---

[397] See chapter vi for details of the Indian policy of the Board of Trade.

[398] Quoted by Egerton in his *History of British Colonial Policy*, 179.

[399] See the letter of F. J. Paris to James Alexander, July 4, 1748, for an account of the keen interest taken by Halifax in New Jersey affairs, in New Jersey *Archives*, vol. vii, 295. See also the numerous representations of the Board to the king, *Ibid.*, vols. viii, ix, *passim*; New York *Colonial Documents*, vols. vi, vii, *passim*.

far as the colonies were concerned.   The governors
were given new and explicit orders to observe their
instructions in all respects.[400] Governor Osborn was
directed particularly to allow no more money bills
to pass in the irregular form which had become customary.   The years 1752 and 1753 are years of resistance by the royal governors; [401] appropriation bills
which were not drawn in the form required by the
instructions were rejected by the councils, and the
Board commended their actions.[402]

The Board also attacked the practice of annual
grants and pointed out their dangers.   Although the
assembly of New York had disavowed any intention
of usurping the government, the Board feared it had
no intention of abandoning its former pretensions.
For

> These annual grants may be employed annually to the pur-
> poses of wresting from the crown the nomination of all officers
> whose salaries depend upon the annual appointment of the
> assembly and of annually disappointing all such services of
> government as may be necessary even to the very existence of
> the colony, which are not entrusted even in their execution to
> such persons as the assembly appoints under the pretense of re-
> ceiving and applying these annual grants.[403]

The outbreak of the French and Indian War
brought the plans for resistance to the claims of the
assemblies to naught.   The governors were forced
to accept money on the terms offered by the assem-

---

[400] General instructions of 1752, in New York *Colonial Documents*, vol.
vi, 760.

[401] Letters of Governors Clinton and De Lancey to the Board, in New
York *Colonial Documents*, vol. vi, *passim*.

[402] New Jersey *Archives*, vol. vii, 365-368; vol. viii, part i, 31 *et seq*.

[403] Letter of the Board of Trade to Lieutenant-governor De Lancey, in
New York *Colonial Documents*, vol. vi, 847.

blies, and did not dare endanger the success of the English arms by entering upon a prolonged struggle with that body. The Board of Trade also realized this necessity and instructed Governor Hardy of New York not to press the question of a permanent revenue,[404] but at the same time it by no means countenanced continued encroachments upon the prerogative. Governor Bernard of New Jersey received the following warning on this point:

> By the nature and form of the laws pass'd in New Jersey, all those powers and prerogatives of the crown on the one hand and the security to the rights and properties of the subject on the other, are set aside. Commissioners are appointed for carrying into execution, independent of the governor, all the purposes of the acts. The treasurers are authoriz'd and directed to issue into their hands whatever sums they shall require, without the warrant or interposition of the governor, and those commissioners and other officers are made accountable to the assembly only. . . Such proceedings as these, must, in the end terminate in a total disarrangement of government.[405]

Other colonies were offending in the same way. Only a few months before the letter just quoted, the Board called the attention of Governor Pownall to irregularities in the Massachusetts laws.

The facts resulting from an examination into the acts

---

[404] The Board instructed him that in the "present situation of affairs, when peace and unanimity and a good understanding between his governor and the people, are so absolutely necessary for the good of the service, to direct that you should not press the establishment of a perpetual revenue for the present, and to allow and permit you to assent to such temporary bills as the Assembly shall, from time to time form and pass for the support of government." — Board to Hardy, March 4, 1756, in New York *Colonial Documents*, vol. vii, 40.

[405] Board of Trade to Francis Bernard, February 8, 1759, in New Jersey *Archives*, vol. ix, 155.

and proceedings of the Council and House of Representatives . . . are such as convince us that the dependence which by the constitution the colony ought to have upon the executive part of the government of the mother country and the sovereignty of the crown stands upon a very precarious foot and that unless some effectual remedy is at a proper time applied, it will be in great danger of being totally set aside.

From these facts it appears that almost every act of executive and legislative power, whether it be political, judicial, or military is ordered and directed by votes and resolves of the general court, in most cases originating in the House of Representatives to which all applications, petitions and representations are addressed and where the resolves are drawn up and prepared, and tho' we apprehend that such resolves are insufficient and invalid, without the concurrence of the Council in the first instance and ultimately that of the governor, yet such concurrence seems to be rather matter of form in proceeding than essential and that the measure whatever it be derives its effect and operation from the judgment and sense of the House of Representatives.[406]

On account of the exigencies of the military situation, however, the Board informed Pownall that the time was not opportune for correcting the dangerous tendencies summarized in its letter.

Illustrations of similar conditions could be drawn from the other colonies,[407] but enough have been cited to show the general movement.   In spite of protests

[406] Massachusetts *Acts and Resolves*, vol. iv, 95.

[407] "It is not only in the laws for providing for temporary services, that they appear to deviate from the principles and practice established in this kingdom; the annual act for the support of government is equally exceptionable in many parts, for we observe, that the salaries are payable to the officers by name, and not for the time being, which has a direct tendency to establish in the Assembly a negative in the nomination of those officers, and that the said act does of itself create appointments of officers, that ought to be appointed by commission from the governor." — Board to Governor Franklin, July 13, 1764, in New Jersey *Archives*, vol. ix, 444.

from governors and from the Board of Trade, and in spite of frequent representations of the state of affairs to the chief ministers, the assemblies steadily extended their power. As long as war lasted no remedy could be applied effectively, and peace was looked forward to eagerly, because of the opportunity it would give for combating the usurpations of the assembly and restoring the constitution to its previous form. This is shown by the frequent expressions found in letters and communications of the governors and of the Board of Trade.[408] The specific remedy which the latter had to offer is discussed in the next chapter.

---

[408] "I hope by the blessing of God we shall soon after this campaign have a glorious peace, and then His Majesty will have no great demands upon this province, which will prevent the encroachments of the assembly upon the prerogative." — Governor Dobbs to the Board, May 18, 1759, in North Carolina *Colonial Records*, vol. vi, 33.

IV. THE IMPERIALISTIC POLICY OF THE BOARD OF TRADE

In the maze of administrative details of colonial government there were the larger questions of the relations of the colonies to the empire. Throughout its history the Board of Trade displayed remarkable consistency in dealing with these questions. Unaffected by changing ministries, and in spite of its varying personnel and its lack of responsibility for long periods of time, the Board held tenaciously to certain principles of imperial government. It sought to preserve the dependence of the colonies upon the home government by retaining control of the executive and the judiciary and by making the colonies conform to one administrative type of government. Closely connected with these schemes were its plans for protecting the colonies by the creation of a central military government in America, which could be used to maintain order and to protect the frontiers.

The question of a fixed civil list

Early in its history the Board realized that imperial interests required the establishment of a fixed civil list in each colony. The question was not prominent when the Board was organized, but soon became so by conditions which developed in New York, where unusual expenditures were required for defense. The main source of income for a colonial

government was the revenue derived from the import
and excise duties.   These were granted to the crown
for terms of years, were lodged with the receiver-general, and could be expended only on warrants issued
by the governor in council.[409] So long as such an arrangement existed, there was no necessity for a permanent law, nor could the payment of official salaries
by a grant of Parliament have made the governor
more independent, since all control of expenditures
was vested in the hands of the direct appointees of the
crown, who were responsible only to the British government for their actions.   Under such conditions
there was no anomaly in the Board instructing the
governor what salary he and the other officers should
receive, nor in specifying exactly what sums each
colony should contribute to the common defense in
time of war.[410]

The revenue act in New York, which had been continued from 1691 to 1709, had never yielded much
more than enough to pay the immediate expenses of
the civil establishment.[411] The encroachments upon
the authority of the governor and council, through
the power of the assembly to control the unusual expenditures caused by the war, had roused the Board to

[409] See the acts of 1692, 1699, 1702. These granted the revenue in
periods of six or three years. That of 1699 did not expire till May, 1706,
yet it was continued by the act of 1702 until 1709. See: New York *Colonial
Laws*, vol. i, 287, 419, 517; New York *Colonial Documents*, vol. v, 111,
545-547. Cf. Spencer's *Phases of Royal Government in New York*, 100-107.

[410] Had the revenue acts been permanent and all expenditures remained
at the option of the governor and council, Hunter's instructions would have
been a proper means for securing the coöperation of the other colonies.
See: New York *Colonial Documents*, vol. v, 138-139.

[411] Report of Bellomont, in New York *Colonial Documents*, vol. iv, 319,
538, 602, 721. Cf. Spencer's *Phases of Royal Government in New York*,
100-106.

a full realization of the danger involved.[412] The remedy was simple enough. If a permanent revenue could be established, the assembly would no longer have the means of extending its authority, consequently Hunter was instructed to insist upon an act for establishing such a revenue.[413]

Hunter arrived in New York in June, 1710, with this instruction and at the first session of the assembly endeavored to secure a law in accordance with it. In spite of all the influence he could exert, however, the assembly would neither provide a permanent revenue nor enact such a temporary law as he was permitted to accept. He reported the refusal of the assembly to conform to his instructions;[414] whereupon the Board at once took up the matter and in a representation to the queen recommended that a standing revenue for the government of New York should be established by act of Parliament.[415] The recommendation met with the approval of the ministry, and the Board was instructed to draw up heads of a bill for that purpose,[416] but for some reason the bill was never presented to either house.[417]

---

[412] See the letters of the Board to Cornbury and its representations to the king, in New York *Colonial Documents*, vol. iv, *passim*.

[413] His instructions, clause 34, provided, "that all laws whatsoever, for the good government and support of the said province be made indefinite and without limitation of time, except the same be for a temporary end, and which shall expire and have its full effect within a certain time." — New York *Colonial Documents*, vol. v, 129.

[414] Hunter to the Board, in New York *Colonial Documents*, vol. v, 177, 183.

[415] New York *Colonial Documents*, vol. v, 190-193.

[416] Order in Council, March 1, 1711, in Board of Trade *Journal*, 22, pp. 254-255. There is a copy of the proposed law in British Museum *Additional Manuscripts*, 33028, ff. 23-31.

[417] Hunter to the Earl of Stair, October 18, 1714, in New York *Colonial*

In the meantime Hunter was encouraged by the Board to persist in his struggle for a permanent settlement and assured that it did not doubt "but proper measures will be taken here for fixing that matter for the future." [418] Soon after Parliament assembled in the following autumn another representation was laid before the queen, which gave a very succinct statement of the conditions in New York and the dangerous example it was setting for other colonies. "And we having reason to believe from their proceedings that they are not likely to settle such a revenue, we humbly offer that provision be made in Parliament here for that purpose." [419]

This representation failed to accomplish its purpose, as did a similar one some months later. No bill was brought in, though the Board continued to encourage Hunter with promises of support. April 1, 1713, the whole matter, with a draft of a bill for a permanent revenue, was laid before Dartmouth who, from his long connection with the Board, must have been familiar with the condition of affairs in the colonies. [420] He approved the bill and directed the Board to lay it before Parliament, but the session was so far advanced that nothing was done. [421] The Board, how-

Documents, vol. v, 451-453. The Board wrote Hunter that the bill could not be presented on account of the early rising of Parliament.

[418] Board of Trade to Hunter, November 13, 1711, in New York Colonial Documents, vol. v, 285.

[419] Representation of the Board of Trade, in New York Colonial Documents, vol. v, 288.

[420] Board of Trade to Dartmouth, in New York Colonial Documents, vol. v, 359. Cf. Spencer's Phases of Royal Government in New York, 137-139.

[421] Board to Hunter, July 20, 1713, in New York Colonial Documents, vol. v, 367.

ever, promised Hunter that the matter would be pushed at the next session.[422]

In the meantime Hunter had despaired of securing any help from England and had been forced to make the best terms he could with his assembly. Early in 1715 he secured a settlement for five years, and the Board said no more about the bill. It is doubtful if there was any intention of enacting the legislation thus constantly demanded by the Board for five years, and even Hunter's friends appear to have questioned the expediency of the measure, since a permanent revenue might have meant his own recall.[423] The Board of Trade, however, was not disposed to abandon its demands and the instructions to Hunter were renewed to his successors, but with no better results.

Instructions similar to those of the governor of New York had been given to the governor of Massachusetts, but the issue was not fought out there until the arrival of Governor Burnet. His instructions, which had originally been prepared for Governor Shute, required the assembly to establish a fixed salary of at least one thousand pounds per annum on

[422] "You may be assured that now we have Her Majesty's commands as aforesaid, we shall not fail at ye beginning of the next Parliament, to take all the care possible that Her Majesty's commands for the future be no more slighted by a people who owe their whole protection to Her Majesty's goodness." — New York *Colonial Documents*, vol. v, 367.

[423] "Meanwhile I was left to beg my daily bread from a hard hearted Assembly here, tho' Her Majesty, upon a representation from the Lords of trade of the state and behaviour of this province had ordered a bill to be drawn and laid before ye Parliament for settling the revenue here during her life, which was accordingly drawn but never presented to either house. Some of my friends wrote me word that they thought it was better for me it should not pass, because if there was a revenue settled I might depend on being superseded." — Hunter to the Earl of Stair, October 18, 1714, in New York *Colonial Documents*, vol. v, 451.

threat of action by Parliament.[424] The assembly refused to comply, and a bitter controversy ensued. Finally the matter was taken up by the Board, which
sustained the governor and, in a representation to the
Privy Council, asked that the matter be laid before
Parliament.

The action of the Board was approved by the ministry, and the impression given out that action by
Parliament was imminent; but it seems more than
probable that Newcastle had no intention whatever
of resorting to such drastic methods, and that the
threat was little more than an attempt to frighten
Massachusetts into doing what the Board demanded.
There is even evidence to indicate that he saw the
bluff would fail, and that the action which was finally
taken was in the direction of "saving the face" of the
administration.[425]

The premature death of Burnet left the matter to
be settled by his successor, Jonathan Belcher, who
arrived in Boston in August, 1730, with even more

[424] Instructions of March 20, 1728, in C.O. 5, 916; Massachusetts *Acts
and Resolves*, vol. ii, 632; Palfrey's *History of New England*, vol. iv, 50;
Greene's *Provincial Governor*, 171-172; Hutchinson's *History of Massachu-
setts*, vol. i, chap. iii; *A collection of the Proceedings of the Great and
General Court or Assembly of His Majesty's Province of Massachusetts
Bay*, 41.

[425] There is in the Public Record Office in London, an unsigned draft of
a letter to Burnet, dated June 26, 1729, which would seem to be from Newcastle, the substance of which follows:

"By my other letter and the copy of the Order in Council inclosed in
it, you will plainly see it is the intention of the crown, that the affair of
settling a salary on you should be laid before the Parliament at their first
meeting, as it undoubtedly will, unless the House of Representation take
care to prevent it in time by complying with what is expected of them.
[It is hoped that things will not come to such a pass; and, as luckily hap-
pens, they have a long time to consider better of it and may improve their

peremptory instructions than had previously been given.   By these he was forbidden to accept any gift or present from the assembly on any account or in any way whatsoever, upon pain of the king's highest displeasure, except under an act fixing a permanent salary of at least one thousand pounds sterling, free from all deductions, to be constantly paid out of such money as should, from time to time, be raised for the support of the government.[426]   If the assembly failed to comply with this instruction, he was directed either to proceed at once to England or send an agent, so that the matter might be laid before Parliament.[427]

The assembly offered Belcher his salary in the customary form of a temporary grant, but his instructions forbade his receiving it in that way.   After considerable delay he secured permission to accept the grant, but was still directed to insist upon a permanent establishment.   This he was unable to get, consequently the annual form of securing special permis-

opportunity.]   Therefore I write you this letter at His Majesty's command, so that you may try to bring them to a better temper, and make them realize that this is the only way of recommending themselves to His Majesty's favor and protection.   Tho you were to insist upon their settling the salaries of all future governors as well as your own, you are now at liberty to accept a settlement for yourself only — but during the whole time of your government, Her Majesty depends upon your skill and prudence to make use of these hints to influence the Assembly to pay due obedience to His Majesty's commands; but whatever you do is to come from yourself in private capacity, so as not to appear like a new overture on the part of the crown, as if it were not really intended to lay the matter before Parliament.   But in case of their voluntary compliance and if it is done before Parliament meets, you may let them know that you will use your endeavors to prevent any Parliamentary Enquiry." — Board of Trade, *America and West Indies*, 5, p. 19.

[426] Massachusetts *Acts and Resolves*, vol. ii, 633; Palfrey, John. *History of New England*, vol. iv, chap. vi.

[427] Massachusetts *Acts and Resolves*, vol. ii, 633; Palfrey, John. *History of New England*, vol. iv, chap. vi.

sion to accept his salary was gone through with until 1735, when the permission was made general.[428]

That the idea of a permanent civil list was no mere whim of the Board, but was one of its most fundamental policies, is seen in the action of Martin Bladen, who according to Belcher, constantly opposed giving permission to accept the temporary grants of the Massachusetts assembly.[429] His opposition may have been based upon personal grounds, but that is not the only possible explanation. No doubt he would have preferred to see the question settled once for all in the interests of the empire, rather than postponed from year to year; for as early as 1726, in his essay on the colonies, he advocated a stamp tax for America, the proceeds of which should go to establish a permanent civil list. In this way the question of salaries could be settled and dangers of further encroachments by the assembly removed.[430] This proposal was not ac-

[428] The reason given by the Board for recommending the withdrawal of the former instruction regarding a fixed salary was that the charter did not admit of any such interpretation as the instruction implied. But in recommending that the clause in question should be omitted, the Board again pointed out that it would be much better to fix a salary on the governor, payable out of some of the royal revenues from the plantations, "By which the governor will become entirely independent of the people, and no longer laid under any temptation of giving up the prerogative of the crown or sacrificing the interest of Great Britain to any private advantage." — C.O. 5, 917, pp. 131-132.

[429] Letter of Belcher to Richard Partridge, in Massachusetts Historical Society *Collections*, sixth series, vol. vi, 81-84.

[430] "All that has been said with respect to the improvement of the plantations will it is supposed signify very little unless a sufficient revenue can be raised to support the useful expence, in order to which it is humbly submitted whether the duties of stamps upon parchment and paper in England may not with good reason be extended by act of Parliament to all the American Plantations." — Bladen's "A Short Discourse on the Present State of the Colonies in America with Respect to the Interest of Great Britain, submitted to Secretary Townshend, 1726," in North Carolina *Colo-*

cepted by the chief ministers, but it shows the attitude of the most active member of the Board of Trade, who was ready to resort to a method which offered the only practical solution of the difficulty.

What has been said concerning a civil list for New York applies in a general way to New Jersey, as the instructions to the governors were essentially the same. Those to Cornbury required the assembly to settle forthwith "a constant and fixed allowance on you, our governour and lieutenant-governour for the time being, suitable to their respective characters and dignity, and that the same be done without limitation of time." [431] Later he was especially instructed to require a settlement for twenty-one years, and failing in that, to demand that it be for not less than eleven years. He was compelled, however, to accept a grant for two years, and afterwards for but one year.[432] Hunter and his successors, Montgomerie and Cosby, were no more successful in securing what their instructions required.

The continued failure of the governors on this point caused the Board of Trade to make the instructions still more specific. When New Jersey was separated from New York in 1738 and Lewis Morris sent over as governor, the Board considered the time opportune for securing its cherished object; therefore Morris was given instructions similar to those sent to Governor Burnet of Massachusetts.

nial Records, vol. ii, 635. This discourse is identical with the one ascribed to Sir William Keith, which was transmitted to the Board, December, 1728, New Jersey *Archives*, vol. v, 214-230.

[431] Special instructions as to salary, 1702, in New Jersey *Archives*, vol. ii, 537-538.

[432] —*Ibid.*, vol. iii, 69-71, 99.

You are therefor to propose unto the Assembly at their first meeting, after your arrival, and to use your utmost endeavours with them that an act be pass'd for raising and settling a publick revenue for defraying the necessary charge of the government of our said province, and that therein provision be particularly made for a competant salary, to yourself as captain general and governor-in-chief of our said province, and to other our succeeding captains-general for supporting the dignity of the said office, as likewise due provision for the contingent charges of our council and Assembly, and for the salaries of the respective clerks and other officers thereunto belonging, as likewise of all other officers necessary for the administration of that government. [The salaries were to be a fixed annual amount payable in sterling, and the governor was forbidden to accept any presents or other remuneration on] pain of our highest displeasure and of being recalled from that our government.[433]

In spite of these peremptory orders, Morris obtained a settlement for only three years. In 1746 the same instructions were given to Belcher, but he found himself helpless on account of the riots in the province, and was even less successful than his predecessors had been. No action of importance was taken by the Board until after the appointment of Halifax as president. The condition of affairs in New Jersey and New York had become so serious that the Board made an investigation and reported its findings with recommendations of proper remedies.

In its report on New Jersey, which appeared in 1750, the Board pointed out that the fundamental weakness of the government was the dependence of the executive upon the financial support of the assembly. In accordance with its traditional policy, it

[433] Instructions to Morris, clause 26, in New Jersey *Archives*, vol. vi, 26-27.

proposed to make the governor independent by granting him a fixed salary out of the British exchequer,
and as the riots in the province would require the
presence of some effective military force, it proposed
to place a sufficient number of regular troops at his
disposal to restore order.[434] The recommendation,
however, was too radical for the ministry of the day
and no positive action was taken.

Within a year the Board made its elaborate report
on New York.   Although the situation there was not
complicated with riots, as was the case in New Jersey,
conditions were serious.   The difficulty there was also
one of revenue, and the Board proposed its regular
remedy of a permanent act, such as had been passed
in Jamaica.   There is an intimation at the close of the
report that the only means of securing such an act
would be by action of the home government,[435] which
was a step which the ministry was not prepared to
take.

Halifax apparently still had hopes of accomplishing the desired end by means of instructions, and in
1752 the governors were ordered not to deviate from

---

[434] See the report of the Board, June 1, 1750, in New Jersey *Archives*,
vol. vii, 466-528.

[435] In commenting on the action of the last assembly the report concludes:
"But, my Lords, they have passed these Acts of supply in the same improper
manner, and with the same usurpations on the prerogative, and liable to
every objection, which induced Mr. Clinton in the year 1748, to dissolve the
Assembly, and leave the province without support rather than in a time of
peace, give his consent and sanction to such destructive encroachments upon
the legal and just prerogative of the crown . . . tho' the Assembly have
agreed to make some provision for the charges of Government, their usurpations on the prerogative are rather confirmed than regained by this last
meeting, and as great a necessity as ever remains for the councils of this
kingdom to interpose and take some measures, for the better settlement of
this most valuable and divided province." — New York *Colonial Documents*,
vol. vi, 638.

them "in any point, but upon evident necessity." The passing of laws in a manner contrary to their instructions was given as the chief cause of the difficulties which had developed in several colonies. "We must therefore in a particular manner insist that in the passing of all laws you have a proper regard to the regulations contained in your instructions." [436]

Clinton was soon relieved at his own request, and Sir Danvers Osborn sent in his place. The instructions to the latter show the temper of Halifax; he was to charge the assembly to recede from the unwarrantable assumptions, and require the enactment of a permanent revenue.[437] Furthermore, his instructions would not have permitted him to accept a temporary grant of revenue in any form,[438] and the assembly was literally to be forced to give way. He was also directed at once to remove any member of his council who should acquiesce in, or who should not actively resist, encroachments from the assembly. On the whole these were the strictest instructions ever given to a governor, but Osborn did not live to carry them out, as he committed suicide soon after his arrival. Lieutenant-governor De Lancey succeeded to the government and attempted to enforce the stringent orders brought over by his predecessor.

---

[436] Circular letter to the governors, June 3, 1752, in New York *Colonial Documents*, vol. vi, 760.

[437] Chalmers, George. *Introduction to the Revolt*, vol. ii, 315.

[438] "We must however beg leave humbly to represent to your Excellencies that it being doubtful whether by the words of the former instruction His Majesty's governor was not tied up from assenting to any law for making provision for temporary services until he should have obtained a permanent revenue." Representation on Hardy's Instructions, April 22, 1755, in New York *Colonial Documents*, vol. vi, 948.

The outbreak of the French and Indian War, however, compelled the Board to allow the governors to accept revenue bills of a temporary character. As the war went on, it became more and more necessary not to arouse the opposition of the assemblies; consequently the Board was compelled to abandon, for the time, its aggressive policy. Governor Hardy's instructions, which were issued in 1755, directed him to accept temporary grants but to continue to insist upon a permanent law.[439] Even this point had to be waived, and the Board finally instructed the governors of Massachusetts, New Jersey, and New York not to insist upon a permanent revenue, but to accept whatever financial aid the assemblies would vote.[440]

The point was not abandoned by the Board but was only waived for the time being, for the general instructions remained as stringent as ever. The continued military necessities only postponed the final solution of the question. The Board had done all it could to secure a fixed civil list so as to make the governors independent of their local assemblies, but could accomplish very little without the intervention of Parliament. The ministry would not ask for that, however, until the failure of the Stamp Act convinced it of the necessity of the step. Then the Board was ordered to lay before Parliament a detailed statement of the cost of the civil establishment in America,[441] but the measure had been postponed too long.

---

[439] New York *Colonial Documents*, vol. vi, 948, par. 19.

[440] New York *Colonial Documents*, vol. vii, 32-33; Massachusetts *Acts and Resolves*, vol. iv, 95; New Jersey *Archives*, vol. ix, 156.

[441] New Jersey *Archives*, vol. ix, 533-534; *Journal of the House of Commons*, vol. xxx, 484.

In Maryland and Virginia permanent laws had been secured, which provided for nearly all the charges upon the civil list in time of peace. In North Carolina the governor and other officers were assigned permanent salaries out of the quit rents; but as these were seldom collected, the regular clause regarding a fixed revenue was inserted in the instructions given to Governor Dobbs in 1754.[442] In Jamaica the assembly was finally induced to yield to the continued demands of the Board of Trade and enact the desired legislation. The crown itself bore the charges of government in Nova Scotia and in Georgia;[443] consequently the struggle over the civil list centered in the three provinces of Massachusetts, New Jersey, and New York. Pennsylvania and New Hampshire should be included, were it not for the fact that the latter occasionally granted the revenue for a period of years, and in the former the proprietaries were sponsors for the salary of the governor. Even then Penn's government was objected to on account of the absence of an established revenue.[444]

From the foregoing account it is clear that the Board realized the fundamental weakness in the im-

[442] North Carolina *Colonial Records*, vol. v, 1114, par. 24.

[443] It is significant that in both of these younger colonies the Board of Trade took no steps to place the governors and other officers at the mercy of the assemblies by asking the latter to pay their salaries. Instead, the necessary sums were annually appropriated by Parliament and the officials thus kept strictly responsible to the home government. For reports on Georgia, see C.O. 5, 672, pp. 26-29, 40-41, 47, 322, 373.

[444] "I shall write to the council to represent how it is taken that there is no settled revenue in the province to answer the exigencies of government, especially for a governor, a judge, and an attorney-general: without this be got in hand with, I fear our own enemies there will have but too plausible a pretence against us here, especially in war time." — Penn to Logan, June 27, 1703, in Penn-Logan *Correspondence*, vol. i, 210.

perial constitution, and throughout a period of sixty years constantly endeavored to correct it by securing a fixed civil list in the colonies. This was its favorite policy, and the one to which it adhered in spite of changing personnel and the rise and fall of ministries. The officers of the later colonies of Nova Scotia and Georgia were paid by the crown; and in every colony in which the government was supported by temporary grants the Board sought to bring about a similar situation or force the colonies themselves to make the salaries permanent. Jamaica, however, is the only colony which yielded.

Control of the judiciary

The question of the control of the judiciary was very closely connected with that of a fixed civil list; but in this case it turned upon the form of the judges' commissions rather than upon their salaries. As to the tenure which the judges were to enjoy, the instructions to the governors during the earlier years of the Board of Trade were not clear. They simply directed the governors not to express "any limitation of time" in any commissions they should issue to judicial officers.[445] This was avowedly to protect the judges from arbitrary removal at the hands of the governors; but what did the phrase, *"no limitation of time,"* mean? It could mean either during good be-

---

[445] See the instructions to Bellomont, in New York *Colonial Documents*, vol. iv, 286; to Cornbury, in New Jersey *Archives*, vol. ii, 518-519. The clause remained unchanged until 1753 and was as follows: You shall not displace any of the judges, justices, or other officers or ministers within our said province, without good and sufficient cause to be signified unto us, and to our said commissioners for trade and plantations; and to prevent arbitrary removals of judges and justices of the peace, you shall not express any limitation of time in the commissions you are to grant.

havior or during the pleasure of the crown. The general practice seems to have been to issue commissions at pleasure during the first third of the eighteenth century, and the question did not become of importance to imperial interests until the administration of Halifax.

The early problem of the Board was to secure able men for the chief judicial positions in the colonies, for the governors found themselves seriously handicapped by the lack of efficient and trustworthy men for chief justices and attorneys-general. Bellomont of New York urgently demanded that such officers should be sent from England. Finally the Board took the matter in hand and secured the appointment of William Atwood as chief justice and Sampson Shelton Broughton as attorney-general.[446] These men were appointed by request of the Board of Trade, after they had been recommended by the attorney- and the solicitor-general in England, as was done in all similar cases of judicial appointments for the colonies where commissions were issued in England.[447]

Similar officers were appointed by the crown for the other colonies,[448] but in some cases the governors appointed when a vacancy occurred. There was no regularity about the procedure. Thus while both Atwood and his successor, Dr. Bridges, were sent from England, Cornbury commissioned Mompesson as chief justice on the death of Bridges, and requested

---

[446] Letters to the Board of Trade, in New York *Colonial Documents*, vol. iv, 667, and *passim*.

[447] Board of Trade *Journal*, 13, pp. 76-94.

[448] Mr. Stephens Thompson was appointed as attorney-general for Virginia in 1703, on the request of Governor Nicholson and the recommendation

the Board to secure his confirmation; but that body replied that he needed no confirmation, "since by the commission given him by your Lordship he is actually chief justice." [449] Numerous illustrations could be cited of appointments by governors, and also many in which they were commissioned in England. [450] The Board, however, does not appear to have controlled the appointments until after 1752, after which date it became less common for the governors to select them.

In its representation of December, 1699, which requested the appointment of a chief justice and an attorney-general for New York, the Board gave an indication of what was to be its later policy toward the judiciary. After pointing out the meager allowance the assembly of New York had granted to previous incumbents of these offices, it said:

We . . . are humbly of opinion that a dependance upon the General Assembly there for a further allowance will by no ways suit with your Majesty's service in the administration of justice against piracy and irregular trade. . . We do therefore humbly represent to your Majesty that much greater allowances will be necessary to invite fit persons to accept of those employments, and that they be assured thereof by an establishment here; which extraordinary charge we humbly conceive will be abundantly recompensed by a very great increase of your Majesty's customs. [451]

of the attorney-general in England. See: Board of Trade *Journal*, 16, pp. 168-197.

[449] New York *Colonial Documents*, vol. iv, 1138-1139. On the death of Mompesson, Governor Hunter appointed Lewis Morris. See: *Ibid.*, vol. v, 400.

[450] See: New York *Colonial Documents*, vol. v, 400, 705, 949, 977; vol. vii, 464, 500; New Jersey *Archives*, vol. ix, 379; Smith, W. R. *South Carolina as a Royal Province*, 333-334.

[451] New York *Colonial Documents*, vol. iv, 599.

Apparently this representation was acted upon in full. Atwood and Broughton were appointed, but it is not quite clear that they received their pay from England. Cornbury says Atwood received three hundred pounds from there and asked a similar salary for Dr. Bridges,[452] but the Board states, in a letter to Bellomont, that the men had received some check at the treasury,[453] and fails to inform us whether or not they overcame the difficulty. The principle laid down by the Board was an excellent one, but required money to carry it into operation. As there was practically no money in the imperial treasury to the credit of New York, the treasury officials resisted any proposal to pay salaries to such officers. In Virginia conditions were a little better as there was a considerable fund arising from the quit rents, and the salary of the attorney-general was paid out of that. In this way he was made independent of the local legislature.[454]

There is but little doubt that the power of the Assembly to fix salaries rendered all the judges practically dependent upon that body, except in the few cases in which they received their salaries from the crown. In New York the salaries were varied from time to time,[455] and in one case apparently for the pur-

---

[452] Cornbury to the Board, New York *Colonial Documents*, vol. iv, 1142.

[453] "Notwithstanding all that we have been able to do, towards the promoting of what your Lordship has so oft desired, in relation to a chief justice and attorney-general for the Province of New York, yet Mr. Atwood and Mr. Broughton met with some stop in the treasury, and we do not see that anything further will be done in that business at present." — New York *Colonial Documents*, vol. iv, 700.

[454] Board of Trade *Journal*, 16, pp. 168-197.

[455] See the appropriation bills in the New York *Colonial Laws*, vols. i, ii, iii, *passim*.

pose of showing disapproval of a decision of the Supreme Court.[456]   These encroachments upon the judiciary, however, did not attract the serious attention of the Board of Trade for many years, and the obscure clause of Bellomont's instructions was continued in those given to other governors.   Governor Clinton of New York was induced to interpret this clause as a direction to make the judges' commissions read during good behavior.[457]   His successor, De Lancey, followed the same custom and governors of other colonies may have issued similar commissions; it is certain that they did in New Jersey.

In 1752 the Board of Trade carefully revised the general instructions to the governors, and the clause regarding the commissions for judges shows the attempt of the Board to check the growing changes in the colonial constitution.   Certain events had called the attention of the Board to the uncertain meaning of the former clause.   The town clerk of Albany had been appointed in 1728 by the crown to hold office during pleasure, but upon his death, in 1750, Governor Clinton appointed Mr. Gansevoert during good behavior.   In the meantime, however, the Board had secured a commission for Mr. Wraxall to hold the office during pleasure.   When the latter arrived at Albany, he found Gansevoert in possession of the office; and, as the latter was not disposed to recognize the commission from England, Mr. Wraxall appealed to the Board.   That body, after a careful investigation, proposed that the attorney-general of

---

[456] Chalmers, George. *Introduction to the Revolt*, vol. ii.

[457] Colden to the Board of Trade, August 12, 1761.   He does not state what the practice was prior to Clinton's administration.

New York should take the proper measures to vacate the commission issued by Clinton.[458]

Another of Clinton's commissions, that to Chief Justice De Lancey, was considered by the Board at almost the same time as that to the town clerk of Albany. This commission had been issued soon after Clinton's arrival in New York and was for good behavior, while that office "had before that time been usually held during pleasure." [459] The Board referred the case of the attorney- and the solicitor-general with the following queries:

> Had Mr. Clinton any power to grant such commission during good behavior, contrary to what had been practised in former cases? Can the crown legally revoke the said commission? if it can what will be the proper method of doing it?

The law officers answered that,

> As the power given by commission is general we apprehend the grant is good in point of law and cannot be revoked without misbehavior.[460]

The Board thus had sufficient information before it to know the limitations of the previous instructions and to change those for the future so as to prevent similar occurrences. In 1754 Governor Dobbs of North Carolina and Governor Reynolds of Georgia were instructed, "that all commissions to be granted by you to any person or persons to be judges, justices of the peace or other necessary officer be granted during pleasure only." [461] This clause was also inserted in the instructions afterwards given to other govern-

---

[458] New York *Colonial Documents*, vol. vi, 768-769.

[459] This would seem to indicate that the practice had been irregular.

[460] New York *Colonial Documents*, vol. vi, 792.

[461] North Carolina *Colonial Records*, vol. v, 1124, clause 62; C.O. 5, 672, p. 163.

ors; [462] and as the governors were strictly enjoined to observe their instructions in all particulars, the question was certain to come to an issue.

The first move came from the assemblies. That of Pennsylvania took advantage of the venality of Governor Denny and secured a judiciary act, by which the judges were to hold their commissions during good behavior instead of at the pleasure of the proprietary. This law was passed in September, 1759, and provided that judges could be removed only on an address of the assembly, [463] but the proprietaries at once complained of the act and asked for its disallowance by the crown. The Board of Trade reported strongly against the law, because its object

> Is to change the tenure by which the judges now hold their offices; not only in the province of Pennsylvania but in every other colony in North America and the West Indies from *"durante bene placitia"* to *"Quamdiu se bene gesserent,"* [464]

and upon this representation the act was promptly disallowed.

This report is interesting as showing that the Board interpreted the early indefinite instruction as meaning that commissions should be during pleasure. It had already announced its policy in the case of a similar law passed by the assembly of Jamaica, upon which the attorney- and solicitor-general were of opinion, that it was not expedient for the interests of either the mother country or the colonies that judges in the plantations should hold their places *quamdiu*

---

[462] Governors Osborn, De Lancey, and Hardy of New York, and was the only clause on the subject in Colden's instructions in 1761.

[463] Pennsylvania *Statutes at Large*, vol. v, 463.

[464] Representation of the Board of Trade, in Pennsylvania *Statutes at Large*, vol. v, 722.

se bene gesserent. The decision on the Pennsylvania act had scarcely been announced when the death of the king terminated all commissions in the colonies and brought the whole question to a head.

The judges in New York refused to act until their commissions had been renewed, and demanded them, as they had formerly held them, on good behavior. In August, 1761, Governor Colden wrote the Board that he might be compelled to issue their commissions in that form in spite of his instructions.[465]   In the preceding June the assembly had sent up a bill providing that the judges' commissions should be during good behavior, and when it met again in the following September, it insisted that the governor should sign this bill, which he had hitherto refused to do.   Colden offered to yield, provided the assembly would grant the judges permanent salaries, so that they would not be too dependent upon the assembly.[466]   The lower house refused to do this, consequently the courts were at a standstill.   In the meantime Colden was waiting anxiously for instructions from the Board.

The question of judges' commissions had also been raised in other colonies.   The assembly of North Carolina passed a judiciary act by which the judges were to hold these during good behavior, and in spite of his instructions, Governor Dobbs allowed this to

---

[465] "I have been informed that the judges design to forbear acting until their commissions are renewed and that they will not accept of them otherwise than during good behaviour as they had their commissions formerly.

"It may be of most dangerous consequence to stop the course of justice, and this may lay me under a necessity of complying in a matter which is so popular, tho the doing of it be against my own judgment (as well as His Majesty's instructions)." — New York *Colonial Documents*, vol. vii, 470.

[466] Letter of Colden to the Board, January 11, 1762, Colden Papers, in New York Historical Society *Collections*, vol. ix, 148.

become a law.[467]   Governor Hardy arrived in New
Jersey late in 1761 and found all judicial proceedings stopped because of the expiration of the judges'
commissions. He met his assembly in a short time,
and having been informed that it would grant no
salaries to the judges if they accepted their commissions other than during good behavior, he renewed
them "in the same manner as they have hitherto been
granted." [468]

In the meantime letters from the governors had
reached the Board of Trade, by which that body was
fully informed of the situation in America. It
realized the importance of the question at issue and
grasped the opportunity to enforce its policy. November 11, 1761, in a long representation to the committee of the Privy Council, it entered into a careful
argument against allowing judges' commissions to be
granted except for pleasure.

> Late years have produced too many examples of governors
> having been obliged for want of such an establishment as
> might induce able persons to offer their service, to confer the
> office on those who have accepted it merely with a view to
> make it subservient to their own private interests, and who
> added to their ignorance, of the law, have too frequently be-
> come the partisans of a factious Assembly upon whom they
> have been dependent for their support, and who have withheld
> or enlarged that support according as the conduct of the judges
> was more or less favorable to their interests.

> That it is difficult to conceive a state of government more
> dangerous to the rights and liberties of the subject, but aggra-
> vated as the evil would be by making the judges' commissions

---

[467] The judges in the Carolinas had previously held only during pleasure.
See: Smith, W. R. *South Carolina as a Royal Province*, 333-334.

[468] Hardy to the Board of Trade, January 20, 1762, in New Jersey
Archives, vol. ix, 346.

during good behavior without rendering them at the same time independent of the factious will and caprice of an assembly, the said Lords Commissioners cannot but consider the proposition as subversive of all true policy, destructive of the interests of Your Majesty's subjects, and tending to lessen that just dependence which the colonies ought to have upon the government of the mother country.[469]

This representation was followed up on December 2, 1761, by general instructions to all the governors in America. These recited the fact that several colonies had passed or attempted to pass laws for commissioning judges during good behavior, and that in several colonies the governors had issued such commissions.[470]

And whereas it does not appear to us, that, in the present situation and circumstances of our said colonies it would either be for the interests or advantage of the said colonies, or of this our kingdom of Great Britain that the judges or other chief officers of justice, should hold their offices, during good behavior; it is therefore our express will and pleasure that you do not upon any pretense whatever upon pain of being removed from your government give your assent to any act, by which the tenure of the commissions to be granted to the chief judges, or other justices of the several courts of judicature shall be regulated, or ascertained in any manner whatever; and you are to take particular care in all commissions to be by you granted to the said chief judges, or other justices of the courts of judicature that the said commissions are granted, during pleasure only, agreeable to what has been the antient practice and usage in our said colonies and plantations.[471]

Before this order reached America, Governor Hardy of New Jersey, as has been noted, had broken through his instructions and renewed the commis-

---

[469] C.O. 324, 17, pp. 133, ff.
[470] North Carolina *Colonial Records*, vol. vi, 591.
[471] C.O. 5, 324, pp. 170-173.

sions during good behavior.[472]   As soon as the news of his action reached England, the Board demanded and obtained his immediate removal from office.   At the same time it asked the attorney- and solicitor-general for an opinion as to the validity of the commissions thus issued in violation of the governor's instructions, and as to the possibility of vacating them by legal process.[473]   It was nine months before an opinion was returned, and then it was that of Attorney-general Yorke alone.   He considered the action of the governor as illegal, because he had committed an act which was not only unauthorized, but was positively forbidden; but as the judges had been *de facto* officers their acts should be considered valid.   The only feasible method of removing them from office, however, was by an appeal to the king in council.[474]   Fortunately such a remedy was not required, for Governor Hardy induced the judges to resign their commissions and accept new ones during pleasure only; but such action came too late to prevent his recall.

While Hardy was yielding to the demands of the former judges, Lieutenant-governor Colden was endeavoring to make terms with his assembly.   Early in

[472] Cf. Beer's *British Colonial Policy*, 191. There is an implication in this that Hardy had received these later instructions before he issued the commissions, which is probably erroneous, as the instructions were not completed until December 2, 1761, and on January 20, 1762, Hardy writes that the commissions had already been granted.

[473] New Jersey *Archives*, vol. ix, 349-351.

[474] "I am of opinion that the appointment of judges of the Supreme Court, during good behavior, instead of during pleasure, contrary to the king's instructions, in governments subsisting solely by his Majesty's authority, is illegal and invalid. The letters patent empower the governor to constitute judges, without prescribing anything as to the form or mode of constituting them; but the instructions, which are referred to by the letters patent, and

1762 he was forced to sign the appropriation bill, which granted salaries to the judges only on condition that they accept commissions during good behavior.[475] In the meantime the situation was further complicated by the arrival of Benjamin Pratt with a warrant under the sign manual, directing the governor to commission him chief justice during pleasure.[476] He received his commission and entered upon his duties, but received no salary. Naturally he could not afford to continue to work without pay, and at the urgent request of Colden, the Board of Trade secured a salary for him to be paid out of the quit rents.[477] The other judges refused to accept commissions during pleasure, for in that case they would receive no salaries; and the governor could not issue commissions in any other manner without danger of being immediately removed from office, consequently Chief Justice Pratt acted alone for some time.[478] Finally, however, the judges gave way and consented to accept their commissions in accordance with the governor's instructions.

---

consequently must be incorporated into them, regulate the mode of the constitution." — New Jersey *Archives*, vol. ix, 380-381.

[475] Letter of Lieutenant-governor Colden to the Board, February 11, 1762. Colden Papers, New York Historical Society *Collections*, vol. ix, 159.

[476] Pratt had been appointed by the Board early in 1761, and arrived in New York in October of the same year. New York *Colonial Documents*, vol. vii, 464, 483.

[477] "We entirely agree in opinion with the lieutenant-governor that if this gentleman be neglected under so singular a hardship, the consequences will greatly affect your Majesty's authority in every part of administration, we cannot but adopt and humbly recommend Mr. Colden's proposition that your Majesty would be graciously pleased to grant Mr. Pratt as chief justice of New York a salary out of your quit rents in that province." — Representation of the Board, New York *Colonial Documents*, vol. vii, 506.

[478] Colden to the Board, February 11, 1762, in New York Historical Society *Collections*, vol. ix, 159.

A similar struggle had occurred in some of the other colonies, but in all cases the Board was successful, and from that time on judges were commissioned only during pleasure. Two acts of North Carolina for regulating judicial procedure were disallowed, largely because the judges were to be commissioned during good behavior.[479] These incidents settled the question of the position of the judges until it again became prominent on the eve of the Revolution.

From the foregoing account it is seen that the attitude of the Board of Trade toward the judiciary was fairly consistent. As early as 1699, it had proposed that the chief judicial officers should be paid by the home government, and at no time did it countenance any movements which would render them independent of the crown. The Board understood its instructions to the governors to mean that judges' commissions should be for pleasure only, and for years most of them appear to have been issued in that form.[480] The first problem was to make them secure from arbitrary removal by the governors, and for that reason judicial officers could be removed only for sufficient cause. The irregular practice of commissioning them during good behavior grew up at a time

[479] The first act was that of 1760, which was disallowed on a representation of the Board of December, 1761. The second act, passed in 1761, was a supplement to the first and had other objectionable features which induced the Board to disallow it. The agent of the colony, Couchet Jouvencal, entered a strong protest against this action of the Board, in which he advanced the reasons for demanding that the tenure of judges' commissions should be changed from pleasure to good behavior. See: North Carolina *Colonial Records*, vol. vi, 587-589, 701, 983-989.

[480] The writer has found no clear cases of commissions which were issued during good behavior before those of Governor Clinton, who commenced his administration in 1744. Certainly all commissions issued by the home government were for pleasure only.

when the Board was most inefficient and the assemblies were making their greatest encroachments upon the constitution.

After 1752 the Board recognized the dangers to the empire from the dependence of all crown officers upon the assembly, and made the instructions so clear that they could not be misunderstood. From that time on commissions could be granted legally only during pleasure. The attempt by the assemblies to regulate commissions by colonial laws was immediately opposed by the Board; and when all commissions were vacated by the death of George II, it compelled the governors to observe their instructions on this point.

As far as this part of its policy is concerned, it must be admitted that the Board scored a brilliant victory, but in doing so it created considerable ill feeling in America. The average man in 1761 was totally ignorant of the form of the judges' commissions thirty years earlier, and to him this action of the Board was an uncalled-for and arbitrary attack upon the independence of the judiciary. This is the view that is presented in the Declaration of Independence, with the blame laid at the door of George III, because the change had been effected at his accession. This was the natural conclusion of men who were familiar only with the conditions after 1740, but it is evident that the charge is an erroneous one. The change in itself was not an attack upon the independence of the judiciary, but an effort to restore an earlier custom of appointing judges during the pleasure of the crown, which for a time had been evaded without authority from the home government, and in direct opposition to what was supposed to be the instructions to the governors. George III could not be responsible for the action of the Board, because the latter had been trying for ten years before his accession to restore the earlier practice, but was hampered by the terms of the existing commissions. There was nothing new in the policy of George III. The Board simply took advantage of the opportunity suddenly offered it by the termination of all existing commissions on the death of George II and carried into execution a policy which it had long before determined upon.

Plans of union

When the Board of Trade was organized, the colonies were engaged in the closing struggles of the first of the French wars, and the immediate administrative problems were those of defense. There were plenty of inhabitants in the northern provinces to protect that region against all aggressions from the French, if they could only be brought to act together. The great obstacles to concerted action were the separation of the colonies, due to geographical situation, and the existence of independent governments over which the crown had no direct control.

In trying to remove the latter difficulty, the Board had before it the previous attempt of the British government to centralize the military power of the northern provinces in the hands of the governors of New York and Massachusetts. Fletcher was governor of Pennsylvania, New York, the Jerseys, and in addition was given command of the militia of Connecticut. Phips was governor of the enlarged

province of Massachusetts and also commander of
the Rhode Island militia.   Neither of these men,
however, had succeeded in enforcing his military
authority over the charter colonies, because the latter
insisted that their charters gave the command of the
militia to their own officers.[481]

The Board, however, challenged this contention,
and after a careful examination of the charters of
Connecticut, Rhode Island, and the Jerseys, it reported that the crown had the power to appoint a
captain-general for all these provinces.   As this opinion was supported by the Board's legal advisers, the
first plan of union was made to hinge on this reserve
power of the crown.   The Board proposed that an
able man should be sent over, commissioned as captain-general of all the forces,

> And all the militia of all the provinces, colonies, and planta-
> tions on the continent of the Northern America, with a power
> to levy arms, muster, command and employ them on all neces-
> sary occasions for the defence of those countries . . . to
> appoint and commission officers to train and exercise at con-
> venient times such of the inhabitants as are fit to bear arms.[482]

In addition to this military power vested in him, the
captain-general was to be given authority to super-
sede any royal governor in whose province he happened to be.

No action was taken at that time; but five months
later the Board submitted another representation, in
which it considered the various arguments for and
against the scheme proposed in its former report, and
again urged the military union under one man.

481 Greene, Evarts B. *Provincial America*, 117.
482 New York *Colonial Documents*, vol. iv, 228.

The distinct proprieties, charters, and different forms of government in several of those neighboring colonies, make all
other union, except under such a military head (in our opinion) at present impracticable, and that what hath yet been done
towards such a military union for common defence (by the
appointment of a quota in the year 1694) hath been so little
complied with, that it requires the exertion of a more vigorous
power than hath hitherto been practised, to make it produce
the desired effect.[483]

The Board proposed, as a proper plan for effecting
and supplementing the military union, that some suitable person should be sent out as governor of New
Hampshire, Massachusetts, and New York, with his
residence in the latter colony.   This recommendation
was acted upon, and commissions granting the necessary civil and military powers were issued to the Earl
of Bellomont,[484] who was thus constituted military
governor over all the colonies north and east of Pennsylvania.

The war closed so soon after his commission was issued that there was no opportunity to test the military
efficiency of the arrangement.   Connecticut and
Rhode Island, as they had done in the case of the
Phips and Fletcher commission, protested vigorously against what they considered an infringement upon
their charters.   In spite of these protests, however,
the Board continued the policy of giving the control
of their military forces to the governors of the other
colonies.   Under Bellomont's commission this military power was annexed to the governorship of Massachusetts.   Upon his death, New York and Massa-

---

[483] Representation of the Board, February 25, 1697, in New York *Colonial Documents*, vol. iv, 260.
[484] — *Ibid.*, 261, 266-273.

chusetts were again separated and the command of the Connecticut militia attached to the governorship of New York,[485] which policy was continued during the administrations of both Cornbury and Hunter.

The command of the Rhode Island militia was left in the hands of Governor Dudley of Massachusetts, who had secured the appointment to that province on the death of Bellomont, but he found considerable difficulty in exercising his commission.[486] Cornbury and Hunter experienced similar difficulties in Connecticut, as both colonies continued to deny the validity of the military commissions of the governors of Massachusetts and New York.[487]

The Board had recognized the impossibility of bringing about any effective union, unless the powers of government which had been granted to the charter and proprietary colonies were restored to the crown. While it aimed to reduce these governments to the same form as the royal provinces as a means of securing administrative efficiency, it also attacked their independent position, because they neither defended themselves nor furnished suitable assistance to the neighboring colonies in the time of war.[488] If they could be deprived of their charter rights, the Board could see its way clear to put all North America under a uniform type of government.

---

[485] Representation of the Board on Cornbury's commission, in New York *Colonial Documents*, vol. iv, 884.

[486] Palfrey, John. *History of New England*, vol. iv, 354.

[487] See their letters to the Board complaining of the action of Connecticut, in New York *Colonial Documents*, vols. iv, v, *passim*.

[488] Representations of the Board, in North Carolina *Colonial Records*, vol. i, 537, 540, 630-633, 889. Cf. Kellogg's "American Colonial Charter," in American Historical Association *Report for 1903*, vol. i, 284-321.

It was one of the constant policies of the Board to oppose the charter and proprietary governments and curtail their privileges as much as possible. The first opposition culminated in the attempt of 1701 to abolish the charters by act of Parliament. This attempt failed, but it was renewed the next year and still again in the years, 1706, 1715, and 1722.[489] In all of these attempts, the Board encountered so much opposition from the colonial governments, as well as from vested interests in England, that the desired legislation failed. Action by *quo warranto* was no more successful as a direct means of attack;[490] but the constant opposition resulted in voluntary surrenders of the proprietary rights of government in the Jerseys and the Carolinas, and weakened the independence of the charter colonies.[491]

[489] Randolph was pushing it in the House of Lords and when it became evident that the bill could not pass that session, he was ordered to take affidavits of such witnesses as could not be present at another session and file them with the Board.

William Penn himself made out a bill for this purpose and submitted it to Manchester, who in turn transmitted it to the Board. That body rejected the bill and insisted upon the former measure. Manchester directed that Mr. Henry Baker, solicitor of the treasury should push the bill before the House of Lords. See: C.O. 5, 1289, p. 12; C.O. 5, 1365, p. 323; Board of Trade *Journal*, 14, pp. 55, 335-338. Cf. Miss Kellogg's admirable treatment of this topic in American Historical Association *Report for 1903*, vol. i, 284-321.

[490] See the Order in Council of June 26, 1706, which states that although the law officers had sufficient evidence for a successful prosecution in the Court of Queen's Bench, it was very doubtful if a peer of the realm, such as the proprietor of North Carolina, could be proceeded against by *quo warranto*. See: North Carolina *Colonial Records*, vol. i, 644.

[491] Cf. the evident desire of Connecticut not to give any cause for complaint, described in "Talcott Papers," in Connecticut Historical Society *Collections*, vols. iv, v, *passim*. See also the urgent letters of Calvert to Governor Sharpe to send over the laws so they could be laid before the Board, in Sharpe's *Correspondence*, vol. ii, *passim*.

The Board had abandoned, for the time, its scheme of consolidating the various governments, except so far as it subsisted in appointing a single governor for New Hampshire and Massachusetts and later for New Jersey and New York. The plan had been brought forward as a war measure, and was based upon military rather than administrative needs. The next plan of union, however, was proposed in time of peace and was intended to secure administrative improvement, as well as military efficiency.

This plan is a part of the representation made by the Board in 1721. After describing the conditions existing in each colony, the report takes up the question of measures which would improve the government in all the colonies. The first great difficulty was the existence of the proprietary and charter governments;

> Nor is it to be expected that either our Indians or European neighbours should pay that respect to your Majesty's subjects, which all those who have the happiness to be under Your Majesty's protection, might otherwise reasonably hope for, until it shall appear, that all the British Colonies in America hold immediately of one Lord and have but one joint interest to pursue; for which reason and many others, we shall first humbly propose, that all the proprietary governments should be reassumed to the crown, either by purchase, agreement, or otherwise, as conceiving this to be one of those essential points, without which your Majesty's colonies can never be put upon a right footing.[492]

After considering means of increasing the trade of the colonies, securing larger returns from the quit rents, and of protecting the woods, the report takes up the question of union.

[492] New York *Colonial Documents*, vol. v, 627-630.

But the most effectual way to put in execution what we have already offered upon this subject to your Majesty's consideration and to render the several provinces on the continent of America, from Nova Scotia to South Carolina, mutually subservient to each others support, will be to put the whole under the government of one Lord-lieutenant, or captain-general, from whom all other governors of particular provinces should receive their orders, in all cases, for your Majesty's service, and cease to have any command respectively in such province, where the said captain-general shall at any time reside, as it is at present practised in the Leeward Islands, where each island has a particular governor, but one general over the whole.

The said captain-general should be constantly attended by two or more councillors deputed from each plantation, he should have a fixed salary, sufficient to support the dignity of so important an employment, independent of the pleasure of the inhabitants; and, in our humble opinion, ought to be a person of good fortune, distinction, and experience.

By this means, a general contribution of men or money may be raised upon the several colonies, in proportion to their respective abilities.[493]

These recommendations were seriously considered and the plan so far matured that the Earl of Stair was offered the office of captain-general; but he refused,[494] and the plan was abandoned. It is of interest chiefly as an indication of the persistence of the ideas which led to the Bellomont commission. The plan, however, shows some improvement over the earlier one. The proposed governor-general would have occupied a position in the colonies as a whole

---

[493] It was in this connection that the Board proposed that the president of the Board of Trade should be charged with the execution of all orders concerning the colonies, which would have made that officer a full-fledged colonial minister. Cf. the similar proposal of Martin Bladen in 1726, in North Carolina *Colonial Records*, vol. ii, 634.

[494] Chalmers, George. *Introduction to the Revolt*, vol. ii, 43.

similar to that of each governor in his respective government. The position of the councilors who were to be delegated from each colony is not clear, as it is not told who was to select them, what their powers should be, or whether they were to have power to bind the colonies which they represented. Confessedly the plan was patterned after the government in the Leeward Islands, where conditions were quite different from those on the continent of America.

Schemes for the formation of some central government for America were also proposed by various persons interested in the welfare of the colonies. One of these was sent from England to Governor Clarke of New York, we are not told by whom. He showed it to his successor, Governor Clinton, who felt under the necessity of writing at once to Newcastle, in order to express his disapproval of the plan.[495] The scheme proposed the raising of a fund by means of a general stamp tax in America, the proceeds of which should be used to defray the expenses of a governor-general and his establishment and to provide for the general defense. The scheme is mentioned in this connection, only because it is so similar to the one proposed by Martin Bladen in 1726 that it may well be considered a paraphrase of his plan.

The Board made no further definite proposals for union, until the approach of the French and Indian War rendered some concerted action necessary. In August, 1753, general instructions were sent to the governors, warning them of the danger from the French encroachments and directing them to main-

---

[495] Letter of December 13, 1744, in New York *Colonial Documents*, vol. vi, 268.

tain regular correspondence with each other.   In case one colony should be attacked, the governors of the others were directed to take prompt measures for its relief.[496]

This was followed by instructions to the governor of New York to call a conference at Albany for the purpose of making a treaty with the Six Nations. Circular letters were also sent to the executives of Massachusetts, New Hampshire, New Jersey, Maryland, Pennsylvania, and Virginia, by which they were notified of the meeting and requested to send commissioners to it.   The purpose of this gathering was solely to arrange a treaty with the Indians, and the commissioners were not asked to consider plans for a confederation.[497] One clause of the instructions to Governor Osborn, however, indicates that the Board no longer looked upon the colonies as isolated governments independent of each other.   He was

> To take care that all the provinces be (if practicable) comprised in one general treaty to be made in His Majesty's name it appearing to us that the practice of each province making a separate treaty for itself in its own name is very improper and may be attended with great inconveniency to His Majesty's service.[498]

The meeting at Albany was held as directed, a treaty with the Six Nations was negotiated, and the plan of union for which it has become famous was promulgated.   Five days before the conference at

[496] New York *Colonial Documents*, vol. vi, 794.

[497] Letter of September 18, 1753, in New York *Colonial Documents*, vol. vi, 802.   In a letter to Governor De Lancey, July 5, 1754, however, the Board expresses a hope that the commissioners at Albany may agree upon some plan of union.   *Ibid.*, 846.

[498] — *Ibid.*, 801.

Albany was opened, Secretary Robinson requested the Board of Trade to prepare a

> Plan of general concert to be ent'red into by His Majesty's several colonies upon the continent [for their mutual defense, in order] that the same may be sent to the several governors of His Majesty's colonies in North America.[499]

The Board had its plan completed in a short time and submitted it to the king, August 9, 1754. Although it could not have been put in operation soon enough to meet the exigencies of the approaching struggle, and the Board held out no delusions on this point, it is of sufficient interest to merit careful consideration.

This plan of union [500] was avowedly based upon military necessity, and the only organs of central government it proposed to create were of a military nature. The governors of each province were to be instructed to secure the appointment by the council and assembly of a commissioner, acceptable to the governor. These commissioners were to meet at New York to formulate details for the military establishment, such as the number of forts necessary for the proper defense of the frontier, the probable garrison required for each, and the cost of maintenance. To enable them to do this, they were to be furnished with authentic copies of each colony's expenditure for twenty years past. Having determined the regular establishment required in time of peace, they were to apportion the cost in men and money upon the various colonies in accordance with the ability of each to bear the burden.

---

[499] New York *Colonial Documents*, vol. vi, 844.
[500] — *Ibid.*, 902-906.

The head of the new military establishment was a commander-in-chief and commissary-general for Indian Affairs, who was to be appointed by the crown and given a fixed salary which was to be charged upon the regular establishment. No central treasurer or taxing machinery was provided, but the commander-in-chief was to be empowered to draw upon the treasurer of each colony for its quota of the regular annual charges. These warrants were to be paid by the treasurer upon whom they were drawn from any moneys in his hands, and if he should not have sufficient funds to pay the drafts, he was required to borrow the amount at once on the credit of the colony. The commander-in-chief was to submit annually to each colony an attested statement of his expenditures, and also transmit a copy of the same to the exchequer in England.

A curious provision was made for emergencies. In all cases of invasion or other grave danger which should require a greater military force than the regular establishment afforded, the colony attacked should furnish an estimate of the probable extra charges required for its defense. Copies of this estimate were then to be sent to the governor of each colony, to be laid before his council and assembly. As soon as such copies were received by a colony, a commissioner should be appointed, who should meet similar commissioners from other colonies wherever the commander-in-chief should designate. Representatives from five colonies constituted a quorum, with power to revise the estimate furnished by the colony in danger and apportion the charges upon each colony. As soon as this was done, the commander-in-chief was authorized to draw upon the several treasurers for the quotas, in which case his warrants had to be honored just the same as those for the regular establishment.

The plan was to be put into operation by action of the colonies themselves. The commissioners, as soon as they could agree upon the financial details of the scheme, were to draw up a formal convention. This was then to be transmitted to each colony

> To be forthwith laid before the governors, councils, and assemblies, who are to take the same into immediate consideration, and having made such alterations therein or additions thereto as they shall think necessary, shall return them to the commissioners within two months, and when all the copies shall have been returned the commissioners shall resume their deliberations: and having finally settled the whole, the convention shall be fairly drawn up and signed by each commissioner and transmitted hither in order to be laid before His Majesty for his approbation.[501]

It should be noted that the final action by the colonies was to be taken by their commissioners, upon whom the various amendments which each colony might offer were not binding. Seven commissioners constituted a quorum and were competent to make decisions which, when ratified by the crown, should be binding upon the whole. Thus seven of the original thirteen colonies could have adopted a form of union, which the other six would have been compelled to accept.

Only as a last resort did the Board contemplate establishing this military government by act of Parliament.

---

[501] New York *Colonial Documents*, vol. vi, 905.

If however it should be found upon trial that this measure should be defeated by any of the colonies either refusing or neglecting to enter into a consideration of the points referred to their deliberation; or, after they are settled, by refusing to raise such supplies as are proposed by this plan to be the fund for the execution of it: We see no other method that can be taken, but that of an application for an interposition of the authority of Parliament.[502]

This plan deviates from that of 1721 by omitting the council for the governor-general and by not giving him any control over civil matters. His powers were limited to military affairs and questions of Indian relations. The plan does, however, show a very clear comprehension of the jealous regard of each colony for its own special privileges. Halifax says:

We have endeavored as much as possible to adapt the plan to the constitution of the colonies, and to form it as unexceptionable in point of powers invested in the commander-in-chief as the nature of the thing, and the design of uniting the colonies under one general direction would admit of,

and adds that the chief executive would not be empowered

To draw upon any province for one shilling more than the commissioners from each colony shall have agreed to be the just proportion of expense which each colony is to bear.[503]

It is evident that Halifax was endeavoring not to arouse any fear on the part of the colonists that their cherished local independence, especially in financial matters, might be endangered.

The absence of a central legislative body is perhaps the strangest feature in the scheme, but the council of commissioners would supply its place. The

[502] New York *Colonial Documents*, vol. vi, 902.

[503] Letter of Halifax to Newcastle, August 15, 1754, in British Museum *Additional Manuscripts*, 33726, f. 243.

whole scheme is very incomplete as a plan for establishing a general government for the colonies, and in
this respect is in strong contrast with the plan of
union which was being drafted at Albany.

Both plans suffered a similar fate; that of the
Board was apparently never submitted to the colonies
for their consideration; and the Board of Trade laid
the Albany plan before the king with the remark,

> The commissioners having agreed upon a plan of union,
> which, as far as their sense and opinion of it goes, is com-
> plete in itself, we shall not presume to make any observa-
> tions upon it, but transmit it simply for Your Majesty's con-
> sideration.

It could not have done more; for the plan was not
officially before the Board and could not be until it
had been adopted by the separate colonies.[504]

From the foregoing account, it is seen that, as far as
devising a central government for the colonies was
concerned, the Board showed very little foresight or
creative genius. Its plans were usually hastily drawn
in the hour of danger, and were really but little more
than temporary makeshifts to meet an emergency.
The plan of 1721, alone, shows evidences of a desire
to create an effective central government, and the first
provision of that contemplated the reduction of all
the colonies to the condition of royal provinces. If
the Board of Trade had any continuous policy on the
question of union, it was that embraced in the Bellomont commission, but it is difficult to trace even that
in the plan of 1754.

---

[504] Representation on the proceedings at Albany, October 29, 1754, in
New York *Colonial Documents*, vol. vi, 917. Cf. McDonald's *Select
Charters*, 252-253; also Beer's *British Colonial Policy*, 22-23.

As compared with its success in dealing with the judiciary, the plans of the Board for securing a union of the colonies must be considered failures.   Its policy in this particular was too imperialistic, as the schemes which it proposed placed all control in the hands of the crown officers, and left so little space for initiative on the part of the colonies that the latter would not accept them.   Judging by its attitude toward the judiciary and a fixed civil list, the Board would have preferred no central government at all to one that might get out of hand, and in that respect its policy was consistent.

V. TREATMENT OF COLONIAL LEGISLATION

The royal veto

None of the colonial governments was complete in itself; all were subordinate to the central power in legislation, as well as in other matters. Colonial laws had to be transmitted to England and submitted to the crown for approval. Royal provinces were expected to transmit their laws rather promptly, while charter and proprietary colonies had special privileges in the matter. Connecticut, Rhode Island, and Maryland were not required by their charters to offer their laws to the crown, nevertheless, each found it convenient to do so when the latter became insistent.

The royal veto fell into disuse early in the eighteenth century as far as laws passed by parliament were concerned, but was continued in regard to colonial laws. In the case of royal provinces, a law could be disallowed by the crown at any time, even many years after it had gone into effect; the only limitation being that laws once approved were forever beyond the royal control. In the charter colonies, where any veto was provided for, the time within which it could be exercised was limited by the terms of the charter, and varied from six months for Pennsylvania laws to three years for those of Massachu-

setts.   A failure to veto within the limited period
had the effect of a positive approval, and tied the
hands of the crown for the future.[505]

Some laws contained a clause suspending the operation of the law until it was formally approved in
England.   In such cases the royal disapproval was
practically the same as a veto by the colonial governor
or by any other executive, except that it could be
postponed indefinitely, and a failure to act had all the
effect of a positive negation of the law.   Because of
the delays accompanying laws so drawn, colonial legislatures consented to such clauses reluctantly and
then only as a last resort in securing the desired legislation.

The great majority of the laws were drawn in the
usual way and, if signed by the governor, went into
immediate operation, and continued in force until
they expired by limitation or repeal.   The royal disapproval of such a law is very different, both in form
and in effect, from what is usually known as a veto.
A veto prevents a proposed law from going into effect, while the great majority of colonial laws referred to here were already in force and would so
continue.   The royal disapproval of such a law consequently had the effect of a legislative repeal: all
acts already done under the authority of a law of this
kind were valid, but the act itself terminated with
the day of its disapproval.   In this respect the action
was also different from a judicial invalidation of a
law; for in such cases no action under color of such
a law is legal, while colonial laws were legal during

---

[505] See the terms of the charters, in Poore's *Charters and Constitutions*.

the period of their operation. The following discussion deals primarily with the royal repeal, which may well be described by the term disallowance, rather than with the veto.

During the period covered by this discussion, nearly four hundred different laws from the continental American colonies alone were disallowed by the crown.[506] As there were probably as many more from the other colonies, it is at once apparent that the British government was pretty active in its consideration of colonial laws.

The Declaration of Independence lays the responsibility for the royal vetoes at the door of the king, but probably unjustly. Although every Order in Council for the disallowance of a law stated that it was done by "the King in Council," the king had nothing to do with the matter personally. The phrase is only one of the numerous fictions of the British government. The real work of considering colonial laws was done by the Board of Trade, and the final action was only recorded as done by the king in the presence of and with the advise of his Privy Council. Hence "disallowed by the King in Council" must be understood to mean by the Board of Trade on the advise of able legal opinion and finally ratified by the Privy Council. As will be shown later, this action corresponded very closely to that of a careful court of record, rather than to the hasty, arbitrary action of an irresponsible individual.

The Board of Trade was thus charged with the

---

[506] This does not include laws which had suspending clauses and which were not approved in England.

consideration of colonial laws, and practically every approval or disapproval was made upon its recommendation. This proved one of its most effective means of enforcing its authority in the colonies. Here was a power to control colonial affairs, far removed from the exigencies of local politics and the petty shortcomings of colonial governors. While every law was considered individually, the Board was evidently guided by general principles in refusing its approval or recommending a disallowance. These were based upon a consideration of the proper field for colonial legislation, the relations of the colonies to each other and to the mother country, and upon a desire to protect the colonists themselves from ill advised legislation.

One of the foremost reasons for the disallowance of laws was that they encroached upon the royal prerogative; that is, they tended to hamper the home government or lessen its authority over local officials or governments. Good illustrations of such laws are the New Jersey and the New York triennial acts,[507] and the North Carolina biennial act.[508] Both were

---

[507] In reporting on the first of these the Board said: "We take leave to observe that this is an Act of so very extraordinary nature importing a great change in the constitution of the province of New Jersey." — Representation of the Board, June 23, 1731, in C.O. 5, 996, pp. 270-273. Repealed, November 25, 1731. See: Privy Council *Register*, "George II," vol. ii, 450, 470, 478-480. In reporting on the second of these Francis Fane said: "I beg leave to observe to your Lordships, that I think this act a very high infringement upon the prerogative of the crown; for it takes away that undoubted right, which the crown has always exercised of calling and continuing the Assembly of this colony at such times and so long as it was thought necessary for the publick service." — Report to the Board, July 20, 1738, in New York *Colonial Documents*, vol. vi, 129-130. This act was repealed, November 30, 1738. See: Privy Council *Register*, "George II," vol. vi, 34.

[508] Repealed, July 21, 1737. C.O. 5, 323, pp. 257-258; Privy Council *Register*, "George II," vol. v, 228, 234, 256.

objectionable because, in providing for regular meetings of the assemblies, they took away from the governor his power to summon, prorogue, and dissolve
the local legislatures.[509]

Inadequate or unnecessary military laws, such as
those passed by Pennsylvania in 1755, come in this
group, because they were looked upon as hampering
rather than aiding the military operations, and were
consequently disallowed.[510]

Other acts which more specifically come under this
general head were those regulating the duties of or
taking away the income of a patent officer,[511] changing his commission,[512] or acts which limited the appointing or executive power of such officers.[513] Others

[509] An act passed by the legislature of Jamaica, in 1741, providing for
triennial assemblies, was also promptly disallowed. See: Board of Trade,
Jamaica, 66, pp. 108-112.

[510] One of these purported to extend to Pennsylvania the provisions of
the Mutiny Act which regulated the quartering of soldiers in England.
The other regulated enlistments in the colony and established rules for the
employment of the provincial troops. C.O. 5, 1295, pp. 218-223.

[511] See the New Jersey Act of 1714 to enforce the ordinance regulating
fees, cited in C.O. 5, 996, pp. 108-110. Repealed, January 20, 1722. See:
Privy Council *Register*, "George I," vol. iii, 463. See also the North Carolina Act of 1740 for the appointment of clerks for the county courts, cited
in Report of the Board, October 14, 1742, C.O. 5, 323, pp. 294-296. Repealed, January 19, 1743. See: Privy Council *Register*, "George II," vol.
vii, 283, 293. The South Carolina Act of 1736 regulating fees of public
officers reduced the income of patent officers, and for this reason was disallowed. See: C.O. 5, 401, pp. 202-204; Privy Council *Register*, "George
II," vol. v, 180-209. Numerous other acts of a similar character were
repealed for the above reason.

[512] The various acts to change the commissions of the judges come under
this head. The North Carolina judiciary act of 1760 is typical of all, and
the objections made to it are similar to those already cited. See the report
of the Board on this act, December 3, 1761, in C.O. 5, 325, pp. 171-185;
Privy Council *Register*, "George III," vol. i, 606, 611, 616.

[513] A Virginia act of 1705 "declaring who should hold office," made
residence within the colony for three years one of the requirements. This

sought to change the charters of towns incorporated by charter direct from the king, as in the case of Norfolk, Virginia.[514] Perhaps oddest of all was the disallowance of Virginia laws appointing and regulating fairs, on the ground that they encroached upon the prerogatives of the governor.[515]

Since most of the encroachments upon the prerogative were through the power of the assembly to control the purse; the efforts of the Board to prevent them usually came to naught, as the assembly could frequently accomplish by indirect means what it was forbidden to do by direct legislation. There were occasions, however, when the Board used its power of disallowance to prevent encroachments of the assembly through its abuse of the money bill. In 1741 the Jamaica assembly passed a triennial act, which the governor refused to sign because it contained no suspending clause.

> After which the assembly compelled him to give his consent to it without such a clause by keeping back an annual bill usually passed for raising several sums of money for defraying the necessary charges of the government, and we are of opinion that this practice which . . . is so fundamentally

was found to restrict the operations of the surveyor of the customs, Wm. Keith, and was disallowed. See: the report of the Board, July 6, 1715, in C.O. 5, 1364, pp. 224-229; Privy Council *Register*, "George I," vol. i, 274.

[514] Representation of the Board, June 14, 1754, in C.O. 5, 1367, p. 67. Repealed, June 21, following. See: Privy Council *Register*, "George II," vol. xv, 148, 153, 161.

[515] Two acts of this character were disallowed, October 31, 1751. The first was entitled, "An Act for allowing fairs to be kept in the Town of Suffolk, and preventing hogs and goats going at large therein, and for altering the times of holding fairs in the Town of New Castle." The second was, "An Act for establishing a town in Augusta County, and allowing fairs to be held therein." See: C.O. 5, 1366, p. 498; Privy Council *Register*, "George II," vol. xiii, 347.

destructive of your Majesty's authority ought to be discouraged whenever it occurs.[516]

Thus the Board could and did prevent forbidden legislation from remaining on the statute books, even though the colonial governors were forced to consent to it.

Ecclesiastical reasons led to the repeal of several laws. Some of these concerned the Church of England, such as laws for the disposal of parish property,[517] laws reducing the revenues of the ministers of the church, as in the famous "Parson's Cause" in Virginia,[518] or laws which provided for the punishment of ministers guilty of immoral conduct.[519] Other laws encroached upon the general freedom of worship in the colonies or gave special privileges to certain sects. An act of Maryland, passed in 1696, was re-

[516] Representation of the Board for the repeal of the triennial act of Jamaica, in Board of Trade, *Jamaica*, 66, pp. 108-112.

[517] A New York act of 1733, which empowered the vestry of Jamaica in Queen's County to dispose of some sixty pounds which it held, was disallowed, August 8, 1734. Other acts permitted vestries to sell real estate. One passed by Virginia allowed the parish vestry of Bruton to sell certain lots it owned in Williamsburg and loan the money on personal security. The Board objected on the ground that the property had been given for the benefit of the poor, and under the proposed plan it might become lost, consequently the act was disallowed, July 20, 1764. See: C.O. 5, 1368, 247-248; Privy Council *Register*, "George II," vol. iv, 6; "George III," vol. iii, 544.

[518] See C.O. 5, 1367, pp. 375-381, for the complaint of the clergy against the four laws changing their pay from tobacco to money, also the action of the Board of Trade in the matter. Repealed, August 10, 1759. See: Privy Council *Register*, "George II," vol. xviii, 101. An act of New York passed in 1700, which divided the parishes of East Chester and West Chester, was also rejected by the Board because it lessened the remuneration of the minister. See: C.O. 5, 1119, p. 362.

[519] Act of North Carolina, passed in 1760, entitled: "An Act for making provision for an Orthodox clergy." The main objections were those of the Bishop of London. See: C.O. 5, 325, pp. 201-207. The act was repealed, June 3, 1762. See: Privy Council *Register*, "George III," vol. ii, 251.

pealed by the king, on the recommendation of the
Board, because it discriminated too severely against
Catholics.[520]   A later law was amended by the legislature on the demand of the Board, for similar reasons.[521]   Other acts passed in 1704 by the same province, one to prevent the growth of popery, and the
other to permit, for eighteen months only, the ministration of Catholic priests in private families were
disallowed because they tended "to depopulate that
profitable colony." [522]

The Board also tried to prevent the persecution of
Quakers.   A law of Virginia, passed in 1663, prohibited the importation of Quakers and punished by
heavy fines their assembling for religious worship.
This law was not discovered by the Board until 1718,
but it was then promptly disallowed.[523]   Six years
later two acts of Massachusetts Bay were repealed by
the king, because they taxed the Quakers in Dartmouth and Tiverton unfairly.[524]   On the other hand

[520] Privy Council *Register*, "William III," vol. vi, 396.

[521] This act in its final form was practically framed by the Board and
enacted by the Maryland Assembly. See: Board of Trade *Journal*, 13, 14.
and 15 for the history of this act.

[522] January 3, 1706, the Board reported on these acts. It stated that the
first of them forbade the exercise of the Catholic religion even in private
families and in the most inoffensive form, "which is not your Majesty's
intention as it would tend to depopulate that profitable colony." See: C.O. 5,
726, pp. 356-357.

[523] This act provided that any Quaker more than sixteen years old, who
should go from his own house and join in any assembly of five or more
persons, should forfeit two hundred pounds of tobacco for the first offense
and five hundred pounds for the second, and should be banished for a third
offense. It also punished by a fine of two thousand pounds of tobacco any
shipmaster who brought into the colony any Quaker more than fourteen years
old. This act was recommended for repeal, because, if enforced, it would
drive out of the colony many industrious persons and because it was not in
harmony with the English toleration act. See: C.O. 5, 1365, pp. 45-46.

[524] Act of 1723. The Board in recommending the repeal of this act held

no unusual privileges were permitted the Quakers, and several laws of Pennsylvania were vetoed because they granted greater freedom in affirmations than were permitted by the laws of England.[525] Thus the Board of Trade not only protected the interests of the established church, but enforced such a degree of toleration for persecuted sects as would not interfere with colonial growth and prosperity.

Any law which affected the material interests of the crown was pretty sure to be disallowed. This fact made it almost impossible for the assembly of North Carolina to frame a quit rent law in such a way that the Board would accept it. As there was little or no coin in the colony, such a law had to provide some equitable rate at which rents could be paid in commodities. This arrangement, however, was open to two objections. In the first place, it infringed the act of Parliament regulating the value of foreign coins; and in the second place, in the opinion of the Board values upon commodities were placed too high. The effect would be to diminish the existing too slender income of the government and still further weaken the independence of the officials whose salaries were paid from the quit rents – perhaps this was what the authors of the acts intended

that, as the charter granted freedom of conscience to all except Catholics, and the regular practice within the colony was to permit each congregation to select its own pastor, it was manifestly unfair to tax a majority of people who were Quakers for the benefit of a Congregationalist minister who was supported by only a small minority of the people in the two towns. See: C.O. 5, 915, p. 400; also the proceedings before the Privy Council, in Privy Council *Register*, "George I," vol. iv.

[525] Acts of this character were repealed in 1711, 1714, and 1719. See: C.O. 5, 1292, pp. 330, 399; 1293, p. 206; Privy Council *Register*, "Anne," vol. v, 293, and "George I," vol. i, 293; Pennsylvania *Statutes at Large*.

to accomplish. Consequently the Board disallowed every such law prepared by the legislature of that colony.[526] Quit rent laws passed by Virginia [527] and by New York [528] met similar fates and for similar reasons. If the Board was unable to secure the enactment of effective laws for the collection of quit rents, it at least stood in the way of their confiscation by action of the colonists themselves.

The Board insisted that colonial laws should not be inconsistent with the laws of England, and always submitted them to an attorney for his opinion on this point. Any conflict between them and those laws of England which extended to America was considered sufficient ground for a repeal. Thus the Board constantly submitted the provincial laws to a kind of constitutional test, and in this way accustomed the colonists to a limitation upon their local legislatures, similar to that which was afterward embodied in the Constitution of the United States. The laws passed

---

[526] The act of 1738, disallowed in 1740, was open to several objections, the most serious of which turned upon the power it gave a small group of men of regulating the value of money, which would have enabled them to manipulate it in their own interests. See: C.O. 5, 323, pp. 273-276; North Carolina *Colonial Records*, vol. iv, 434-435; Privy Council *Register*, "George II," vol. vii, 162, 177. The act of 1748, repealed in 1754, besides regulating the payment in commodities, was especially unfair to the remaining proprietary interest. It also made twenty years' occupancy of land a valid title. See: Report of the Board, March 25, 1754, in C.O. 5, 323.

[527] In recommending the repeal of the Virginia act of 1720, the Board said that it "deminished His Majesty's revenue, and weakens the process for the crown in the recovery of forfeitures and arrears of quit rents." — Representation of the Board, July 18, 1723, in C.O. 5, 1365, p. 253; also Privy Council *Register*, "George I," vol. iv, 327.

[528] The main reason for recommending the repeal of the New York acts of 1744 was that they made the collection of quit rents more difficult. See: New York *Colonial Documents*, vol. vii, 504; Privy Council *Register*, "George II," vol. viii, 86, 96.

by Parliament and binding upon all the colonies corresponded to the Constitution and the acts of Congress. The work of the Board of Trade and its officers in maintaining the supremacy of the general law, when a local law conflicted with it, corresponded to the action of the Supreme Court of the United States. The question at issue was largely a judicial one – were the laws in conflict? If they were, the local one must give way.

The parallel between British colonial practice and present day United States practice is clear in the case of laws from chartered colonies, as the charter was a written constitution. The local legislature was limited by the terms of the grant; if a power had not been granted, it could not be exercised legally. The law of Rhode Island establishing an admiralty court illustrates this point. The Board submitted the law to Attorney-general Northey for his opinion,[529] who reported that he had examined the act and the charter of the colony and was of the opinion that the charter gave the legislature

> Power to erect only courts for determining all actions, causes, matters, and things happening within that island which doth not impower them to erect a Court of Admiralty, the jurisdiction of such court being of matters arising on the high sea, which is out of the island.[530]

Although the charter did not provide for a royal veto, on the basis of this report the Board recommended the act for disallowance, which was promptly done by an Order in Council.[531]

---

[529] December 2, 1703, C.O. 5, 1290, p. 387.
[530] Northey to the Board, December 24, 1703, C.O. 5, 1262.
[531] February, 1704, C.O. 5, 1290, p. 422.

The above is rather an uncommon case, but it brings out very clearly the American idea of a constitutional test of laws passed by a subordinate division of the government. The settlement of conflicts between laws passed by Parliament and acts of colonial legislatures, unlimited by a specific charter, involved just as strictly a constitutional test as in the case cited from Rhode Island. Tests of this kind had to be applied by the legal advisers of the crown instead of the administrative officers; consequently the Board simply took the advice of its counsel in such matters. If their opinion was adverse to a law, the Board promptly asked for its repeal.

The legislatures of all the colonies [532] were made to feel this check upon their law-making powers. The judiciary act of Massachusetts was objected to on the ground that it infringed the right of the Admiralty Courts to try cases without a jury,[533] and that of Virginia because it did not specifically recognize the right of appeal to the king in council.[534] Pennsylvania, New Jersey, and several other colonies attempted to establish rules for affirmations different from those in the acts of Parliament, and many of their laws received the royal veto.[535] Other attempted

---

[532] With the possible exception of Rhode Island; Delaware was not recognized as a separate province by the British government.

[533] "The Act entituled, An Act for establishing of Courts, providing, amongst other things, that all matters and issues in fact shall be tried by a jury of twelve men, has, in that particular, been looked upon to be directly contrary to the intention of the act of Parliament . . . by which it is provided that all causes relating to the breach of the acts of trade may, at the pleasure of the officer or informer, be tried in the Court of Admiralty, etc." — Board to Bellomont, February 3, 1699, in Massachusetts *Acts and Resolves*, vol. i, 287.

[534] Chalmers, George. *Introduction to the Revolt*, vol. i, 318.

[535] Objections were made to both Georgia and South Carolina laws be-

variations from English law, to which the Board objected, were laws establishing novel rules of procedure in the courts,[536] laws defining the privileges of freemen,[537] and criminal laws with uncommon methods of punishment.[538]

The two great classes of laws, however, which were repealed because they conflicted with the laws of England were those creating bills of credit or regulating their value in coin, and laws governing the

cause they departed from the rules laid down in the Toleration Act. Georgia sought to extend the privileges granted to Quakers to all protestants and dissenters by an act passed in 1756, but the act was disallowed. See: Pennsylvania *Archives*, first series, vol. i, 155-158; C.O. 5, 673, pp. 228-229.

[536] A great variety of laws of this character were disallowed. A South Carolina act of 1759, regulating the proof of wills, permitted methods of proof not allowed by the laws of England [C.O. 5, 404, pp. 59-61]. Methods of selecting jurors, unfamiliar to English lawyers, were attempted by several of the colonies with the usual result. The treatment of the Georgia act of 1756 is typical of all [C.O. 5, 673, pp. 224-231]. Several colonies passed laws greatly extending the jurisdiction of county courts. These were objected to because of the ignorance of the county judges. The North Carolina act of 1755 illustrates both the laws and their treatment [C.O. 5, 324, pp. 299-308]. Pennsylvania attempted to limit grand jury presentments, but the Board objected [C.O. 5, 1291, p. 266; Privy Council *Register*, "Anne," vol. iv, 451]. In 1726 South Carolina attempted to make the first action in civil cases a capias instead of a summons, but the British lawyers objected to the innovation [C.O. 5, 401, pp. 28-30].

[537] Three acts of Pennsylvania for this purpose were repealed in 1706, 1714, and 1719 because they were held to interfere in some measure with the work of the admiralty courts. See: C.O. 5, 1291, p. 283; 1292, p. 399; 1293, pp. 206, ff.

[538] More laws of Pennsylvania than of any other, or perhaps all of the other colonies, were objected to because of the unusual punishments provided. These included divorce for the injured husband or wife as a punishment for adultery, marriage for those guilty of fornication, castration for rape and bestiality, selling for fourfold the value of the property destroyed for incendiarism, the death penalty for manslaughter, and the same penalty for false swearing as the person against whom the evidence was given would have suffered had he been convicted. Some of these were reënacted with amendments so as to meet the objections of the Board, but others were again repealed by order of that body. See: C.O. 5, 1291, pp. 254-289; Privy Council *Register*, "Anne," vol. iii, 99-101; Pennsylvania *Statutes at Large*.

descent of property. The first class of laws violated the act of Parliament regulating the value of foreign coins in the colonies. Nearly every colony had some of its acts disallowed for this reason, because all were confronted with the problem of securing some form of circulating medium.[539] The second class is well illustrated by Connecticut's intestate law and by that of North Carolina which allowed illegitimate as well as legitimate children to inherit property. The last was ordered repealed and the first held invalid, although that decision was finally reversed.[540] Other colonies attempted to pass similar laws, but the Board uniformly interposed the royal veto.[541]

It was in dealing with laws which were intended to regulate commerce, or which laid duties upon imports, that the Board exercised its greatest control. While its attitude was greatly influenced by the prevailing mercantilist doctrines, its reasons for repeal in many cases are actuated by administrative, as well

---

[539] See: New York *Colonial Documents*, vol. v, 67 and *passim*; Chalmers, George. *Introduction to the Revolt*, vol. i, subject, bills of credit.

[540] Connecticut Historical Society *Collections*, vol. iv, 114-115, 143-150, and *passim*; vol. v, 74-87, 489-494, and *passim*; Trumbull. *History of Connecticut*, vol. ii, chap. iv.

[541] A Pennsylvania act of this character was disallowed in 1706 because it was contrary to the English law of inheritance [C.O. 5, 1291, p. 267; Privy Council *Register*, "Anne," vol. iii, 99-101]. Two laws of New Hampshire met a similar fate the same year, and for similar reasons. An additional objection was made to one of these acts, namely, that it not only altered the law of descent but it also applied to persons residing in England as well as to those in the colony [C.O. 5, 912, pp. 186-190; Privy Council *Register*, "Anne," vol. iii, 269]. A North Carolina act of 1762 for the distribution of intestate estates was apparently drawn so as to be in entire agreement with the laws of England; yet, because it failed to make provision for the legal representation of the heirs of a dead child, the act was disallowed, July 20, 1764 [C.O. 5, 325, pp. 240-241; Privy Council *Register*, "George III," vol. iii, 514, 544].

as commercial, motives. The merchants in England were extremely sensitive about any burdens whatever being laid upon their commerce with the colonies, consequently they were always prepared to urge the repeal of any provincial law which they found objectionable. Usually the Board was very prompt in taking such action as the merchants demanded, but sometimes it refused. The following are the kind of acts which were objected to.

In 1700, the Board reported against a law of Massachusetts, which included a clause establishing sea-ports, on the ground that it encroached upon the power granted to the commissioners of customs "to appoint ports in all His Majesty's plantations for the lading and unlading" [542] of enumerated goods. The power to appoint ports was thus denied to the colony, because the exercise of such a power might interfere with the enforcement of the acts of trade. An act regulating the building of ships was repealed at the same time as the above act, on the ground that it might subject British merchants who had ships built in the province to inconvenient regulations.[543]

Eight years later the Board condemned a Virginia revenue law because it laid a tonnage duty in such a way as to discriminate in favor of ships wholly owned within the province, and made use of a scheme for estimating the tonnage of vessels which the merchants claimed was unfair. The act was promptly disallowed.[544] A little later two acts of Maryland,

[542] Massachusetts *Acts and Resolves*, vol. i, 336, *note*.
[543] — *Ibid.*, 353, *note*.
[544] Representation of the Board, January 5, 1708, in C.O. 5, 1362, pp. 275-278; Privy Council *Register*, "Anne," vol. iii, 519.

one of which regulated the size of tobacco hogsheads,
and the other forbade cutting and defacing them in
loading upon ships, were disallowed: the first on the
complaints of ship-owners that the special size of
cask required was different from that in use in Virginia and consequently would not pack to advantage
in the holds of the ships; and the second because it
required a bond from the shipmaster to observe its
provisions and so laid a burden upon British shipping.[545]

The next year the Board had before it the acts of
both Virginia and Maryland establishing ports and
towns.[546] It had previously advised the enactment of
such a law in Virginia, but not the kind of a law
which was passed. Ports were desired but not towns.
The colonial legislatures, however, sought to develop
towns as well. The ports were erected into boroughs,
with markets, fairs, merchants' guilds, and special
exemptions from a portion of the duties regularly
paid by persons not residing within their limits. To
encourage immediate growth in population, the residents were also exempted from the poll-tax of tobacco for a period of fifteen years. The Board found
two serious objections to these laws. By encouraging

---

[545] Many of the papers relating to Maryland are included with those of
Virginia, as in this and the following cases. The bond required was two
hundred pounds sterling. The penalty for defacing a cask was three pounds
for each cask or hogshead so injured. As the casks were of such a size
that screws had to be used in loading them into the holds of vessels, defacing was almost unavoidable. Representation of the Board, March 23,
1708, in C.O. 5, 1362, pp. 291-293; Privy Council *Register*, "Anne," vol. iv,
45.

[546] The Virginia act was passed in 1706. There were three Maryland
acts; the first passed in the same year as that of Virginia, and two additional and supplementary acts passed in 1707 and in 1708.

the growth of towns they might finally lead to the development of manufacturing, especially of woolens, and thus reduce the English exports of goods of that kind. By attracting persons to the towns they would diminish the number engaged in the production of tobacco, lessen the total crop, and so diminish the export trade of the provinces. Thus English trade would suffer a double injury. The usual veto followed.[547]

In 1717 two more acts of Virginia received the royal veto. One, passed in 1713-1714, was to prevent frauds in tobacco payments and was held to impose a "great burden" upon trade.[548] The other, passed in 1714, regulated the Indian trade, excluding unauthorized persons from such trade. The Board held that this act infringed acts of Parliament preserving to all British subjects the right to trade with the Indians, and hence was essentially illegal.

Other colonies found the Board obstinate in resisting attempts to monopolize the Indian trade for their own inhabitants. In 1729 a series of ten acts, which had been passed by New York since 1720, was disallowed.[549] A few years later a South Carolina ordinance, which was designed to assert the rights of the

[547] This whole incident started from a petition of the merchants who traded to Virginia, asking the commissioners of customs to have certain places designated as ports. The matter came before the Board of Trade in 1705 and it recommended that such action was desirable on account of the scattered settlements and large navigable rivers in that colony. Instructions were sent to the governor to secure the necessary legislation, and the acts described above were passed. Representation of the Board, November 30, 1709, in C.O. 5, 1362, pp. 432 ff; Privy Council *Register*, "Anne," vol. iv, 491.

[548] See the report of Solicitor-general Thompson and the representation of the Board, June 29, 1717, in C.O. 5, 1364, pp. 463-464.

[549] Privy Council *Register*, "George II," vol. ii, 97-106.

people of that colony to the trade with the Creek and
Cherokee Indians, also met the fatal objection of the
Board.[550] This opposition to colonial laws regulating
the Indian trade probably did not assist in the solution of that vexed problem, but did prevent any one
colony from solving it in its own favor.

A Massachusetts revenue act of 1718 laid higher duties upon English goods than upon those from any other country or province,[551] and also double duties upon
wines and other products not imported directly from
the place of their production,[552] provisions which
were discriminations against English commerce. The
law also discriminated against English ships by requiring all such vessels to pay the powder duty, while
the ships of that and the neighboring provinces were
exempted from such tax.[553] Such a law not only laid
a burden upon English merchants, but was clearly an
attempt to regulate foreign commerce. The Board
lost no time in laying it before the king with the
recommendation that it be disallowed.

> And forasmuch as this act seems designed to be an annual
> one, we would propose that in case it shall have been re-
> enacted this year before the said governor receives Your
> Majesty's orders on this head, he may be enjoined forth-
> with to declare your Majesty's disapprobation thereof and

[550] This act was objected to because of the way it was passed. See the
report of the Committee of the Privy Council, March 18, 1738, in Privy
Council *Register*, "George II," vol. v, 499.

[551] English merchandise was taxed at the rate of twenty shillings for
every hundred pounds, cost value. Other goods were taxed but one penny
per pound. See: Massachusetts *Acts and Resolves*, vol. ii, 108, sec. 1.

[552] The double duties had to be paid by all importers who were not bona
fide residents of Massachusetts.

[553] Act passed, June 28, 1718, in Massachusetts *Acts and Resolves*, vol. ii,
107-112.

not to permit the said act or any part of it to be put in execution.[554]

The recommendation was promptly approved by the king in council and orders issued in accordance therewith.

In the meantime other colonies had attempted to pass similar laws, which caused the Board to issue its first special instruction to the governors not to enact any law which would affect the navigation of the kingdom.[555] The New York revenue act of 1715 had laid a tariff duty on all European goods. The Board examined the act and wrote Hunter that it considered that particular clause objectionable, and that if he could not secure its repeal, the law would be disallowed.[556] Hunter obtained the desired amendment, but protested against a regulation which was opposed to former practice.[557]

A North Carolina revenue act laid a direct import duty of ten per cent upon all goods of British manufacture. It was not regularly submitted to the crown for confirmation, but had been transmitted to the Board of Trade by the customs officers, and without

[554] Representation of the Board of Trade, April 24, 1719, in C.O. 5, 915, pp. 267 ff.

[555] Instructions sent to Governor Hunter, September 27, 1717, in New York *Colonial Documents*, vol. v, 501.

[556] "We have considered the Revenue Act and have some objections to it particularly that it affects the shipping and navigation of this kingdom as you will see from the inclosed paper of observations, however we would not lay it before His Majesty to be repealed, because you say the repealing it would ruin the trade of the province; you must therefore move the Assembly to pass a new act not liable to the said objections, otherwise we shall be obliged to lay this act before His Majesty for his disallowance, for no acts are to be passed in ye plantations whereby the shipping and navigation of this kingdom are affected." — Letter to Hunter, February 25, 1718, *Ibid.*, 500-502.

[557] — *Ibid.*, pp. 517-519.

waiting for further information the Board laid it before the king for disallowance. At the same time the
proprietors of the colony were directed to reprimand
their governor for consenting to a law, so "repugnant
to the laws of Great Britain and no ways warranted
by the charter." They were also informed that a
repetition of the offense would be sufficient ground
for annulling their charter.[558]

The New York revenue act of 1720 again laid a
two per cent duty on European goods, but had a
clause suspending its operation until it had been confirmed.[559] In 1724 the Board of Trade recommended
that the act should be "passed into law," although it
objected to the principle of the tax; but it was over-
ruled by the Committee of the Privy Council which
insisted upon the disallowance of the act.[560]

In order to prevent the enactment of similar laws
for the future, instructions were at once sent to all
the governors forbidding them to consent to any law
which laid any duty whatsoever on European goods
imported in English vessels.[561] The Board did not

[558] Representation of the Board to the king, May 1, 1718, in C.O. 5, 1293,
pp. 148-152. The act was annulled by an Order in Council, May 14, 1718,
in Privy Council *Register*, "George I," vol. ii, 141.

[559] New York *Colonial Laws*, vol. ii, 32.

[560] The Board of Trade reported in favor of confirming the law, July,
1722. The report was opposed by the London merchants and the committee
did not take any action on it for two years. Finally, in 1724, it took up the
report of the Board and the petition of the merchants, heard counsel for and
against the act, "And do agree humbly to offer their opinion that the said
act is not fit for your Majesty's royal approbation." — New York *Colonial
Documents*, vol. v, 706; Privy Council *Register*, "George I," vol. iv, 46, 76,
501, 502, 507.

[561] This instruction was issued at the demand of the Committee of the
Privy Council. See: Order in Council, April 30, 1724, in New York *Colonial
Documents*, vol. v.

recommend the disallowance of all laws which violated this instruction; but it refrained from doing so, only because of the confusion which might result from the repeal of a revenue law after the taxes had been collected and in some cases expended. In such cases, however, it demanded that the law should be amended so as to remove the objectionable features.[562]

The Board did not even permit evasions of this rule by indirect methods of taxation. Massachusetts attempted to do this in 1752 by an excise tax levied upon retailers of certain goods. The retailers had to have licenses and importers were forbidden to sell to any but licensed retailers. As this was considered a burden upon the import trade, the act was disallowed.[563]

The jealous care with which the Board of Trade excluded the assemblies from all legislation which in any way burdened British commerce is also seen in its attitude toward laws, other than those imposing ordinary tariff duties. A Massachusetts act of 1718 "for the better regulating of the culling of fish" was objected to by certain merchants and recommended by the Board for repeal, on the ground that it imposed upon British traders undesirable restrictions in purchasing fish.[564] Virginia and New Jersey attempted to prevent the importation of convicted

---

[562] Representation of the Board of Trade on the New York revenue law, August 6, 1755, in New York *Colonial Documents*, vol. vi, 33-36.

[563] C.O. 5, 918, p. 276; Privy Council *Register*, "George II," vol. xiv, 146.

[564] The merchants complained that the fish were badly culled by the persons appointed under this act, and as they had to be accepted, even though inferior, the trade was injured. Before the passage of this act the merchant had his own culler present while the fish were being culled, and so could control the quality of his purchase, which under the new law was impossible. See: Representation of the Board, May 4, 1721, in C.O. 5, 915, p. 324.

criminals, but the acts were promptly vetoed in England.[565] Other colonies tried with equally ill success to exclude paupers and other indigent persons,[566] the Board interposing a steadfast objection.

Pennsylvania passed a series of laws which laid heavy burdens on the importation of convicted criminals, paupers, and other indigent persons. Some of these were not transmitted to England for some time and so escaped the vigilance of the Board. One passed in 1738 was objected to and recommended for disallowance, but the Privy Council was so dilatory that the six months expired before any action was taken,[567] which had the effect of confirming the act.

In 1746 the Board considered the acts of 1742-1743, one of which laid an import duty upon criminals and paupers. Although Francis Fane reported that he had no objection to the act "in point of law," the Board recommended that it should be disallowed and also three similar acts passed in 1722 and 1729.[568] The reason for the repeal of the act of 1742 was that

[565] The Virginia Act was passed in 1722 and vetoed the next year. See: C.O. 5, 1365, p. 252. For the New Jersey Act see the representation of the Board, March 17, 1732, in C.O. 5, 996, pp. 283-284; Privy Council *Register*, "George II," vol. ii, 624.

[566] A South Carolina act of 1738, regulating the coasting trade, included this among its provisions. Another reason for its disallowance was the attempted special privileges given to vessels owned wholly within the province. See: Representation of the Board, May 9, 1755, in C.O. 5, 403, pp. 6-8; Privy Council *Register*, "George II," vol. xv, 452.

[567] The duties and penalties were held to be sufficient to prevent the transportation of felons. The Board reported for repeal, February 21, 1739, but no action was taken by the Privy Council until 1747. See: C.O. 5, 1294; Privy Council *Register*, "George II," vol. xi, 127.

[568] This report provoked an indignant protest from the Penns against the proposed repeal of laws which had been so long in force, and against which no objection had previously been made. This protest saved the act of 1722 and the two acts of 1729, as two of them had been repealed several years

the duties and the amount of security required of the importer of indigent persons made the act virtually prohibitory. The report also indicates that the vital objection to this and the other acts was that they imposed duties in such a way as to regulate immigration, although they specifically exempted from their operation such persons as could be legally imported according to the laws of England. But as the exemptions did not include the penalties imposed upon masters of ships for violating the acts, which would "probably deter them from importing" such persons, the Board concluded that the acts were clearly regulative and intended to evade the acts of Parliament.[569] In 1746 Pennsylvania passed another act, laying duties only on persons "Convicted of heinous Crimes," but the Board secured the repeal of this act, just as it had the others and on similar grounds.[570]

The question of the slave trade early attracted attention. The colonies attempted to regulate the importation of slaves, just as Pennsylvania did that of criminals, by means of tariff duties. In doing this, they were actuated by different motives. The southern colonies usually desired nothing more than revenue, but at times they attempted to regulate the quantity and quality of the slaves imported; the northern colonies more frequently intended that their

before by the assembly. See: Petition of the Penns against a Representation of the Board, in C.O. 5, 1271, v, 38; Privy Council *Register*, "George II," vol. xi, 51-52, 79.

[569] Representation of the Board, December 5, 1746, in C.O. 5, 1294, pp. 252 ff. See, also: Pennsylvania *Archives*, vol. i, 721, and Pennsylvania *Statutes at Large*, vol. iv, 509-511.

[570] This act was supplementary to the act of 1742. See: Representation of the Board, July 29, 1748, in C.O. 5, 1294, p. 355; Privy Council *Register*, "George II," vol. xii, 107.

laws should be exclusive. In either case the laws could be and frequently were regulative. The Board conceded that the assemblies might lay a tax upon negroes for purposes of revenue; but it insisted that such a tax should not be so laid as to amount to a regulation or impose a burden upon commerce.

Virginia had passed three different acts between 1710 and 1718 which laid an import duty of five pounds per head on negroes; but, as no one complained, the Board paid little attention to them. In 1723, and again in 1728, new laws were framed which levied but two pounds duty per head. Both of these, however, received the royal disapproval, on demand of the Board, because they laid a burden upon British merchants.[571] Another reason was that the tax would increase the value of slaves, make it practically impossible for poor planters to purchase them, hence delay the settling up of the country, and so indirectly reduce the potential quantity of tobacco for export.[572] The action in the case of the Virginia laws indicates that it was not the amount, but the principle of the taxation, which was opposed by the Board.

The difficulty was solved in 1735 as a result of the Board's consideration of the last five-year revenue act of New York, which had been passed in 1732 [573] and contained a clause laying a heavy import duty on slaves. The act had been in operation three years,

[571] The tax was to be paid by the importer. The most serious objection, however, was the indirect effect upon English trade of an increase in the cost of slaves, and the consequent limitation of the tobacco fields.

[572] See the representations of the Board of January 29, 1723, and May 23, 1729, in C.O. 5, 1365, pp. 269-271; 1366, pp. 28 ff. See, also: the Privy Council *Register*, "George I," vol. iv, 546; "George II," vol. ii, 47.

[573] New York *Colonial Laws*, vol. ii, 768-787.

and had been complained of so often by the merchants
that finally the Board sent the governor instructions
to have the law amended at once so that

> No duty be laid on any slaves imported payable by the im-
> porter . . .   also to signify our royal intention to our
> council and the Assembly of our said province that if they do
> not immediately comply with this our instruction we shall re-
> peal the act now complained of.[574]

Similar instructions were issued to other governors,
and from that time on, colonial laws which imposed
duties on negroes had to specify that the tax should
not be paid by the importer.[575]

The Board of Trade also took exception to acts of
the colonial assemblies which were intended to place
restrictions upon intercolonial trade; but in practice
did not demand the repeal of very many laws for that
reason.   A law of North Carolina levying a duty
upon Indian traders from Virginia who traded with
the Indians to the south and west was repealed in
1709.[576]   The Massachusetts tariff act which laid re-
taliatory duties on the products of New Hampshire
was passed in 1721.   Mr. West, the attorney for the
Board, gave an opinion on this law in 1725, in the
course of which he said,

> If any province injures another by any undue tax on their
> trade the remedy I think ought to be by application to the

[574] Additional instructions to Governor Cosby, August, 1735, in New
York *Colonial Documents*, vol. vi, 33-34.

[575] See the instructions to Francis Bernard, 1758, in New Jersey *Archives*,
vol. ix, 52-53; to Arthur Dobbs, 1754, North Carolina *Colonial Records*,
vol. v, 1118.   Cf. Du Bois's *Suppression of the Slave Trade*, chaps. ii-iv.

[576] Order in Council of September 26, 1709, in C.O. 5, 1316, O, 40.   In
1711 this act was renewed by North Carolina in the form of an export duty,
as it was claimed that the Virginia traders passed through North Carolina
territory in going to and from the Indian country.   The Board at once de-

crown to prevent any such acts being pass'd into law, and not by way of reprisals enacted among themselves.[577]

The Board was evidently of the same opinion as Mr. West; for in 1731, when the residents of Albemarle County, North Carolina, complained of Virginia's laying a heavy import duty upon their tobacco, it at once ordered the secretary to prepare the draft of a representation for the repeal of the acts.[578] Four years later, when Massachusetts excluded New Hampshire bills of credit, the Board ordered the act to be laid before the king for his disallowance.[579] Other cases could be cited in which the Board showed a similar attitude. Thus when Governor Dobbs complained of a South Carolina statute which taxed naval stores imported from the northward, the Board wrote him that it must be in its consequence destructive to

> The commerce of His Majesty's subjects in North Carolina and have an improper effect thereupon and therefore we shall lose no time in enquiring into this matter and taking such measures as shall appear to us to be proper.[580]

---

manded that the act be disallowed. See: Representation of the Board, December 19, 1712, in C.O. 5, 1363, pp. 437-438.

[577] Massachusetts *Acts and Resolves*, vol. ii, 235.

[578] There were two of these acts, one passed in 1705 and the other in 1726; both intended to prevent the importation of tobacco from North Carolina. In recommending the repeal of these laws the Board pointed out that the only good port in North Carolina was near the southern boundary, and that it was therefore necessary that the planters use those of Virginia. If the planters to the northward were cut off from Virginia by both land and sea, as these laws contemplated, they would be placed under difficulties so great that they might be forced to give up the production of tobacco and go to manufacturing. See: Representation of the Board, July 29, 1731, C.O. 5, 1366, pp. 76-78. The acts were disallowed, November 25, 1731. See: Privy Council *Register*, "George II," vol. ii, 477.

[579] Massachusetts *Acts and Resolves*, vol. ii, 747.

[580] Letter of November 9, 1757, in North Carolina *Colonial Records*, vol. v, 786-787.

The policy of the Board on the subject of inter-colonial commerce is just as clear as it was on the question of external trade, although there are fewer instances of its use. The few instances of action, how-ever, were effective in preventing the growth of dis-criminating trade laws. The most striking illustra-tion of this is the rapidity with which commercial retaliation of all kinds developed as soon as the colo-nies threw off British control, and the absence of such controversies during the preceding century. After the colonies became independent they were unre-strained, there was no body to disallow their laws, they had no common superior, nor was there any place where unfair and discriminating laws of other colonies could be effectually impeached. The little which the Board did in this field made a world of dif-ference – the difference between commercial har-mony and commercial anarchy.

Efforts to prevent conditions in any colony which might lead to a retardation of its development, or which might cause a depopulation of neigh-boring provinces, are closely related to the Board's commercial policy. Overlarge individual land holdings hindered rapid growth in population, consequently the Board insisted upon laws break-ing the exorbitant land grants in New York, and refused its consent to land grant, seating, and cultivation laws in other colonies because they would encourage the growth [581] of large hold-ings. It also put its stamp of disapproval upon laws

[581] In 1707 the Board secured the repeal of a Virginia law regulating land grants and their seating. This act permitted anybody to take up two hundred acres of land for each taxable servant above five in number, be-

offering to newcomers temporary exemption from prosecutions for debts contracted in other provinces.[582]

Another important class of acts which the Board very frequently offered for the royal veto included those which affected private property. A wide range of laws could be included under this general head; but the most common can be grouped into two general divisions. The first and larger class included laws which in some way affected credit transactions,

---

sides the fifty acres he could take up for bringing a servant into the colony. Not more than four thousand acres could be granted in one patent, but a person could take out as many patents as he chose. Under this law any person with one hundred slaves could patent nineteen thousand acres of land, or other areas in proportion. The Board maintained that this was far more than any one man could cultivate, and would enable a few rich men to secure control of all the good land. Thus the law would delay the actual settling of the colony.

The provision in regard to seating was equally objectionable. Building a house twelve by twelve, clearing, planting, and tending one acre was sufficient for "seating and planting," without any provision as to the number of acres. The Board insisted that this should suffice for but fifty acres, instead of a possible four thousand. See: Representation of the Board, March 27, 1707, in C.O. 5, 1362, pp. 117 ff.

The repeal of the above law left a law of 1666 in force which defined "seating" as building a house and keeping stock for one whole year, without mentioning the number of acres. This too was disallowed in 1711, having been in force forty-five years. See: Representation of the Board, February 22, 1711, in Privy Council *Register*, "Anne," vol. v, 227.

Other colonies attempted to change the terms of granting lands and failed. North Carolina in 1738 tried to reduce the requirement by one half, but the law was vetoed in 1740. See: C.O. 5, 323, pp. 279-281; Privy Council *Register*, "George II," vol. vii, 257. A number of other acts of North Carolina affecting land grants were repealed in 1754. See: Representation of the Board, March 25, 1754, in C.O. 5, 323; Privy Council *Register*, "George II," vol. xv, 118-121.

[582] The act of North Carolina, vetoed in 1707, is a good illustration. By this act persons coming from other colonies were not to be proceeded against for debts due in places from which they came for a period of five years after coming to the colony. See: Representation of the Board, November 12, 1707, in C.O. 5, 1292, pp. 17-19.

such as acts giving the claims of resident creditors precedence over those of non-residents,[583] various forms of bankruptcy laws,[584] legal tender acts,[585] stay laws,[586] statutes of limitations,[587] and usury laws.[588] The second class embraced those which affected land titles, such as cultivation laws, and acts regulating the method of recording deeds and proving titles, especially if such acts were retroactive.

As the colonies grew and the population flowed

[583] See: North Carolina *Colonial Records*, vol. iv, 844; Pennsylvania *Archives*, first series, vol. i, 157.

[584] "It is easy to foresee that such a law can be beneficial to the very small part of the creditors resident in the colony only and that the nine-tenths of them who reside here would be exposed to frauds and difficulties of every sort and might be greatly injured in their properties.

"For these reasons we beg leave to lay the said act before your Lordships, with our humble opinion, that it should forthwith receive His Majesty's disallowance." — Report of the Board to the Privy Council, June 29, 1758, on the Massachusetts bankruptcy law, passed August 31, 1757, in Massachusetts *Acts and Resolves*, vol. iv, 44.

The Maryland act for the relief of poor debtors, repealed in 1709, comes under this head, although it affected English merchants less. The Virginia insolvency law of 1762 was a bankruptcy law in all but name, and affected English creditors almost as much as did that of Massachusetts. It was disallowed in 1763, after a full hearing of the complaints and objections of merchants who might be affected. C.O. 5, 727, p. 132; 1368, pp. 234-241; Privy Council *Register*, "George III," vol. iii, 54.

[585] New Jersey *Archives*, vol. viii, part ii, 101, 125, and *passim*; New York *Colonial Documents*, vols. vi, vii, *passim*.

[586] New Jersey act for the suspension of civil actions from February to September, 1748. See: Representation of the Board, July 21, 1749, in New Jersey *Archives*, vol. vii, 307-308.

[587] See the representation of the Board on a Virginia act fixing a limitation of obligations for judgments, bonds, etc., March 21, 1729, in Board of Trade *Journal*, 39, pp. 60-61; Privy Council *Register*, "George II," vol. i, 509.

[588] New York act to prevent the levying on specialties more than the principal, interest, and cost of suit; disallowed, August 12, 1731. See: Privy Council *Register*, "George II," vol. ii, 402. Maryland act to limit damages upon protested bills of exchange to ten per cent; passed, December 11, 1708; repealed, December 15, 1709, because the limit did not permit

westward and filled up the back country, it became
necessary to increase the original number of civil divisions. In Massachusetts it had been the custom,
when a new town was created, to allow it to send delegates to the House of Representatives the same as the
older towns. In 1743 the Board of Trade instructed
the governor not to give his assent to any similar law
in the future, on the ground that

> This practice of erecting new towns and vesting them with
> this privilege, having formerly by its frequency been found to
> produce many inconveniences and particularly that of contin-
> ually increasing the number of Representatives.[589]

Although the lower house of the Massachusetts legislature objected to the instruction as an illegal attempt
to limit the legislative privileges granted by the
charter, it observed the new order, in form at least,
until 1757. In that year Danvers was erected into a
town with the privilege of sending representatives to
the House; but the act was disallowed at the request
of the Board in 1759, because it was clearly in violation of the governor's instructions on this point.[590]

In the meantime the same question had arisen in
North Carolina in a somewhat similar form. From
time to time, new counties had been created with the
privilege of sending two delegates to the assembly.

even ordinary interest on protested bills, when unavoidable delays were
considered. See: C.O. 5, 727, p. 141; Privy Council *Register*, "Anne,"
vol. iv, 491.

[589] Representation of the Board, July 31, 1759, in Massachusetts *Acts and
Resolves*, vol. iv, 5. The above quotation is the Board's own reason for
issuing the instruction. Cf. the report of the Board on laws creating townships passed in 1739-1740, *Ibid.*, vol. ii, 1006-1007.

[590] Massachusetts *Acts and Resolves*, vol. iv, 5, 93-94; C.O. 5, 919, pp.
40-41. Notice of the disallowance apparently never reached Massachusetts,
and Danvers continued to send representatives to the General Court.

Some of the older counties claimed the right of sending five representatives, consequently there was dissatisfaction in the other counties. In 1746, Governor Johnson, by some shrewd parliamentary practice, secured the enactment of a law rearranging the representation. This act was considered by the Board between the years 1750-1754 and finally recommended for disapproval, together with all the previous acts creating counties.[591] Governor Dobbs was then instructed to incorporate the counties by charters, issued with the consent of his council, and at the same time directed what representation he should permit each county to have in the assembly. This arrangement failed, and he was finally instructed to reënact the laws creating counties, but such acts should not confer upon them the right to elect members of the assembly.[592]

Probably the Board had no real conception of the growth of an American commonwealth, else it would not have taken the hostile attitude it did toward an increase of the representative body. Possibly the members were so profoundly impressed with the evils of the "rotten borough" that they feared its introduction into the colonies. The constantly increasing numbers of local units, and the automatic acquisition of representation, tended to make some of the lower

[591] Representation of the Board of Trade on the condition of North Carolina, March 14, 1754, in North Carolina *Colonial Records*, vol. v, 81-108. March 25, the Board recommended the repeal of thirteen different acts for the creation of counties, precincts, and townships, which was done, April 8, 1754. See: C.O. 5, 323; Privy Council *Register*, "George II," vol. xv, 118-121.

[592] Instructions to Arthur Dobbs, in North Carolina *Colonial Records*, vol. v, 340-341, IIII.

houses unwieldy. As they had steadily encroached
upon the council, the growing disparity in numbers
between the two houses only added to the powers and
authority of the popular chamber; hence the Board
felt justified in checking further additions to that
body.[593]

Except in Massachusetts, the Board interfered only
when the governor and his legislature disagreed, and
in the case of New Hampshire [594] and North Carolina it finally permitted the colonists to settle the question for themselves. Even the objection to the practice in Massachusetts was finally withdrawn as illegal, so that the colonies were left to work out the
problem, each in its own way.[595]

In its attempt to eliminate irregularities in colonial
legislation, the Board of Trade made an attempt to
introduce into the colonies a system of private bill
procedure similar to that in use in England. The
first instruction to the governors of Massachusetts on
the subject was issued in 1715 to Governor Burgess.
It provided that every private law should have a
clause saving the rights of the crown and all persons
other than those mentioned in the act.[596]

No further instructions appeared until 1723, when

---

[593] By the letters of Governor Shirley it appears to us that there have
been no fewer than thirty-three new townships since 1692, each of which has
a right to send one or two representatives to the assembly. There are now
one hundred and sixty towns in the province, most of which send two representatives. We think this enough. This destroys the balance between the
assembly and council. — Representation of the Board on a Massachusetts
act creating new townships, June 8, 1743, in C.O. 5, 918, pp. 93-95.

[594] See the representations of the Board of July 9 and December 22, 1752,
on the acts of New Hampshire, in C.O. 5, 941, pp. 277-280, 293-294.

[595] Massachusetts *Acts and Resolves*, vol. iv, 94, 452.

[596] — *Ibid.*, vol. vi, p.v.

the governor was directed to require all such laws to have a clause suspending their action until they were approved by the crown.[597] In addition he was directed

> Not to give your assent to any private act until proof be made before you in council (and entred in the council books) that publick notification was made of the parties' intention to apply for such act in the several parish churches where the premises in question lie, for three Sundays at least, successively, before any such act shall be brought into the Assembly; and that a certificate under your hand be transmitted with and annexed to every such private act signifying that the same has pass'd thro' all the forms above mention'd.[598]

The House of Representatives in Massachusetts refused to follow the above instructions, and no private acts were passed until 1742,[599] when one was attempted. As there was no evidence, however, that the instructions had been observed it was disallowed.[600] Six more private acts were passed in the next fifteen years, but as all were for the purpose of granting divorces and did not especially affect property, no attention was paid to them.[601] In 1757 another attempt was made to evade the instructions, but the Board secured the disallowance of the one act of that year, as

---

[597] This instruction was added at the request of the Committee of the Privy Council. Previous to 1722 such instructions had only been given to the governors of Jamaica, Bermudas, Barbadoes, and the Leeward Islands. See: Privy Council *Register*, "George I," vol. iv, 183.

[598] Massachusetts *Acts and Resolves*, vol. vi, pp. iv, v. The same instruction was issued to all the governors in America. See that to Governor Lewis Morris, in New Jersey *Archives*, vol. vi, 24. Cf. Todd's *Parliamentary Government*, private bill procedure.

[599] Massachusetts *Acts and Resolves*, vol. vi, p. iv.

[600] — *Ibid.*, 161. Private Act, no. 80, passed, June 18, 1742; disallowed, May 28, 1746.

[601] — *Ibid.*, 163-177. Private Acts, nos. 81, 82, 83, 84, 85, 86.

well as one which passed the following year.[602] Between the years 1760-1767, eight more private bills were passed, three of which were repealed. Apparently the forms of procedure required by the governor's instructions had not been followed; but that was not the only cause for disallowance, as the Board considered the laws objectionable in themselves.

While the Board failed to induce Massachusetts to follow the forms laid down for legislation of this kind, it did successfully stand in the way of the enactment of many laws in violation of its orders. It should be noted, however, that the real objection of Massachusetts to the instruction was that it was an unwarranted infringement of its charter, and without legal force.

The safeguards thrown about private bills were certainly reasonable, for in most cases such laws were extrajudicial in character, affected property rights, and might easily do great injustice to innocent parties. The Board was quite inexorable when such a law failed to indicate that due notice had been given of the application for such a bill,[603] and that the rights

---

[602] Both of these laws were to expedite the settlement of estates. After reciting the limitation in the governors' instructions, the representation of the Board concludes: "These regulations have ever been esteem'd essentially necessary for the security of private property in His Majesty's plantations; and as they have not in either respect been observed in the passing of the two private acts above mentioned" they should be disallowed. See: Representation of the Board, July 31, 1759, in C.O. 5, 919, pp. 41-44; Massachusetts *Acts and Resolves*, vol. vi, 178-180.

[603] See the representation of the Board of May 16, 1760, for the repeal of three private acts of Virginia, passed in 1758-1759. "In these acts there is no certificate of any previous notification, in the parish church, of the intention of the respective parties to apply for such act," etc. See: C.O. 5, 1367, pp. 401-405. Many other illustrations are found in the Virginia and Carolina *Entry Books*.

of minor heirs had been conserved.[604] In practically
all of the royal provinces these regulations were followed without complaint. Where they were evaded,
a repeal was almost inevitable. The southern group
of colonies made more extensive use of such laws than
did the northern, as there were more occasions there
to break through entails of land.[605]

The Board was not only particular of the procedure in such bills, it carefully looked into their contents to see that no great innovations were creeping in.
Private divorce acts different from those in England
were objected to but not repealed, for obvious rea-

[604] An act of Pennsylvania passed in 1718, placing the property of
William Clark, deceased, in the hands of trustees to be sold for the payment
of his debts, is typical of several which the Board rejected. William Clark,
the son, had become bound for £220. Afterwards his father died, leaving
property valued at £3000 to his son and his son's wife for life, after which
it was to go to their children. The son died, leaving a wife and three
children, who were still minors and were living in Barbadoes. The act
proposed to sell a portion of the property left by the elder Mr. Clark to
pay his debts without any notice to the minor heirs to whom it belonged, nor
any saving of their rights. Needless to say, it met the royal veto. See:
Representation of the Board, November 26, 1719, in C.O. 5, 1293; Privy
Council *Register*, "George I," vol. i, 364.

[605] The *Entry Books* for Virginia and the Carolinas contain many entries
like the following: "We have consulted Mr. Fane, one of your Majesty's
council, upon the several acts, who has no objection to any of them in point
of law; and as they have pass'd thro' the forms in Virginia prescribed by
Your Majesty's instructions for the enacting of private laws, and no complaint has been offered to us against any of them during the six months in
which they have lain by in our office," we recommend their confirmation.
See: Representation of the Board, June 29, 1733, for the confirmation of
thirteen private acts of Virginia, passed in 1730-1732, in C.O. 5, 1366, pp.
103-107.

"This Act appears to have been passed with the consent of all the parties
concerned, and in exact conformity to the regulations prescribed by Your
Majesty's Instructions." — Representation of the Board for the confirmation
of a North Carolina act of 1761 "to dock the entail of Lands therein mentioned," March 15, 1763, in C.O. 5, 305, pp. 224-225.

sons.[606] If a party had an easy remedy at law, the private bill was frequently repealed.[607] Laws, public in form but private in application, were not tolerated, if they were detected;[608] nor were private bills of an unusual character, such as permitting a married woman to sell her real estate during the lifetime of her husband without his consent,[609] or exempting par-

---

[606] Three divorce acts of Massachusetts, passed in 1755, 1756, and 1757, were considered by the Board in 1758. Two of these divorces were for adultery on the part of the husband, and the wife in each case was given the divorce and permitted to marry again. Matthew Lamb said they were "the first of their kind he ever saw in the colonies or elsewhere." Only one recited a previous divorce from bed and board, the other two contained no evidence that the charges recited had been proved before a competent tribunal, and all three acts were defective because they dissolved the marriage on one side only. As the laws had already had their effect, the Board did not recommend a disallowance; but as it was doubtful whether any colony had power to pass laws of that nature, and consequently an open question whether the laws were not in themselves "null and void," they were sent to the attorney- and solicitor-general for their opinion. This was done "to the end that proper instructions may be form'd for the governor of this and other His Majesty's colonies to regulate their conduct in the like cases." These acts, however, were not disallowed. See: Representation of the Board, June 6, 1758. C.O. 5, 918, pp. 486-490.

These are not the first divorce laws, for general divorce laws existed in several colonies, but are the first private divorce acts of a particular character. See the Pennsylvania laws for the punishment of adultery, of 1702 and 1705-1706. The first was repealed because it was not specific in regard to the kind of divorce it allowed. The other specified "from Bed and Board" and was not objected to. See: C.O. 5, 1291, p. 260; Pennsylvania Statutes at Large, vol. ii, 180. Cf. Channing's History of the United States, vol. ii, 235.

[607] Five private acts of New Hampshire were repealed at one time for this reason. Representation of the Board, July 10, 1764, in C.O. 5, 942, pp. 268-284.

[608] See the action of the Board in regard to a Georgia law of 1759 confirming titles to certain lands. Representation of the Board, June 23, 1761, in C.O. 5, 674, pp. 192-196.

[609] A Virginia act of 1732 enabled Frances Greenbill to dispose of her lands and other estate by either will or deed, even though her husband were living. Francis Fane in his report to the Board said: "This is the first instance wherein the legislature in any of the colonies abroad have taken

ticular individuals from prosecution for debt for a term of years.[610] Much less did the Board tolerate private acts which were in effect only bills of attainder.[611] It was as scrupulous about innovations contrary to the law of England as any court, and the importance of a private bill as a dangerous precedent was frequently considered, and led to many vetoes.[612] On the whole the Board's private bill policy was a success from an administrative standpoint, and of very considerable value to the colonists themselves.

In addition to the kinds of laws mentioned above, the Board of Trade found reasons for disallowing many others. Some were of an ecclesiastical nature, such as laws regulating riotous sports,[613] the action of

upon themselves to alter the law in so settled and known a point as giving a power to a *femme couvert* to sell or dispose of her real or personal estate in the supposed lifetime of her husband." — Representation of the Board, March 21, 1745, in C.O. 5, 1366, pp. 371-372. The act was promptly disallowed. A Massachusetts act of 1762 was disallowed for similar reasons. See: Privy Council *Register*, "George II," vol. viii, 527; C.O. 5, 920, pp. 149-151.

[610] See the Board's report of May 12, 1758, on an act of Pennsylvania for the relief of George Croghan and William Trent, passed in 1755, and disallowed in 1758, in C.O. 5, 1295, pp. 249-251.

[611] Six private acts of Massachusetts for the punishment of six individuals for trading with the French were disallowed in 1707. See: C.O. 5, 912, pp. 356, 388.

[612] A South Carolina act of 1733, or 1723 (the date is variously given), was repealed in 1734, largely because of the precedent it might establish. The act altered a will by taking property from one son and giving it to another, and changed several other provisions. See: Representation of the Board, April 18, 1734, in C.O. 5, 401, p. 95.

A New Hampshire act of 1742 changed an estate from an estate tail to one in fee simple by changing the terms of a mortgage. It was repealed because it might create a dangerous precedent. Representation of the Board, June 14, 1754, in C.O. 5, 941, pp. 351-354. The effect of several of the laws cited above as precedents for others was also a reason for their disallowance.

[613] Pennsylvania *Archives*, first series, vol. i, 155, 157.

vestries,[614] and the observance of the Sabbath. Some were badly drawn, uncertain in their meaning, or absurd in their provisions.[615] Many others were in violation of instructions, repealed laws formerly confirmed,[616] or reënacted laws already disallowed. Still others attempted to change slaves from real to personal property.[617]

The foregoing account shows that the Board, through its power to secure the repeal of colonial laws, was able to mould and develop certain phases of the provincial constitutions. The power to regulate external commerce was carefully retained in the hands of the home government, and restrictions placed upon the power of the colonies to regulate commerce of a purely intercolonial nature. Trade was given a chance to expand by the Board's preventing the colonial legislatures from laying legal obstacles in the

[614] North Carolina *Colonial Records*, vol. vi, 716.

[615] February 7, 1706, thirty-five acts of Pennsylvania were disallowed, mainly for one of these defects. See: C.O. 5, 1291, pp. 254 ff.

[616] The Virginia acts of 1705 for the better regulation of William and Mary College and to prevent the "tending of seconds" were disallowed for this reason. See: Representation of the Board, August 6, 1731, in C.O. 5, 1366, p. 502. Scores of similar cases could be cited.

[617] Slaves had been declared real estate by an act of Virginia, passed in 1705 and confirmed by a later one about 1725. The Board steadily refused to permit any changes from that definition. In a letter to Governor Fauquier, May 6, 1763, the Board said: "The royal negative has been twice given to the proposition of making slaves personal estate, and after fullest consideration, both by this Board and by His Majesty in council, so it would not become us, whatever our opinion might be, to revive the discussion of it; but as we are convinced of the rectitude of that principle of policy which has made slaves real estate, and annex'd them to the plant's, in all British colonies which depend on slave labor, we cannot approve this bill, and are at a loss to guess what motive could have induced the Virginia legislature to attempt to subvert a policy long established, which has after forty years experience been found so beneficial and advantageous as this is represented to have been." — C.O. 5, 1368, p. 226.

way of the collection of debts, private bills were carefully hedged about with legal restrictions, judicial procedure was kept closely patterned after that of England, and much was done to prevent the introduction of innovations of uncertain value.

Under the threat of repeal if they refused to comply, the assemblies were forced to consent to modifications of revenue measures which the governor and council had been unable or unwilling to secure; and in case of the Pennsylvania law taxing the proprietary estates, the agents of the province, in order to prevent its disallowance, entered into bonds before the Board to secure certain amendments.[618] Last but not least, the Board was able to prevent the enactment or secure the repeal of unjust or discriminating laws thus affording the residents of the colonies some protection against the action of an ignorant or partisan assembly.

Method of disallowance

Having examined the causes for repealing colonial legislation, let us now consider the method of pro-

---

[618] "We the undersigned, Benjamin Franklin and Robert Charles, agents for the province of Pennsylvania, do hereby consent, that in case an act passed in the said province in April, 1759, entitled 'An Act for granting to His Majesty the sum of one hundred thousand pounds and for striking the same in bills of credit . . . and for providing a fund for sinking the said bills of credit by a tax on all estates real and personal and taxables within this province' shall not be repealed by His Majesty in council, we, the said agents, do undertake that the assembly of Pennsylvania will prepare and pass and offer to the governor of the said province of Pennsylvania, an act to amend the aforementioned act according to the amendments proposed in the report made by the Lords of the Committee of Council this day . . . and will indemnify the proprietaries from any damage that they may sustain by such act not being so prepared and passed by the assembly and offered to the governor. Witness our hands this twenty-eighth day of August, 1760." — Pennsylvania *Statutes at Large*, vol. v, 656-657.

cedure by which a law was finally disallowed. The
laws were transmitted to England and could come
before the Board of Trade in any one of four ways.
They could be delivered to one of the principal secretaries of state, who would either transmit them to the
Board or lay them before the council. In the latter
case they were referred to the Committee of Council,
which in turn referred them to the Board.[619] As the
crown lawyers had held that the time clause limiting
repeals dated from the time the laws were submitted
to the Privy Council, it was to the interest of the
colony to submit them to the council with the least
possible delay. The most expeditious way to do this
was to deliver them to the clerk of the Privy Council.
In such cases the laws went by reference to the committee and thence to the Board, which was the third
method and the one most frequently used by the Massachusetts agents. Lastly, the laws could be delivered directly to the Board of Trade. This practice
was abandoned by Massachusetts and Pennsylvania
because the Board claimed the power to have a law
disallowed at any time, unless it had been before the
Privy Council.

No matter how and to what officers the laws were
submitted in the first instance, they were always ultimately referred to the Board of Trade for consideration. The first point to be settled was, whether a
law conflicted with any act of Parliament. The members of the Board did not presume to pass on questions of that kind, but referred them to its legal advisers. Whatever laws affected the customs or the
admiralty in any way were referred to the comission-

---

[619] Before 1721 the reference was usually directly to the Board of Trade.

ers of customs or to the admiralty board respectively for their opinion. These officials confined their observations wholly to the effect of the law upon their own field of activity.[620]

The Bishop of London was always consulted in regard to laws which in any way might affect his ecclesiastical jurisdiction, or which concerned religious conditions, or regulated morals. He was quite ready to give his opinion and even insisted upon being heard. The *Journal* of the Board frequently has entries like the following:

> The Lord Bishop of London desired the board when the acts of New York and of the Leeward Islands shall come under consideration, that they would be mindful of his objections against the particular acts mentioned in the minutes of June 15th last.[621]

> The Lord Bishop of London desired that an act past in the Massachusetts Bay entitled An Act more effectually providing for the support of Ministers . . . may not be confirmed by His Majesty 'till he be heard thereupon.[622]

> Ordered that the Bishop of London be notified that the Board wish to speak with him, Tuesday morning next.[623]

Many other illustrations could be cited, but enough have been given to show the general custom of the Board in the matter.[624]

If a law did not seem to affect any particular de-

---

[620] See the correspondence in regard to the Massachusetts act of 1716, fixing fees in the admiralty offices, in Massachusetts *Acts and Resolves*, vol. ii, 68 69.

[621] Quoted from the *Journal* of December 3, 1702, in Pennsylvania *Statutes at Large*, vol. ii, 461.

[622] Board of Trade *Journal*, May 24, 1704; Massachusetts *Acts and Resolves*, vol. i, 505.

[623] *Journal*, November 10, 1727; Massachusetts *Acts and Resolves*, vol. ii, 481.

[624] Cross in his *Anglican Episcopate and the American Colonies* does not discuss this important phase of the Bishop of London's work.

partment of the home government, it was sent to one of the crown lawyers for an opinion "in point of law," and there it was likely to remain until some one paid that officer his fee and saw that he made his report. If no one looked after the act, it might remain in his hands for years. This was especially true of private acts, and the Board frequently reminded the governors that interested parties should have an agent on hand to attend to such matters.[625] For the same reason it insisted upon each colony maintaining a representative to look after public laws, and in the course of time this was done.[626]

As it was to the interest of each colony to secure a favorable report from the attorney to whom the laws had been referred, an active agent began his campaign for their confirmation with that official. By calling on him and explaining the purpose and the necessity of each law, he could frequently secure a favorable report, which otherwise might have been adverse.[627]

---

[625] June 4, 1719, the Board commented on a private act of Massachusetts, and after stating that the act itself was unobjectionable added: "Some persons should be appointed here to solicit the dispatch of this and all other private acts, and to pay the fees in the several offices, when His Majesty's pleasure is declared upon them." At the same time it wrote Governor Shute: "It will be necessary for the future that when any private bills are sent over, the parties concerned in those acts do appoint some person here to solicit the dispatch of them, otherways they will lie unconfirmed." – C.O. 5, 915, pp. 20, 276.

[626] September 4, 1701, the Board wrote Governor Blakiston of Maryland, "We wonder the Assembly should not think fit to constitute an agent for soliciting their affairs here. There are occasions (tho' not at our Board) in which business cannot be done without some charge: and inconveniences have arisen by the delay of reports upon some laws, and otherwise; all of which will grow worse and worse if some fit person be not appointed to look after such like matters." – C.O. 5, 726, p. 99.

[627] "The fate of the act depends in a great measure on this gentleman's

When the opinion of the attorneys had been received the Board was ready for the serious consideration of the law. Here again the work of a friendly agent was of the utmost importance. The Board could not possibly know the local demands for a law, which on its face appeared objectionable, and had to depend upon such information as the legislature or its representative might furnish. On several occasions the Board had already prepared a formal representation for the repeal of acts, when the appearance of some one familiar with conditions in the colony from which the acts came changed the whole appearance of things, and caused the Board to abandon its representation, and allow the acts to remain in force.[628]

The whole method of procedure can best be seen, however, in a typical case, such as the repeal of the Massachusetts Act of 1722 which laid a tax on the Quaker towns of Dartmouth and Tiverton for the

report; and which report must again entirely depend upon the idea, and information he receives of the reasons, circumstances and views with which the act was passed in the provincial Assembly. Here is the heavy and useful part of the duty of an agent; to attend the reporting counsel, to explain circumstances, and lead his opinion to a report favorable to the wishes of the province for which he acts; as a person in the reporting counsel's situation must be unacquainted with a thousand things an agent can explain, and consequently without his information be liable to many mistakes." — North Carolina *Colonial Records*, vol. v, 747.

[628] May 28, 1754, the Board ordered a representation prepared for the repeal of nine acts of South Carolina. June 26, Mr. Crockatt, agent for that colony, was called in and allowed to present reasons why one of the acts should be allowed to stand. After he was gone, the Board agreed to allow the act to "lie by probationary." June 3, 1763, Governor Ellis of Georgia, who had just returned to England, appeared before the Board and presented facts justifying a Georgia law for the speedy collection of small debts, a representation for the repeal of which was already drawn. After he withdrew the Board decided not to repeal the act, and ordered changes to that effect made in the representation. See: Board of Trade *Journal*, 62; 69, pp. 281-283.

support of Congregational ministers. The assessors of the two towns refused to assess the tax and were consequently thrown into prison. They at once prepared a petition to the king, which complained of the injustice of the act in question and asked that they be released. The Lords Justices in Council referred the petition to the Committee of Council, which in turn referred it (October 24, 1723) to the Board of Trade for consideration.[629]

In the meantime, the act in question had been re-enacted, and this fact was stated in the petition. The Board considered the matter on November 14, and as the act of 1723 had not as yet been received, that of 1722 only was sent to Mr. West for his "opinion in point of law." On November 20 the agents for the Quakers attended the Board, and were informed that the act was with Mr. West and that it would be considered as soon as his opinion should be received.

December 10, Mr. West reported that he had been attended by the agents for the Quakers, as well as that for the province, and thinking "the whole of the complaint was not within the intention of your Lordship's reference to me, as no circumstance of what they alledged did in any manner appear upon the face of the act itself, and that therefore my duty in obedience to your Lordship's commands was only to certify that upon consideration of the act as it stands simply upon the record I have no objection in point of law to its being confirmed." [630]

This report was received by the Board the same day, and two days later the agents were notified that

---

[629] Massachusetts *Acts and Resolves*, vol. ii, 251-257, 272-273.
[630] — *Ibid.*, vol. ii, 272-273.

the act would be considered at the meeting one week
hence. The meeting was held on the appointed day
and was attended by Mr. Richardson and Mr. Partridge with their solicitor, Mr. Sharpe, in behalf of
the Quakers. The province was represented by its
agents, Mr. Sandford and Mr. Sanderson, assisted
by their solicitor, Mr. Bampfield. Each attorney
presented proofs and arguments in support of his side
of the case, and was given a chance to reply to the
proofs and arguments of his opponent. After the
formal hearing the agents and their attorneys withdrew, and the secretary was ordered to prepare the
draft of a representation to the Lords Justices for the
repeal of the act of 1722, which was agreed to and
signed the following day, and transmitted to the office
of the Privy Council.

January 14, 1724, an Order in Council referred
this representation to the Committee of the Privy
Council to be considered and reported upon. As that
committee delayed action, Mr. Partridge petitioned
the Board that the act of 1723 should also be sent up
to the council, and in accordance with this petition,
a representation was at once prepared for the repeal
of that act. This representation, like the previous one,
was referred to the Committee of Council. That
body then took the two representations into consideration and recommended that the acts of both 1722
and 1723 should be disallowed and that the taxes of
the two towns should be remitted, which was promptly done by an Order in Council.[631]

What was done in the above case is fairly typical
of the action in other instances, although the proced-

---

[631] Massachusetts *Acts and Resolves*, vol. ii, 273-277.

ure varied with the amount of opposition the interested parties offered each other.   The contest over the
above act might well have been carried to the Committee of Council, where the hearing was by counsel
only.

Motions before the committee were regularly of
three kinds, to confirm a report of the Board, to oppose it, or to have it recommitted.   If the latter motion should be successful, the whole question might
be gone over again before the Board, and the second
report of that body would go through the same forms
as did the first.   If on the other hand the motion to
oppose was successful, the committee made a report
different from that of the Board, which amounted to
a reversal of the action of that body.   Such occurrences were not frequent, although they did happen.[632]

Sometimes a representation was dropped in the
Privy Council at the request of the Board itself, as
was the case of one for the repeal of the various acts
of New Hampshire for the creation of counties.[633]
At other times they were pigeonholed or lost by the
committee to which they were referred,[634] and in some

---

[632] An illustration of this has been given in the case of the report of the
Board on the New York revenue act of 1720. On the whole the Board was
very slow to disallow an act that would cause any great amount of inconvenience in a colony. It preferred to warn the governor of the irregularity
of the law, and depend upon him to secure its modification. See the action
on the New York revenue acts, in New York *Colonial Documents*, vols. v, vi,
passim. Also the action on the Massachusetts bankruptcy law, in Massachusetts *Acts and Resolves*, vol. iv, 443-444.

[633] This representation was made July 9, 1752, and referred to the Committee on Plantation Affairs. No further action was taken, as the Board
informed the Council on December 22, following, that the disorders in New
Hampshire had apparently ceased; consequently the matter was dropped.
See: C.O. 5, 941, pp. 277-280, 293-294; Privy Council *Register*, "George II,"
vol. xiv, 180.

[634] This appears to have been true in the case of the New Jersey act of

cases they were referred to the committee and a day set for a hearing, but no further action taken.[635] Consequently a considerable number of acts which the Board recommended for disallowance were never repealed, simply because no positive action was taken by the Privy Council.

Such a method of repeal could not be called arbitrary, for it had thrown around it at every point all the forms of legal procedure. No law could be disallowed except after an opportunity had been given all parties concerned to oppose such action. The Board really gave to every person concerned due process of law: each party had his day in court; and after the Board had acted, it was always possible to carry the case up to the committee, where a judicial review of the action of the Board could be had. In fact it was very similar to a system of repeals by the action of a superior court. It is no exaggeration to say that our own Supreme Court declares state laws unconstitutional with even less ceremony than the Board used in disallowing colonial acts.[636]

1748 for determining its boundary with New York. Such also appears to have been the final disposition of the Massachusetts act of 1735 to prevent the use of paper money in that colony which had been issued by a private corporation in New Hampshire. See: Privy Council *Register*, "George II," vol. iv, 473, 484, 485, vol. xiv, 442, 456, 499.

[635] A South Carolina act of 1731, for the remission of quit rents, was recommended for repeal by the Board, November 1, 1732. The representation was opposed by the agent for the colony, and the whole matter referred to a committee as usual. July 25, 1733, the committee set "Wednesday next" for a hearing on the question, but the record fails to show any action whatever on "Wednesday next" or any later day, nor is any reason given for the nonconsideration of the matter. See: Privy Council *Register*, "George II," vol. iii, 73, 74, 81, 210.

[636] What has been said of the method of disallowing colonial laws applies equally to their confirmation. There was no difference whatever in the procedure.

If one were to criticise the methods of repeal, it would have to be on the ground of too much red tape. The almost numberless references from one board and from one officer to another, and the possibility for delays and dilatory motions, make the procedure seem cumbersome.   Yet it may have been better that these delays should exist, for they gave the colonies a better opportunity to justify their legislation.   In case of urgent necessity, however, the Board could secure prompt action; so that the red tape was not always a hindrance to efficiency.

When a law was disallowed, notice of the fact was sent to the governor of the province, who saw that it was entered in the law books.   It is possible this was not always done, and no doubt the notice sometimes failed to reach the colony,[637] for Governor Colden in a letter to the Board in 1761 says,

> I am told that several acts in Basket's edition of the acts of New York in 1718, are noted to be repealed, of which repeal not the least evidence appears anywhere in this province. This may deserve your Lordship's attention, as I make no doubt the judges continue to proceed upon them as of force.[638]

It does not appear from the record whether Colden was correctly informed or not, but it is not improbable that such things as he mentions could have happened.

Considerable confusion sometimes resulted from the repeal of laws which were in force, and often the Board refrained from recommending a royal veto solely because of the inconvenience it would produce

---

[637] Cf. the disallowance of the Massachusetts act of 1757 creating the town of Danvers, in Massachusetts *Acts and Resolves*, vol. iv, 93-94.

[638] New York *Colonial Documents*, vol. vii, 454-455.

in the colony affected. But serious irregularities could not be allowed to grow, and the Board felt compelled to act at times, regardless of the results to the persons who had disregarded ordinary restrictions. As it said in regard to a series of extraordinary laws of New Hampshire:

> The practice of passing laws of this nature, without clauses suspending their execution until Your Majesty's pleasure can be known, is of such a dangerous tendency and example, and many of the laws are themselves so unconstitutional and unjust, that we fear it will be necessary, that Your Majesty's disallowance of them should be made public in order to deter the legislatures of Your Majesty's colonies from assuming powers and taking cognizance of matters that do constitutionally belong to the Courts of Justice alone.[639]

The control exercised by the Board over legislation was no doubt often irritating to the colonists, just as the invalidation of laws by the courts is irritating to both state and nation, at times, in the United States. Some of the restrictions imposed by the Board were evaded by means of temporary laws, but the importance of these has probably been overrated, as they could be successful only to a limited extent. They could not be used for the regulation of courts and judicial procedure, for private acts, nor for the regulation of commerce. Taken all together, the royal veto proved a pretty effective check upon even the charter colonies, as witness the action of Massachusetts in regard to its bankruptcy law.

An examination of the laws of Pennsylvania shows that the legislature of that colony tried very seriously

---

[639] Representation for the repeal of sixteen laws (mostly private acts) of New Hampshire, July 10, 1764, in C.O. 5, 942, p. 266.

and honestly to correct such laws as were repealed because they were defective, arbitrary, or absurd in their provisions.   The members of the legislature evidently made a serious effort also to have their laws conform to the laws of England when inconsistencies were pointed out.[640]   Probably no other part of the British administrative machinery worked so effectively as did that for the control of colonial legislation, especially when one considers the common willingness of the provincial governors to evade their instructions and permit forbidden practices.

Appeals to the King in Council

There is an obvious difference between repealing, or disallowing, a law and declaring it null and void. The latter action was not taken very frequently, the most familiar instance being that of the action of the Privy Council in the case of Winthrop *vs.* Lechmere. The charter of Connecticut did not reserve to the crown the right of a royal veto of the laws passed by the colonial legislature, and the colony steadily resisted any attempt by the home government to exercise such authority.   The charter did, however, require all colonial laws not to be contrary to the laws of England.   When the intestates' law came before the Privy Council, in the case mentioned above, it was declared null and void because it was opposed to the common law of England.   This action amounted to more than a disallowance of the law, for

---

[640] See: Pennsylvania *Statutes at Large*, vol. ii, 191, 438. Note how carefully many of the laws, repealed in 1706 on the recommendation of the Board, are changed when reënacted so as to meet specific objections. Note especially how the law of 1706 providing for the succession of authority in

all settlements previously made under color of the act were invalidated.

The Board of Trade was not even consulted in the above transaction, but the entire proceedings were conducted before the Committee of the Privy Council. As the decision was afterwards reversed in the case of Clark *vs.* Tousey, several explanations for the first decision have been offered. Ferdinando John Paris, who was present at the time, offers an explanation quite different from those usually given. He lays no stress whatever upon the question of confirmation or lack of confirmation, as, according to the Connecticut charter, that question should have made no legal difference. He ascribes the whole success of Winthrop to the fact that the attorneys for Lechmere were grossly incompetent.

In the course of the hearing before the committee, the attorneys for Winthrop,

> Boldly put it upon Mr. Lechmere's Coll to shew that that distributory act had ever, once, been followed or carried into execution in Connecticut; and they were so very poorly instructed that they did not in return, offer to shew that it had.[641]

The attorneys for Winthrop on this occasion were Attorney-general Yorke and Solicitor-general Talbot.

Yorke afterwards became Lord Chancellor Hardwicke and as such gave the decision in the case of Phillips *vs.* Savage, which was in form a reversal of

the absence of a governor, which was disallowed in 1709, was reënacted in 1712 with exactly the changes required, and how it was confirmed in 1714.

[641] Letter of Paris to Jeremiah Allen, July 26, 1738, in Connecticut Historical Society *Collections*, vol. v, 78.

the case he had won for his client, Winthrop.   Paris
says that in giving his opinion in this case he said,

> That he had been of council for Mr. Winthrop in his case
> formerly.   That as his Coll, he had at such time, offer'd all
> that he cou'd for his clyent, to get the Connecticut Act re-
> pealed and yͤ Ordͬˢ reverst.   That thô he had prevail'd
> therein for his clyent, yet, with very great deference to those
> Lords who judged in that case, he was not satisfied in his
> own private opinion with that determination in Winthrop's
> case.[642]

It thus appears that Lechmere's counsel allowed
themselves to be bluffed and so lost the case, and that
even the attorneys who won considered the decision as
not in accordance with sound legal principles.   Besides this irregularity, there was another innovation
in the decision.   Winthrop's petition only asked for
general relief; but on the failure of Lechmere's counsel to show that the law had ever been carried into
execution, it was declared void, "At once, without
any Reference to the Board of Trade" a thing that
"was never done in any one case, before or since, to my
knowledge." [643]

This case illustrates the close connection between
the Board of Trade and the Committee of Council
which passed upon appeals from the colonies.   If an
appeal involved a purely judicial question, such, for
instance, as a claim that the colonial courts had erred
in giving a decision, it was settled by the committee
without a reference to the Board; but if the appeal
turned upon a colonial law or the official action of an
officer, it was regularly referred to that body for

---

[642] Connecticut Historical Society *Collections*, vol. v, 81.
[643] Paris to Allen, July 26, 1738, *Ibid.*, 78.

consideration. Such, for instance, was the case in the appeal of the Quakers of Dartmouth and Tiverton cited above, which could not be decided without passing upon the law under which they had been convicted. The consideration of the law and the expediency of repealing it was the legitimate work of the Board, and the final decision of the whole matter rested upon the report of that body.

As Paris points out, the action on Winthrop's appeal should have followed the regular lines of procedure in similar cases. The attorneys for Lechmere should have petitioned, in case the legal question was decided against their client, that they be heard in favor of the law. Such a motion would have separated the purely judicial question from the question of policy involved in the repeal or disallowance of a colonial statute. The second question would have gone to the Board for consideration, and the effects of the actual operation of the law would then have been brought out. This action was taken in the case of Phillips *vs.* Savage, and the petition was granted; but as the decision of the committee was contrary to the contention of Phillips, it was not necessary to enter into any particular defence of the law itself.

During its earlier years, especially, the Board was frequently called upon to decide whether an appeal from the colonies should be admitted. When a demand was made for an appeal and there was some doubt as to whether it should be admitted, the case was referred to the Board of Trade for investigation; if it decided the case was properly one of appeal, steps were taken to admit it. This was the action in the case of John and Nicholas Hallam's appeal from Connecticut,[644] the Atwood and Bayard case from New York,[645] and numerous others.

It is thus seen that Miss Kellogg's statement that,

The judicial functions of the council in hearing appeals from the colonial courts and taking action thereon were never transferred to the new administrative body, thus the Privy Council remained throughout the entire period of American colonial history what it still is for the British imperial system, the final and supreme court for colonial appeals,[646]

is true for purely legal questions only.

If an appeal from a colonial court involved, as many did, the validity of a colonial law or some misconduct on the part of a royal officer, the Board of Trade considered that portion of it which involved a question of administration.[647] In some cases it was difficult to separate these two points, which accounts for such decisions as that of Winthrop *vs.* Lechmere. The distinction is one of considerable importance, for a question which came before the Board was decided upon its merits, while the committee in considering an appeal did not pass upon the merits of the case,

[644] "Upon the Petition of John and Nicholas Hallam, complaining that the governor and company of Connecticut had refused to admit them to appeal to your Majesty in Council here from a sentence past in a Court of Assistants of that colony in the month of May, 1700, relating to the last will and testament of John Liven of the said colony, deceased" we advised with your attorney- and solicitor-general "and humbly offer that your Majesty be pleased to admit the Appeal." — Representation of the Board, May 27, 1701, in C.O. 5, 1289, pp. 99-100.

[645] See the Board of Trade *Journal* [14, pp. 453-454, 15, pp. 1, 135] for April and May, 1702, for the action in this case.

[646] "The American Colonial Charter," in American Historical Association *Report for 1903*, vol. i, 209.

[647] Cf. Hazeltine's "Appeals from Colonial Courts" in American Historical Association *Report for 1894*, 350.

but only upon the regularity of the procedure in the lower courts.

The above point becomes clearer if one considers the kind of appeals which the Board instructed the governors to permit.

> It appears upon a retrospective view . . . that from the first institution of government under commission and instructions from King James the Second, down to the year 1753, the liberty of appealing to the governor and council from the judgments of the Inferior Courts of Common Law was expressly confined, first by a clause in the commission, and in later times by an article in the governors' instructions, to cases of error only.[648]

This article was revised in 1753, and the clause confining appeals to cases of error only was omitted. Although the instructions on this point were the same to all the governors, no question arose as to their meaning until 1764. In that year Governor Colden of New York admitted an appeal from a judgment of an inferior court, which was founded upon the verdict of a jury. This was an extension of the right of appeal which neither the judges of the Supreme Court of New York nor the members of Colden's council were willing to admit; consequently they protested to the Board of Trade.[649]

That body compared the clause in Colden's instructions with the earlier ones on the subject, and rendered the following decision:

> We do conceive that the alteration was solely intended to avoid an ambiguity in the expression that might have admitted a doubt whether liberty of appeal did not extend to

---

[648] Report of the Board of Trade on appeals from the New York courts, September 24, 1765, in New York *Colonial Documents*, vol. vii, 762.

[649] Letter of Colden to the Board, November 7, 1764. *Ibid.*, 676-677.

criminal cases, though it was apparently intended to be confined to civil causes; and we conceive that the confining such appeals to cases of error only, was upon the principles of law a rule so absolute of itself and so well established by the usage and constitution of this kingdom, that it was thought unnecessary to point it out by express words in the instructions.[650]

The instructions to Governor Moore were made so clear that they could not be misunderstood. He was to allow appeals to himself in council from any of the common law courts, in cases of error only, and when the sum in dispute exceeded three hundred pounds. An appeal could then be taken to the king in council, if the sum in dispute exceeded five hundred pounds, and the appeal were taken within fourteen days after sentence had been pronounced. In both cases the appellant was required to give security for the payment of all charges that might be assessed against him, in case the decision of the lower court should be affirmed.

There was but one exception to the above regulations. If the matter in question related

To the taking or demanding any duty payable to us or to any fee of office or annual rent or other such matter or thing where the rights in future may be bound,

an appeal was to be allowed, even though the sum in controversy should be less than five hundred pounds.[651]

The Committee of the Privy Council, when sitting as a court, thus confined itself wholly to the question of legality of procedure in colonial courts. It was

---

[650] New York *Colonial Documents*, vol. vii, 763.

[651] Instructions to Sir Henry Moore, in New York *Colonial Documents*, vol. vii, 764-765.

a court. The Board of Trade was an administrative body with certain extrajudicial functions. Each respected the special field of the other's activity, and kept within its own limits.

Complaints

The question of complaints was very closely connected with that of appeals, as they were begun in the same way by a petition to the king in council. After being read there, they were referred to the Committee of Council and thence to the Board of Trade. As these complaints were founded upon some breach of the constitution of the colonies, the operation of some unjust law, or the arbitrary or illegal procedure of some official, it was no easy task for any body of men to give a fair opinion upon them. In some cases it was even difficult to distinguish between an appeal and a complaint, which accounts for the Board's being called upon for an opinion in some cases of appeals.

Although the slowness of communications made it impossible to avoid frequent and annoying delays before an opinion could be given, the Board tried to furnish justice to all parties concerned. It proceeded as follows. The complaints having been lodged in its office, the party against whom they were made was notified. If he was in America, copies of the complaints were either sent to him or delivered to his agent.[652] If he was present in London, as was Fletcher for instance, he appeared in person before the Board, examined the charges and the proofs against him and

---

[652] See the letter of Popple to Secretary Burchett, in North Carolina *Colonial Records*, vol. iii, 349.

was furnished copies of the same. All charges and complaints had to be supported by written proofs, which were usually authenticated by the seal of the colony from which they came.

Having received copies of the charges against him and the proofs in support of the same, the person against whom they were made was given whatever time he needed to prepare a defense,[653] and was furnished with full means for securing proofs from the colonies in the preparation of his case. Governors were not permitted to refuse access to official records, and a governor might even be ordered to have damaging evidence against himself authenticated with the seal of the colony.[654] The counter case, when it was prepared, was filed with the Board and copies furnished to the plaintiff, and the latter might then ask time for the presentation of further proofs in support of his case.

After the charges, counter charges, and proofs were filed, the case was given a formal hearing at the Board. Each party was present in person or was represented by his agent, unless he chose to let the case go by default, and frequently each party was also assisted by legal counsel. The procedure, in fact, was almost identical with that followed when a colonial law was being considered. In the course of time the Board submitted its findings in the case to the Privy Council with recommendations.

It was possible for either party to oppose the report before the Privy Council or its committee; but the hearing before that body was almost like an appeal

[653] See the complaints against Governor Fletcher and the prosecution of them, in New York *Colonial Documents*, vol. iv, 178, 443, 479.

[654] North Carolina *Colonial Records*, vol. ii, 162.

to a superior court on a writ of error. No additional proofs could be presented, but only argument by attorneys for or against the report of the Board. The committee reported its findings to the king in council, which report might or might not be in accordance with the report of the Board, but usually the latter was sustained. The final decision was announced by an Order in Council, which, after the committee had reported, was a mere legal formality.

The methods of the Board of Trade in dealing with complaints were too slow and complicated and allowed of too many delays. The whole procedure illustrates the Englishman's sense of judicial fairness; no man should be condemned without a hearing, but the very fairness to one party often meant absolute injustice to the opposing party, especially was this true in the prosecution of complaints against a governor. It seldom happened

> That such oppressions can be fully proved without depositions of witnesses, and as there is no law by which witnesses can be compelled to depose in such extrajudicial cases, or any power in the plantations, except the governors themselves to take their depositions and return them authentically to Britain, if they were willing to be examined, for this reason it often happens that the greatest wrongs done there cannot be proved in Britain.
>
> And where the persons oppressed can prevail with witnesses to come over from the plantations, they must bear the expense of it, and likewise pay them for their trouble, hazard, and loss of time, which with their own charges in the prosecution may amount to above a thousand pounds. That is what few of the planters can bear, and several have been ruined by it.[655]

---

[655] From a scheme for the improvement of colonial administration submitted to the Board by Secretary Stanhope in 1715. See: North Carolina *Colonial Records*, vol. ii, 162.

VI. BOUNDARIES, TRADE, DEFENSE, AND INDIAN AFFAIRS

Besides the work discussed in the preceding chapters, the Board of Trade had important duties to perform in dealing with questions which especially concerned the external relations of the colonies. As the representative of the English government the Board had charge of boundary disputes, Indian relations, and defense; it also assisted in the administration of the laws of trade and supervised the schemes for fostering certain industries in the colonies.

Boundary disputes

When the Board of Trade was organized, the territorial limits of the various British colonies were vague and indefinite. Some reached far into the interior of the continent, regardless of the claims of colonies established by other nations; others overlapped their English neighbors on either side. To add to the confusion, no one appeared to know just where any described line ran, and residents of adjoining colonies were not agreed upon the location of rivers and ocean inlets named in the descriptions of their boundaries. Under such circumstances it was a slow, tedious process to settle the various disputes between the individual colonies. It was even a harder task to determine the boundaries between English and foreign colonies. Both of these tasks fell to the lot of the Board of Trade, and it dealt with them as best it could.

The Board was the one information bureau for the commissioners who were appointed to negotiate boundary treaties with foreign nations, as the papers upon which the various English claims were based were principally deposited in its office. When treaties were to be drawn up, it was required to furnish to the envoys full descriptions of the claims of the particular colonies affected, instruct them what demands to make, suggest what compromises might be accepted, and correspond with them as the negotiations proceeded. Naturally the most of this work came at the close of the wars with France and Spain, although some of the negotiations occurred during periods of peace.

In 1700, when France and England were attempting to settle their disputed boundaries in America, especially those of the Hudson's Bay Company, the various proposals of the French were submitted to the Board for consideration,[656] and on another occasion the envoys met with the Board to hear the claims of the company presented by its own representatives.[657] When a treaty with France was under consideration in 1709, the Board was called upon to supply Secretary Boyle with a full history and description of the claims of Hudson's Bay, Nova Scotia, New York and the Five Nations, Island of St. Christopher, New Foundland, Tobago, St. Lucia, and Dominico. Copies of the most important documents

---

[656] Board of Trade *Journal*, 13, p. 19.
[657] June 12, 1700. Board of Trade *Journal*, 13, pp. 70-73.

bearing on these claims were prepared at the same time.[658] Similar action was taken in 1714 when the peace negotiations were on.[659] And in 1719, when the instructions were prepared for Martin Bladen, one of the envoys to Paris, the description of the southern limits of the Hudson's Bay Company's claims were defined substantially as the forty-ninth parallel, the present boundary of the United States.[660]

Boundary disputes between the several colonies were of even more pressing importance than were those with foreign nations. In 1700 none of the colonies had its limits so well defined that it was free from such controversies, and as time went on these questions had to be settled. It was difficult for the interested parties to arrive at a satisfactory agreement without recourse to some outside party; consequently the Board of Trade was the body to which, as a last resort, all these controversies were referred.

Such disputes were nearly always complicated by the question of private interests, as the titles to land along the contested line rested upon grants from one or the other of the claimants to the region. When the line was finally determined, property owners who had deeds from one colony might find themselves occupying land which had legally been granted to other parties. The crown also had interests to be considered in disputes between a royal and a proprietary province; since in one case the quit rents belonged to the crown, and in the other to the proprietary. Conse-

---

[658] C.O. 324, 9, pp. 294-394.

[659] Board of Trade *Journal*, 24, p. 277.

[660] —*Ibid.*, 29, pp. 41, 135. A copy of the chief instruction to Martin Bladen on this point has already been given in *footnote* 109.

quently any change in the boundary line meant an increase or a loss of royal revenue.

As all settlements of a boundary controversy were, of necessity, ratified by laws passed by the colonial legislature, any such settlement could be invalidated by the action of the Board of Trade. If private individuals were injured in their property interests, they had just grounds for a complaint to the king, and such a complaint would involve the boundary dispute and its settlement. If, on the other hand, the interests of the crown were at stake, it had to be made a party to the settlement or it would refuse to recognize its validity. Thus in either case the question would come before the crown for ratification.

The part which the Board of Trade played in a boundary controversy is illustrated by the settlement of the dispute between New York and Connecticut, which dated back to the time of Charles II. In 1664 a commission appointed by the king had heard both parties and agreed upon a settlement, which was concurred in by the representatives of both New York and Connecticut. It was afterwards discovered that the distances stated in the report were not accurate and that the towns of Rye and Bedford, which were intended to be included in New York, were actually located in Connecticut.[661] Finally, in November, 1683, Governor Dongan for New York and Governor Treat, assisted by three commissioners for the colony of Connecticut, went over the division line and settled it from place to place.[662] By this action the towns of Rye and Bedford were again included in New York,

---

[661] New York *Colonial Documents*, vol. iv, 625.

[662] "In prosecution of this last agreement an exact survey was made, and

but in 1697 they revolted from that colony to avoid the payment of taxes, and insisted upon being annexed to Connecticut.[663] The latter colony supported their contentions and the question finally came before the Board, where the whole matter was reviewed.

The agents for Connecticut attacked the validity of the settlement of 1683 on two grounds: in the first place, the commission had exceeded its powers by changing the boundary when it was only authorized to survey a line previously agreed upon; and in the second place, the agreement was to have been submitted to the king for his confirmation, which was never done. The Board decided that the commission of 1683 was fully authorized by both colonies, especially as both had acquiesced in its decision for fourteen years, and recommended that the crown at once confirm the agreement which the commission had made, which was done by an Order in Council, March 28, 1700.[664]

In this action the Board was not deciding the question of boundary, it was only passing upon the validity of a settlement already mutually agreed upon by the two contending parties. It should also be noticed, that the line had formerly been determined by a royal commission created for that purpose, which was the method which the Board always insisted should be followed, unless the two parties could agree upon a line without recourse to a commission. Even

---

the bounds or mears accordingly fixed and distinguished by certain landmarks." — Representation of the Board of Trade, March 13, 1700, in New York *Colonial Documents*, vol. iv, 625.

[663] Letter of Governor Fletcher to the Board, in New York *Colonial Documents*, vol. iv, 276.

[664] Report of the Board of Trade. *Ibid.*, 626-627.

in that case, if either of the colonies was a royal province, the agreement would have to be confirmed by the crown to make it binding.

The regular method of procedure in settling a dispute was to secure the appointment of a royal commission. All the important boundary controversies, such as those between North Carolina and Virginia,[665] North and South Carolina,[666] New York and Massachusetts,[667] and the latter province and New Hampshire [668] and Rhode Island,[669] were settled in this way. These commissioners were appointed by the Board of Trade upon the authority of an Order in Council, were composed of men selected from the neighboring colonies, and were usually paid by the two parties to the controversy. This method of payment required the consent of both parties, but it seldom happened that a colony refused to bear its share of the charges.[670] In some cases the Board secured authority to pay the expenses of such commissions from the quit rents of

---

[665] The commissions for settling this boundary were joint tribunals, appointed partly by the crown and partly by the proprietaries. See: North Carolina *Colonial Records*, vol. i, 703, 716, 735, 750, vol. iii, 12, 17.

[666] — *Ibid.*, vol. iv, 28.

[667] Proposed but not carried into execution. See: Pratt's *Boundaries of New York*, vol. ii, 88-225.

[668] Commission of 1737. See: New York *Colonial Documents*, vol. vi, pp. 823, 953.

[669] The commissioners in this case were Cadwallader Colden, Abraham Vanhorn, Phillip Livingston, Archibald Kennedy, and James De Lancey of New York; John Hamilton, John Wells, John Reading, Cornelius Vanhorn, and William Provost of New Jersey; and William Skeene, William Shirreff, Henry Cope, Erasmus James Phillips, and Otho Haymilton of Nova Scotia. See: Board of Trade to Governor Clinton. *Ibid.*, 167-168.

[670] In regard to a commission for settling the boundary between Massachusetts and Rhode Island, the Board says the "charges of which and the execution thereof the agents for the Massachusetts Bay and Rhode Island have agreed are reasonable equally to be bourne by both provinces." — Letter to Clinton, August 1, 1740. *Ibid.*, 167-168.

the provinces concerned, as was done in settling the southern boundary of Virginia in 1711 and again in 1729.[671]

In 1748 New Jersey attempted to settle the line between herself and New York, which had been in dispute for many years, by the authority of an act of her own legislature. In 1719 Governor Hunter, acting under color of a New York law which had been concurred in by New Jersey, issued a commission to survey the line. Disputes arose, however, and the commission never completed its work, consequently the question remained unsettled until New Jersey passed the act mentioned above. Governor Belcher instructed his agent, Mr. Partridge, to secure its confirmation as soon as possible,[672] and that gentleman laid the act before the Board the same day he received it.[673] The New York agent opposed the confirmation of the act, delays ensued, and it was not reported upon until 1753, when the Board asked that it be disallowed.[674]

The reasons for recommending this action are illustrative of the attitude of the Board, at all times, on such questions.

[671] North Carolina *Colonial Records*, vol. iii, 13, 17, vol. iv, 28.

[672] As the act had a suspending clause, it had to be confirmed before it was valid. See: Pratt, Daniel J. *Boundaries of New York*, vol. ii, 605, 642-645.

[673] Letter of F. J. Paris to James Alexander, November 4, 1748, in New Jersey *Archives*, vol. vii, 168.

[674] Representation of the Board, July 18, 1753, in C.O. 5, 997, pp. 386-406. The representation was referred to the Committee of the Privy Council, which sent copies of it to the solicitors on both sides, who in turn petitioned for it and against it. These petitions were referred to the committee, but the *Register* fails to show that any further action was taken. As the act, according to Pratt, had a suspending clause, no action amounted to a refusal to confirm it. See: Privy Council *Register*, "George II," vol. xiv, 442, 456, 499.

The Province of New Jersey in its distinct and separate capacity can neither make nor establish boundaries; it can as little form regulations for deciding differences between itself and other parties concerned in interest. . . The legal method of proceeding we conceive must be derived from the immediate authority of the crown itself, and be signified by a commission from His Majesty under the great seal.

The agents for New Jersey contended that the case was similar to that of the New York and Connecticut boundary line, and that all that was necessary was a confirmation by the crown. To this the Board replied:

It appears to us that Governor Hunter ought not to have issued his commission for running the line above mentioned without having previously received the royal direction and instruction for that purpose; and that a commission issued without such authority can be considered; with respect to the interests of the crown, in no other light than a mere nullity.[675]

The New Jersey agents urged that the crown had confirmed the New York act of 1717, and thus had become a party to the transaction; but the Board looked upon that act as a necessary revenue measure which had been accepted without any consideration of the involved dispute.[676]

In December, 1754, New York passed a law by

---

[675] Representation of the Board, in C.O. 5, 997, pp. 386-406.

[676] New Jersey *Archives*, vol. viii, part i, 148-149. The act in question is a very long one, entitled, "An Act for Paying and Discharging Several Debts due from this Colony to the Persons therein named and for Raising and Putting into the hands of the Treasurer of this Colony Several quantities of Plate to be apply'd to the Publick and necessary uses of this Colony and to make Bills of Credit to the value of forty-one Thousand five hundred and Seventeen Ounces and a half of Plate for that purpose." Only two clauses concerned the boundary, and these could easily have been overlooked by the Board. See: New York *Colonial Laws*, vol. i, 938-991; Pratt, D. J. *Boundaries of New York*, vol. ii, 605.

which the whole question in dispute was to be left to the determination of the crown,[677] but the following June the Board recommended that this act also should be disallowed for the following reasons:

> It is improper as the method of determination which it proposes is unusual and contrary to the constant practice in cases of like nature: questions of disputed boundary, whereby private property may be affected, having never been determined by the crown in the first instance but always by a commission from His Majesty with liberty to all parties which shall think themselves aggrieved by the judgment of the Commissioners, to appeal to His Majesty from their decision.[678]

In order to bring the controversy to a close, the Board proposed that the governor of New York should be instructed

> To recommend it to the Assembly of that province to make provision for defraying one half the expence of obtaining and executing such commission, as aforesaid, whenever his Majesty shall be graciously pleased to issue it,[679]

which was approved and the instructions issued in accordance therewith. The proprietaries were ready to bear their half of the expense of the proposed commission; but on account of its heavy military expenditures, the New York assembly refused to bear the added charges of running the line. In 1764, however, it gave its consent, the commission was issued in 1767, and the boundary finally settled.[680]

The work of the Board in settling the line between New York and Massachusetts offers a seeming exception to its policy announced in the above case. That

---

[677] New York *Colonial Laws*, vol. iii, 1036-1038.

[678] Report of the Board, June 12, 1755, in New Jersey *Archives*, vol. viii, part ii, 109.

[679] — *Ibid.*, 110.

[680] Pratt, D. J. *Boundaries of New York*, vol. ii, 734, 750-801.

boundary had long been in dispute and the two colonies had failed in all their attempts to arrive at an agreement. Finally, in 1756-1757, the question came before the Board of Trade. After a careful examination of the records in its office, it gave its opinion,

> That a line to be drawn northerly from a point on the south boundary-line of the Massachusetts Bay, twenty miles distant due east from Hudson's River, to another point twenty miles distant due east from the said river, on that line which divides the Province of New Hampshire and the Massachusetts Bay, would be a just and equitable line of division between Your Majesty's provinces of New York and the Massachusetts Bay.[681]

The agents of the two colonies were given copies of this decision and both accepted it. The Board then reported its decision to the king and asked that the proposed boundary should be established by an Order in Council.[682]

This looks on its face like an actual settlement of a boundary by the Board, but that was not the case, as all that the Board did was to determine the meaning of certain grants. After its decision the boundary was still unsettled; and a commission had to be appointed to survey and mark out the line according to the determination of the Board. New York provided for the expense of such a commission in 1764; but as the two colonies could not agree upon the way the line should be surveyed, the question remained unsettled until after the Revolution, and the final de-

---

[681] Report of the Board, May 25, 1757, in New York *Colonial Documents*, vol. vii, 224.

[682] They were given two months to consider the decision of the Board before the latter embodied it in a representation to the king. See: Pratt, D. J. *Boundaries of New York*, vol. ii, 147-150.

termination of it was made in 1787 under the authority of Congress.[683]

Not only a colony but an Indian tribe could have recourse to the Board of Trade for the settlement of disputed lands. The best illustration is the controversy between Connecticut and the Mohegan Indians, to settle which a commission had been appointed in 1704. It heard all parties and made a decision the next year; but Connecticut considered its findings unfair, and appealed to the king in council.[684] After hearing the agents for Connecticut, the Board proposed that a commission should be appointed to review the work of the former commission. An order was issued for its appointment, but for some reason it was never carried into effect. At the instigation of Mason, the order was revived in 1737 and a commission appointed to review the decision of 1705. There was a slight irregularity in its report, and on the petition of Mason, acting in behalf of the Indians, another commission of review was issued in 1740.[685]

It is thus seen that the Board of Trade acted as a high court of arbitration for disputes as to territory or jurisdiction. It did not settle disputes on its own authority, but it provided a way by which such controversies could be determined by special commissions. These were in reality special courts of arbitration, which had power to settle the questions at issue, but from which an appeal would lie to the

[683] Pratt, D. J. *Boundaries of New York*, vol. ii, 149-218.

[684] Connecticut Historical Society *Collections*, vol. v, 20-21; Palfrey, John G. *History of New England*, vol. iv, 364-365.

[685] Connecticut Historical Society *Collections*, vol. v, 21, 263-265, 274-280.

Board.[686] If either party were dissatisfied with the decision of such a commission, it could prosecute a complaint in the usual manner; and if its work should appear irregular, another commission was issued to rehear the case. In all this there was an evident attempt to do justice to all parties concerned. In some cases it was a slow and extremely tedious method of procedure, but it never deprived a colony of its territory without first securing its consent to the transaction, until after the expulsion of the French when the question of western limits was raised. Even then it is doubtful whether the proclamation of 1763 and the policy which followed it can be interpreted as determining boundaries in any final and legal sense. The clause in the Constitution regarding changes in state boundaries is but a recognition of the constant practice of the Board of Trade in settling disputes of this character.

Trade Relations

The Board of Trade was only indirectly concerned with the enforcement of the laws of trade and navigation, as the real work of executing those laws belonged to the officers of the customs and the admiralty.

Considerable information regarding illegal trade found its way to the Board of Trade from one source or another,[687] but the Board itself was practically powerless in such matters. It could pass the infor-

---

[686] In form it was an appeal to the king, but as all such complaints and appeals were heard by the Board of Trade, it was in reality an appeal to that body.

[687] Note the action of the Board on April 17, 1707, in suspending the prosecution of Vetch and others for trading with the enemy, in Board of

mation on to the colonial governors and instruct them to enforce the law, and could also transmit the intelligence to the customs and the admiralty; but it could not directly prevent violation of the trade laws by means of revenue officers and patrol boats. In 1710 the Board received testimony of a considerable illegal trade between Carolina, Curaçoa, and St. Thomas. It wrote a very sharp letter to the proprietors – it was the fashion just then to threaten them on every plausible occasion – insisting that steps be taken to break up the practice.[688]   At the same time it wrote a much more sensible letter to the commissioners of customs, transmitting the evidence it had received, and advised that two revenue cutters on that station would effectually check the smuggling operations.[689]

Trade *Journal*, 19, p. 125. The next year Mr. Lloyd, a New England merchant, gave information of a contraband trade from Carolina to Portugal by way of Rhode Island. In this case ships loaded with rice in Carolina, gave bonds to discharge the cargo in an English port, cleared for Rhode Island, unloaded and discharged their bonds, then reloaded and sailed for Portugal. See: Board of Trade *Journal*, 20, 233-234.

[688] Copies of the testimony were sent to the proprietors, not only of the trade to Curaçoa, but also of an illegal trade to Martinique by means of flags of truce. (Flags of truce were ships carrying prisoners to exchange with the enemy. The masters of such vessels also carried considerable cargoes for trading purposes on such trips, and in some cases the presence of the prisoners was only a cloak to cover prohibited voyages and give the appearance of legality.) The proprietors were ordered to investigate the facts and to prosecute offenders, if the evidence warranted it, and to give orders not to permit any trading by flags of truce which might touch at Carolina ports. See: C.O. 5, 1292, pp. 204-205.

[689] "Their Lordships being of opinion that the said illegal trade may in a great measure be prevented by two brigantines of ten or twelve guns each, to cruise off of these islands, upon proper stations, with power to examine and seize such vessels as shall be found trading contrary to law; they have commanded me to desire you will lay the matter before the honorable the commissioners of His Majesty's customs, and to let me know whether they have any objection to the sending of such brigantines, or whether they have any other remedy to propose that may more effectually prevent such

Proof of illegal trade usually reached the Board some time after the violations had occurred. Thus in 1750 it heard a very considerable amount of testimony which proved that there had been systematic violations of the Molasses Act and other trade laws for years,[690] and that colonial ships had traded with both French and Spanish colonies during the wars.[691] The data from the customs as to the amount of duties which the Molasses Act had yielded told the same story.[692]

During the wars trade with the enemy was especially profitable, hence the temptation to violate the trade and navigation laws was vastly increased. These violations were especially flagrant during the French and Indian War, yet the Board says the first information it had received of illegal trade by way of

Illegal Trade." — Popple to Burchett, February 3, 1710, in Board of Trade *Commercial Series II*, 645, p. 50.

[690] Even as early as 1722 information reached the Board of fraud in connection with the trade with the sugar islands. See the letter of Captain Brand, describing the methods of changing rum and molasses from the French casks to those made by coopers carried by the vessels, in C.O. 323, 8, L. 35. The testimony of Admiral Knowles, Captain Tyrrell, and Mr. Tomlison shows that the frauds had extended over a long term of years. Much of Admiral Knowles' testimony dealt with conditions as far back as 1737. See: Board of Trade *Journal*, 58, November and December, 1750.

[691] Admiral Knowles testified that there were forty-two vessels from the northern colonies at Hispaniola with fictitious flags of truce at one time during the war of 1744-1748. He testified that he had sent full accounts of the violations to Newcastle, but received no orders in the matter; then, on his own responsibility, he ordered the ships in his squadron to capture all vessels which appeared to be violating the trade laws. See: Board of Trade *Journal*, 58, December 6, 1750.

[692] C.O. 5, 38, Appendix no. 4. A copy of this has already been given in *footnote* 253. C.O. 5, 872, no. 191, shows largely increasing sugar importations from New England and Carolina. No doubt much of this was from the French sugar islands, although it was entered as from the English islands.

Monte Christi had been in letters from the governor of Jamaica in 1759.[693] As for the gross abuse of cartel ships, or flags of truce, the Board asserted in 1760 that it had received no information of their use "during the present war," although it did not doubt but they had been so employed. As soon, however, as the existence of illegal trade was reported, the Board proposed a general proclamation and particular instructions to the governors of all the provinces as the proper means of breaking it up.[694]

The Board busied itself more with questions affecting the growth of the commercial interests of the empire than it did with the enforcement of customs regulations. It spent much more time and energy looking after passes for vessels than it did in preventing smuggling.[695] During the War of the Spanish Succession commercial relations with the colonies were seriously interfered with, and it was unsafe for merchant vessels to venture on a voyage without a convoy. The Board tried to arrange the convoys so

[693] In 1760 the treasury sent the Board proof of illegal trade, both by means of flags of truce, and by way of Monte Christi, and asked it to supply any information it had received of similar violations. In answer to this the Board wrote: "We have not, during the present war, received information of any trade carried on with the enemy by means of cartel ships. . . We think the only remedy is not to allow any exchange of prisoners in America by means of cartel ships. . . With respect to the trade to Monte Christi, we first heard of it through the lieutenant-governor of Jamaica, in a letter dated March 28, 1759." — Letter to the secretary to the commissioners of the treasury, March 7, 1760, in C.O. 324, 16, pp. 175-181.

[694] Representations on the testimony of illegal trade by way of Monte Christi, submitted by the governor of Jamaica, August 31, 1759. See: Board of Trade *Jamaica*, 67, pp. 448-457; also: Beer, Geo. L. *British Colonial Policy*, chaps. vi and vii.

[695] The determination of when and to whom passes should be issued was left almost wholly to the Board. See: Board of Trade *Journal*, 25, pp. 343-347; C.O. 324, 10, p. 91.

as to secure the best commercial relations, both for Virginia and Maryland and for the English merchants. The ministers were planning to have the convoy sail for Virginia in June, but that was earlier than many of the ships could be ready for a voyage of that kind. They were also planning for its early return from Virginia, which was objected to by the merchants; for if the ships were not ready to return with the convoy, they would be compelled to remain until the next year, which would involve heavy losses to ships and crews. The time for the convoy to return was also placed at a bad season, for the new crop of tobacco would not be ready to ship; and as there would be no other opportunity for a year, the planters would practically lose one crop, and the nation the revenue on it.

The Board proposed either two convoys or one; if only one could be sent, it should sail for Virginia in September, arrive there about December, and return the next May. In that way each crop of tobacco could be brought away at the proper season, and British goods would arrive in the colonies at the time they were most needed.[696]

The chief work of the Board in promoting the interests of British commerce was to furnish information concerning the trade situation and to recommend ways of improving it. Each of the governors was expected to furnish annual reports of the population, the manufactures, the trade, and the finances of his province.[697] From these returns the Board compiled

---

[696] Representation of the Board, April 26, 1706. C.O. 5, 1362, pp. 44-51. See also the letter to Secretary Hedges, February 1, of the same year.

[697] See the circular letters sent to the governors, in New York *Colonial*

reports on the conditions of the provinces, somewhat similar to those which are published in the "blue books" at the present time. The well known report of 1721 is a good illustration of what these reports contained.[698] In addition to such reports, the Board had to be ready to furnish Parliament with information on a variety of subjects when called upon. The information it secured was much like that supplied by our own consular service, and the merchants of England looked upon the Board in much the same light that our manufacturers do the United States consular officers. Any measures or conditions which in any way affected their trade with the colonies were promptly reported, or rather complained of, to the Board.[699]

The Board of Trade was thoroughly imbued with the mercantilist doctrines of the time, but its constant correspondence with those who were familiar with conditions in the colonies made it favor a generally liberal policy. Its conception was that the colonies should be both a source of supply for raw materials and such products as could be made most advantageously there, and that they should also furnish a growing market for England's manufactured goods. In this way colonies and mother country could be mutually helpful to each other.

The value of the colonies as a market was very

Documents; New Jersey *Archives*; Sharpe's *Correspondence*; Pennsylvania *Archives*; North Carolina *Colonial Records*.

[698] New York *Colonial Documents*, vol. v, 591-630.

[699] See extracts from Board of Trade *Journal* in North Carolina *Colonial Records*, and in Pennsylvania *Statutes at Large*, Appendices. See also the extensive reports of various officers respecting trade conditions in different places in Board of Trade *Commercial Series I.*

thoroughly impressed upon the Board by the English merchants and manufacturers, as well as by the royal governors. The two principal items of British export in the first three decades of the Board's activity were woolen and linen goods. These made up considerably more than one half of all the exports to the colonies, and in 1721 wool alone constituted one half of the annual exports of goods of British manufacture,[700] consequently the wool trade was very dear to the financial heart of every Britisher. During the earlier years the Board nursed this market as carefully as it could, and constantly demanded information regard-

[700] September 8, 1721, the Board [C.O. 324, 10, p. 385] reported the exports to the colonies as amounting to the following annually:

In British Manufactures & Products

Woolen Manufactures	. . .	£147,438	11s.	7d.
Silk wrought and thrown	. .	18,468	7	1
Linens and Sail Cloth	. . .	11,464	9	0
Cordage	. . . . .	11,284	5	9
Gunpowder	. . . .	2,392	15	5
Leather wrought and Saddles	. .	15,161	12	6
Brass and Copper wrought	. .	2,265	6	7
Iron wrought and Nails	. .	35,631	13	6
Lead and Shot	. . . .	2,850	9	3
Pewter	. . . . .	3,687	6	11
In many other Goods	. . .	43,941	5	6
		£294,586	3s.	1d.

In Foreign Goods

Linens	. . . . .	£ 86,413		
Calicoes	. . . .	10,102	4s.	
Prohibited East Indian Goods	. .	10,523	12	9d.
Wrought Silks	. . .	1,189	11	1
Iron and Hemp	. . .	6,152	5	11
Other Foreign Goods	. . .	21,760	19	9
		£136,141	13s.	6d.
		294,586	3	1
		£430,727	16s.	7d.

ing conditions which might in any way jeopardize this much prized export trade. The act of 1699, which was intended to prevent the development of a colonial wool manufacture, should be looked upon as an effort to preserve the American wool market.[701]

The colonists were not averse to using English woolen goods when they could get them. As Governor Dudley wrote to the Board, they were proud enough to wear clothing made of the very best goods England could produce, and were determined to do so if saving, chopping, and ship-building could pay for it.[702] But clothing they had to have, and they could only buy when goods were to be had at reasonable prices and in return for the products they had to sell. When these failed, as they did during Queen Anne's War, the colonists generally were forced to resort to such goods as they could make. A considerable clandestine trade within the colonies soon developed, and Yankee inventiveness was directed toward devising means of evading the act of 1699. Perhaps the most ingenious method of keeping within the law regarding transportation was the Rhode Island scheme of driving the sheep to the place where the wool was wanted, shearing them there, and then driving them back to the owner's pasture.[703]

The reports which reached the Board indicated there was every reason to fear that the colonial mar-

[701] This act made it illegal to load any wool or wool products upon any ship, wagon, horse, or other means of transportation for the purpose of carrying it to any other point. Instructions to the governors strictly enjoined them to enforce this law. See: trade instructions to Governor Nicholson of Virginia, October 16, 1702, in C.O. 5, 1360, p. 308.

[702] Dudley to the Board, March 1, 1709, in C.O. 5, 913, pp. 95-96.

[703] Letter of Larkin to the Board, December 5, 1701, C.O. 5, 726, p. 117.

ket for wool was in permanent danger. From Massachusetts came news that sheep raising had spread from the islands to the mainland, and that soon there would be a thousand sheep where there were not a hundred before; [704] that wool cards and combs were being imported in great quantities; [705] that the wool trade was greatly abated due to the excessive cost of English goods; [706] and that unless a lumber and shipbuilding trade could be developed, the use of English goods would decrease each year.[707] From Maryland came letters stating that "pinching want" had

This letter was written from Maryland and is included in the correspondence from that province. He also adds that the people of Connecticut and Rhode Island made as good "Druggets" for four shillings a yard as he ever saw in England in his life.

[704] Letter of Jahleel Brenton to the Board, March 30, 1703, C.O. 5, 863, N. 33. He also adds that most of the lawyers interpreted the act of 1699 as not intended to check transportation of wool from one part of the colony to another. The residents of the islands had formerly bought their clothing from England, but since the scarcity they had commenced to work their wool up into clothing for the market.

[705] Letter of Bridger to the Board, March 5, 1706, C.O. 5, 912, p. 127. He states that since the previous December 3, one hundred fifty-five dozen wool cards had been imported into New England besides great quantities of wool combs, and the importation of wool had greatly decreased. The Board at once wrote to the attorney-general to inquire if there was any law to prevent the trade in cards and combs, and was informed that the trade was legal. See: Board of Trade *Journal*, 18, pp. 262, 356; C.O. 5, 912, p. 178.

[706] "I must add that the woolen trade from England also is to a great measure abated, the people here clothing themselves with their own Wool. . . Nothing is here sold at less than one hundred and fifty pounds per cent advance, most goods more, so that country men cannot purchase them." — Governor Dudley to the Board, March 1, 1709, C.O. 5, 913, pp. 95-96.

[707] "The woolen manufacture for the supply of the inhabitants here will prevail every year, unless the people are put to building ships for the royal navy, or that we get into a further masting and providing of spars and boards, such as are not either for length or breadth to be had in the Baltick." — *Ibid.*

forced the inhabitants to resort to spinning and weaving their own clothes from such materials as they could get, but that supplies from England would cause most of them to abandon the new industry.[708] The governor of Virginia wrote that similar conditions existed in that colony, and that in one of the best counties for the production of tobacco more than forty thousand yards of cloth had been made in one year.[709] Purely repressive legislation would hardly meet the situation. Convoys for the fleet which supplied Virginia and Maryland were secured, and with the fresh supply of English goods the domestic cloth manufacture declined in those colonies.[710] New England, however, could only be diverted from its wool manufacture by directing the energies of the inhabi-

---

[708] "Pinching want has put some few on making of a little linnen and woollen, but not sufficient to supply their own family's and that too would be quickly laid aside were they supplyed from Great Britain at any reasonable price, but few goods of late years have been sold under three hundred per cent." — Governor Seymour to the Board, 1708, in C.O. 5, 727, p. 87.

In April, 1713, the president and council of Maryland complained of the hard times the province had been having: "So that most of us labour under great difficulty's, and had not many people applyed themselves to spinning the little wool their small flocks of sheep afford, and likewise some small quantity of flax, they would have suffered very much for want of necessary clothing, which too many, not so careful and industrious have too fully experienced." — C.O. 5, 727, pp. 334-335.

[709] Letter of Governor Spotswood to the Board, March 20, 1711. He adds that no doubt the quantity of cloth was greater in the poor counties, that it was necessity and not inclination which caused them to resort to the manufacture, but that increased skill would make it necessary to divert them into other lines of effort. See: C.O. 5, 1363, pp. 318-319.

[710] "This province is highly obliged to your Lordship's just consideration of their great necessity in that you have been pleased to recommend to the merchants to supply it with English manufactures, which they have by this fleet in some measure complied with, so that the little manufacturing of linnen and woollen will fall of themselves." — Letter of Governor Seymour to the Board, 1708, C.O. 5, 727, p. 92.

See also the admission of the Virginia merchants that conditions in Vir-

tants into channels as remunerative to them and more valuable to the empire.

Conditions favored the production of naval stores as the most convenient way of accomplishing this result. In spite of the covert, and at times open, hostility of the naval officials,[711] the Board secured bounties for American-made tar, pitch, resin, and turpentine more than sufficient to counterbalance the excess in freight rates from the colonies over those from Sweden.[712] In addition, the Board had Mr. Bridger sent over as surveyor of the woods, and di-

ginia were largely the result of the failure of the regular convoy in 1707, in Board of Trade *Journal*, 20, pp. 329-330.

It is not improbable that there was more or less unfairness and fraud in connection with the convoys. In explaining the causes for excessive freight rates from America, the Board stated that the officer in charge of the convoy would announce the precise day upon which he intended to sail; but that certain masters of vessels would induce him to postpone his departure without public notice, then they would demand excessive freight rates, which the planters would refuse to pay until about the time for the fleet to leave, when they would pay the rates demanded, rather than miss a shipment to England. After which the convoy would delay for the masters to complete their cargoes. See: Representation on Trade, February 14, 1710, in Board of Trade *Commercial Series II*, 645, p. 67.

[711] During the first few years of the bounty there were many complaints from merchants of hostile action on the part of the navy, such as severe grading and prejudice in favor of Swedish tar. In March, 1708, Bridger complained that the navy did not pay the premiums according to the act of Parliament. The same year merchants complained that the premiums had been paid in noninterest-bearing bills, by which they would lose two thirds of the premiums. January 5, 1711, the Board wrote a letter to the admiralty asking the opinion of the officials in that office as to the proper premiums for spars, boards, and other naval stores. Burchett replied for the admiralty, January 16, that no advice could be given as to the amount of the premiums which should be paid, that the navy officials had no objections to such importations, but thought the bounties should be paid by some other department. See: Letter to the Board, C.O. 5, 912, p. 431; Board of Trade *Journal*, 20, p. 230; C.O. 5, 913, pp. 308-309, 317.

[712] The premiums paid under the act of 1706, which was continued for twenty years, were four pounds per ton on tar and pitch, three on resin, six

rected him to instruct the colonists in the art of making tar. He evidently did as well as he could for several years, going from point to point and distributing printed directions to those who might engage in the new industry. He had much prejudice to contend with, the New Englanders refusing to believe his argument that tar making was so profitable that a person could earn enough at it to buy two coats in the same time he spent in the actual manufacture of one, until he demonstrated the fact to their entire satisfaction.[713]

The new industry was soon established, and under the influence of the bounties paid in England, a plentiful supply of the very best tar, pitch, and turpentine was secured for the navy.[714] At the same time shipping was stimulated by the additional carrying trade,

on hemp, and one on masts. The freight rates from Sweden in 1709 were £3 per last of twelve barrels, while the rate from America was £7 10s. per ton of eight barrels. This rate, however, was abnormally high because of the war. See: C.O. 324, 11, p. 73; Representation on trade, in Board of Trade *Commercial Series II*, 645, p. 67.

[713] "The country people or planters are entered so far into making their own woolens, that not one in forty but wears his own carding, spinning, etc. — they are so fond of their own ways and thoughts that nothing can draw them off but that which must tend to their present interest and advantage." The claims of profits in the tar and pitch making "they would not believe — unless they see it tried before their faces." — Bridger to the Board, March 13, 1708, in C.O. 5, 912, pp. 431-432.

[714] February 25, 1717, the Board heard a considerable amount of testimony in regard to the tar produced in America. The agents for Carolina asserted that New England and the West Indies were supplied from that province, and that there was plenty of the best quality to supply Great Britain. A Mr. Allen claimed that there were not two hundred barrels of Swedish tar to be had in London. A Mr. Hughs said it was fully as good as Swedish, and that Finland, where the tar had formerly been produced, was becoming depopulated. See: Board of Trade *Journal*, 26, p. 203. March 13, 1707, Bridger stated that the previous year New England had shipped 2,190 barrels of tar, 2,275 of pitch, 68 of resin, and 4,924 of

and a portion of New England's dangerous energies diverted to ship-building, shipping, and tar making. Thus the precious wool trade was protected.

The development of naval stores, however, was not a mania on the part of the Board. All of America was not to be set to making tar, but only such portions of the inhabitants as could not be advantageously employed in other industries which were profitable to England. The production of naval stores was not to be encouraged in Virginia and Maryland, but was to be discouraged there, for it was not so profitable to England as was the tobacco trade.[715] Nothing was to be done which should in any way interfere with or retard the growth of the tobacco industry. The refusal of the Board to permit colonial laws to limit the importation of negroes, or to encourage the development of cities and towns, and its hostility to excessive grants of land, all turn upon the effect such measures might have in diverting people from tobacco culture. That industry was profitable to England; and if the colonists were not engaged in that, they would of necessity engage in something else, possibly manufacturing, which would reduce England's colonial market by the amount of goods they supplied.

The thoroughness with which the Board was im-

turpentine. Even after the bounties were removed, the importations in 1733 amounted to 6,123 lasts of tar and pitch. See: C.O. 5, 912, p. 431; C.O. 323, 10, N. 42.

[715] "Tho' the encouragement of the production of naval stores in the plantations being of the highest importance to England, yet it is not fitting to be encouraged in those places which are proper for the production of tobacco, and therefore you will take care therein; but that the production of naval stores may be in such parts of your government, as are only proper for them." — Letter from the Board to Governor Seymour of Maryland, March 26, 1707, in C.O. 5, 727, p. 129.

pressed with the idea that the colonial market could only be protected by inducing the colonists to engage in noncompetitive industries is seen in its various reports on trade conditions. In 1714 it advised:

> That as the provinces on the continent of America are of late years very much increased in their numbers of people, particularly the northerly ones, who have applyed themselves to the manufacturing of coarse woolen goods, and thereby prejudiced our woolen trade here, and therefore we humbly propose that these people particularly in New England and New York should be diverted from that undertaking by being encouraged in the production of naval stores, since in return of such stores, they would take off considerable quantities of woolen manufactures from hence, which would be a double advantage in this Kingdom.[716]

In 1717 it informed the king that the people at the north had been "under the necessity of applying themselves" to woolen, linen, and other manufactures, and the only way to prevent it was to get them to turn their attention to some other profitable industry.[717] And again in 1721, it said:

> It is therefore to be presumed that necessity and not choice has put them to erecting manufactures. Hence the proper remedy would be proper encouragement of importation of naval stores and minerals of all kinds. The trade of most importance to them and the one for which they are best fitted is shipbuilding.[718]

[716] Representation of the Board, November, 1714, in Board of Trade *Trade Papers*, 23, No. 79.

[717] Representation on Naval Stores, March 28, 1717, in Board of Trade *Trade Papers*, 23, no. 85. The Board goes on to argue that such an industry would not only enable England to sell its wool, but also enable it to purchase naval stores without paying out bullion. It would also increase the shipping of the colonies and diminish that of the "northern countries," especially as it was feared that the Tsar was about to limit such exports to Muscovite bottoms.

[718] Representation on the state of His Majesty's plantations in America,

The Board never favored a policy which might lead to the depopulation of any colony; [719] and as the presence or the growth of population rests primarily upon economic conditions, it sought to bring about such changes in the laws of trade as would favor each particular section, and in such a way as to extend the British market as much as possible, and reduce it as little as possible. Thus it favored allowing South Carolina rice to be shipped directly to Portugal, where it competed to some extent with English wheat, but more with Italian products, because it would build up a market for English manufactured goods in two ways. South Carolina would be a better market, because the planters would have more to buy with. [720] Portugal also would be a better market for the English, because it could pay for its rice in its own products, and the improved communications would be a direct aid to commercial relations.

The ship-building industry in New England was directly favored by the Board of Trade. It also sought to engage the farmers there in the production

September 8, 1721, in C.O. 324, 10, pp. 320-321. A representation on naval stores accompanied this report which advocated direct encouragement to the production of raw iron and mineral ores of all kinds. It also proposed that whenever bounties were paid on any commodity it should be included among the enumerated products.

[719] This has already been treated in connection with the disallowance of colonial laws. The Board would not even favor a British law to prevent wool manufactures, as it might make it very difficult for the poor people to clothe themselves; although it was willing to prohibit the exposing for sale of domestic-made woolens. See: Representation of the Board, December 5, 1728, in C.O. 324, 11, pp. 141-142.

[720] Representation of 1721, in C.O. 324, 10, pp. 371-373. The Board pointed out that the chief reason Carolina rice was sold so little in Portugal was because of the double freights, and that with direct shipments the Italians would be driven from the market.

of hemp,[721] but with rather ill success. It did what it could to encourage the trade in lumber, as far as it did not endanger the forests which were most useful to the royal navy. It also favored the encouragement of the colonial production of iron, but in doing so it encountered pressure from English iron manufacturers, and proposed that the production of raw iron only, or at most pig and bar iron, should be permitted in the colonies. As much partially manufactured iron from foreign countries found its way into the plantations on account of the drawbacks permitted on iron reëxported from England, the Board recommended that Parliament take off the drawback, in the interests of the British manufacturer.[722] Its recommendation that colonial crude iron should be allowed to enter England free of duty was rejected in 1721 and again in 1738,[723] but became a law twelve years later.

[721] See the proposal of the Board that the government should send five hundred bushels of hemp seed to New Hampshire, Representation of September 4, 1735, in C.O. 5, 917, pp. 135-136.

[722] These importations were chiefly from Holland. In 1705 a drawback had been taken off of manufactured iron and steel, but continued on the unwrought, which proved to be a direct encouragement to iron manufacture in America. See: Representation of the Board, January 26, 1711, in Board of Trade *Commercial Series II*, 645, p. 436. The reëxportations of iron and steel increased from eighty-nine tons in 1704-1705 to five hundred and thirty-four tons in 1708-1709. See: Report of commissioner of customs, in C.O. 323, 7, K. 7.

Sir Ambrose Crowley testified before the Board that exportations of manufactured iron had decreased greatly during the same years, and that if the drawback were removed the iron merchants could sell so cheaply that they could prevent the development of a colonial manufacture. See: Board of Trade *Journal*, 22, pp. 173-174.

[723] Sir Joshua Gee, in 1718, advocated bounties on colonial bar and pig iron. The Board, in its recommendations of 1721, proposed the removal of all duties on pig iron. It had favored both bar and pig iron, and had a bill brought into Parliament taking the duty off of both, but the bar iron was opposed and the bill dropped. See: C.O. 324, 10, pp. 212, 433-434.

At this time, however, the iron interests in England secured concessions in the form of prohibitions of steel manufacture, slitting mills, plating mills, and forges with tilt hammers.[724]

A portion of the iron bill was forced upon the Board of Trade by the merchants, through their influence in the House of Commons.[725]   Other industries, when they felt the effect of a diminishing trade to the colonies and discovered that it was in part due to the colonists supplying their own needs, appealed to the House of Commons for such legislation as would enable them to retain their markets.   Legislation in such cases was due to the direct pressure from those engaged in an industry, and not to any policy agreed upon by the Board of Trade and presented as a desirable measure.   The hat bill [726] and the attempt to prevent wool manufactures in the colonies are good illustrations.

The Board did not advocate a selfishly narrow trade policy, but believed that the colonies and the home country should form one commercial unit, as nearly independent of all others as possible.   It sought to retain the colonial market for England's more important products, and to open markets and encourage profitable industries within the colonies so

[724] The law provided penalties for the erection of such prohibited furnaces or mills; declared those already established common nuisances; and required the governors to enforce the law for their destruction and the prosecution of their owners, under penalty of a fine of £500 for neglecting to do so. See: 23 George II, cap. 20; Pickering. *Statutes at Large*, vol. xx, 30.

[725] House of Commons *Journal*, vol. xxii, 772, 776, 777, 780, 788, 791, 793, 810, 828, 850.

[726] House of Commons *Journal*, vol. xix, 245, 249-250, 252, vol. xxi, 802, 824.

as to make them rich and able to buy liberally of English goods. To this end it advocated a policy of bounties for infant industries, and a policy of preferential tariffs in favor of the colonies. This is seen in the reports on trade conditions, especially that of 1721, in recommending a direct export trade for Carolina rice, and free trade for lumber, iron, and minerals.[727] It is also seen in its policy of bounties on naval stores, and its direct encouragement to the potash,[728] sugar, indigo, and silk industries.[729] The manufacturers looked upon the colonies primarily as markets for their goods, and as they were a class constantly growing in influence, they could make their demands felt. The old mercantilist theory was that colonies were primarily sources of supply for goods which could not be produced at home. The Board

---

[727] It is evident that the Board had much more in mind in this recommendation than merely using the colonies as a source of supply. The one thing which hampered the British trade most was to find an adequate market for colonial products. As the Board said in regard to the great mineral resources of New York and Pennsylvania, it had good reason to believe, "that, if proper encouragement was given in Great Britain, to take off that, and their timber, the people would be diverted from the thoughts of setting up any manufactures of their own, and consequently the consumption of Great Britain considerably advanced." – New York *Colonial Documents*, vol. v, 604. Beer in his discussion of the commercial policy of England possibly makes too much of what he calls the new conception in British colonial policy of colonies for markets instead of sources of supply. See: *British Colonial Policy*, 139 ff.

[728] See the letter of Popple to Lowndes of the treasury, asking financial assistance for John Keble and his potash enterprise in West Jersey, in New Jersey *Archives*, vol. iii, 347-349; also the letter of Partridge to Governor Greene of Rhode Island, July 30, 1754 [Rhode Island *Colonial Records*, vol. ii, 142], in regard to Thomas Stephens' plans for a potash manufacture in America, and the encouragement the Board had given him. He adds that the British import duty on potash had lately been removed.

[729] The import duty on silk was removed in 1750. 23 George II, cap. 29, Pickering. *Statutes at Large*, vol. xx, 97.

tried to reconcile these two doctrines and make the colonies preëminently a market as well as a source of supply.

The attempt of the Board to preserve the forests in America, particularly those which could be of direct use to the royal navy, although it belongs rather in the field of defense than in that of trade policy, was one of its pet measures for many years. At first it sought to secure its ends by the enactment by the colonial assemblies of laws for the protection of mast trees, but apparently New Hampshire was the only one which complied. The Board then appealed to Parliament, which passed the White Pine Bill.[730] Then followed a long and apparently futile attempt to enforce the various provisions of the act, during which the Board secured the appointment of a surveyor of the woods, supported him as best it could, but finally encountered serious difficulties in regard to his salary, gradually lost its enthusiasm for the work, and allowed the subject to be forgotten after the ascendency of Newcastle.[731]

Aside from the danger of competitive industries, the most pressing commercial question before the Board of Trade was that of the colonial bills of credit, which had been issued in several of the colonies after 1690, the practice having been started by Massachu-

[730] This failed the first time it was introduced, but became a law in 1711. See: C.O. 5, 913, pp. 238, 321.

[731] Mr. Bridger was the first surveyor of the woods. He was followed by Armstrong, after which the duty was made a part of that of the lieutenant-governor of New Hampshire. Both Bridger and Armstrong reported much difficulty in enforcing the law, as frauds of every description were practiced by those engaged in the lumber industry. Each was accused of corruption in the exercise of his office, in the form of selling licenses to cut timber, and

setts in that year.[732] Other colonies adopted the plan
either of issuing bills of credit or of lowering the
value of the coin and in a few years the merchants
began to complain. The Board consulted the law
officers and decided that the evil could be remedied
by a royal proclamation fixing the value of foreign
coins in America, which was issued in 1704,[733] but
proved entirely inadequate for the purpose. In New
York it was suspended for a time, and in almost no
colony was it carefully observed; consequently an act
of Parliament was passed in 1708, which aimed to do
what the proclamation had failed to accomplish.[734]

The Board of Trade sought to enforce this act by
instructions to the governors and by disallowing such
colonial laws as contravened it, but the evil continued
to grow. Governor Hunter of New York consented
to the striking of bills of credit as a means of getting
a revenue settled for five years.[735] The assembly
passed another paper money act in 1717,[736] which
went into effect before it was considered by the Board
of Trade. The latter disapproved of the act, but as

accepting fees to permit the loading of timber marked with the great arrow.
Lieutenant-governor Dunbar encountered almost open rebellion when he
tried to break up illegal timber cutting. The letters to and from New England in the Board of Trade papers are filled with information connected
with the preservation of the forests. See: C.O. 5, vols. 861-882, 908-918.

[732] Palfrey, John G. *History of New England*, vol. iv, 20.

[733] New York *Colonial Documents*, vol. iv, 1131.

[734] This bill was drawn up by the Board of Trade at the request of a
committee of the House of Lords. It was sent to the attorney-general for
his opinion and then passed by Parliament. See: Board of Trade *Journal*,
37, pp. 156-157; C.O. 324, 908, p. 155; 6 Anne cap. 30, Pickering. *Statutes
at Large*, vol. xi, 412.

[735] New York *Colonial Laws*, vol. i, 847.

[736] — *Ibid.*, 938. This is the law which figured in the boundary controversy with New Jersey.

the bills had come into the hands of third parties, a
disallowance would have produced a great deal of
confusion; consequently, in 1720, the Board recommended that it be confirmed, but that no similar laws
should be passed in the future. Circular letters were
accordingly prepared and sent to all the governors, by
which they were strictly enjoined not to consent to any
act creating additional bills of credit, except it have
a suspending clause, or be a law establishing a permanent revenue.[737] Thus the Board evidently considered
the advantages of a fixed civil list more important
than the evils of a paper currency.

The exception clauses furnished a loophole sufficiently large to enable the assemblies to evade the
limitation. New Jersey, in 1723, passed an act which
established the revenue for ten years, but did it only
as a device for creating a larger amount of bills of
credit.[738] Other colonies adopted the same expedient,
although few of them found it necessary to establish
the revenue for a longer period than had been customary before that time. The Board, however, objected
to the new acts; and in 1726 Secretary Popple wrote
to the governor of Pennsylvania the following sentiments in regard to the paper money acts of that province:

> Their Lordships have found by experience, that bills of credit
> have been of very ill consequence in other places where they
> have been issued, particularly in Carolina, where not only the
> province but the merchants have sustain'd great losses there-
> by.

---

[737] Order in Council, May 19, 1720, in New York *Colonial Documents*,
vol. v, p. 539.

[738] Letter of Burnet to the Board, December 16, 1723, in New York
Colonial Documents, vol. v, 700.

Were it not for the disorders and inconveniences of such action, the acts would be repealed.

And if any further acts are pass'd for creating more bills of credit than those already issued, their Lordships will certainly think themselves oblig'd to lay them before His Majesty for his disallowance.[739]

The Board insisted more and more that provision should be made for sinking the bills of credit within a reasonable time. An act of New Jersey which made current forty thousand pounds in bills of credit had a provision for loaning these bills on good security at five per cent interest, which was to be set aside as a fund for sinking them; but as the interest continued to accumulate in the treasury, the assembly decided that it would be better to use it for current expenses. Governor Burnet gave his consent to the appropriation act, although forbidden to do so by his instructions.[740] His successor, Montgomerie, had special directions to secure the repeal of this act, but the assembly refused to concur with the wishes of the Board; whereupon the latter had the act disallowed.[741]

Massachusetts always refused to add a suspending clause to an act; and in spite of the governor's instructions on that point, the assembly (1733-1734) passed laws creating bills of credit in excess of the sum allowed for annual expenses, which laws were considered by the Board in 1735 and allowed to expire

[739] Pennsylvania *Archives*, first series, vol. i, 186-187.

[740] Letter of Burnet to the Board, December 20, 1726, in New York *Colonial Documents*, vol. v, 810.

[741] Letter of the Board to Montgomerie, July 21, 1731, in New Jersey *Archives*, vol. v, 302.

without being disallowed.[742] The Board, however, instructed the governor as follows:

> We do hereby strictly enjoin and require you upon pain of our highest displeasure and of being immediately recalled from that our government not to give your assent for the future to any act whatever for issuing new bills of credit except only thirty thousand pounds for annual support of the Government or to any act for re-issuing old bills or that shall continue any bills current beyond the time limited by the acts for emitting them, without inserting in every such case a clause for suspending the execution of every such act until our pleasure shall be declared thereupon.[743]

The war from 1744 to 1748 still further increased the amount of the outstanding issues. In the meantime, the Board had concentrated its attention on another phase of the paper money question. Most of the colonies had endowed their paper currency with legal tender qualities, to which the Board was especially opposed; and soon after Halifax became head of the Board, it was decided to ask Parliament to abolish all colonial paper money. The attempt was made in 1749; the House of Commons gave leave to bring in a bill, and a committee of nine, five of whom were members of the Board, was appointed to draw up the measure.[744] The bill passed its first reading, was considered in the committee of the whole, of which Fane was chairman, but failed to pass. The House, however, ordered the Board to present, at the beginning of the next session, a full report of the extent of bills of credit in the plantations, which it did;

---

[742] Massachusetts *Acts and Resolves*, vol. ii, 701.

[743] — *Ibid.*, vol. ii, 745.

[744] House of Commons *Journal*, vol. xxv, 746. The bill was strongly opposed by the colonial agents, who presented petitions in behalf of their constituents and were heard before the House by counsel.

and in 1751 an act was passed prohibiting such bills in the New England colonies.[745]

The Board sought to secure its object in the other colonies by peremptory orders to the governors; but the French and Indian War compelled the latter to disregard their instructions, and even forced them to permit the new issues to be made legal tenders.[746] The assemblies did, however, provide for the sinking of their new emissions within a reasonable time. Seeing that it must either change the instructions or tacitly acquiesce in their violation, the Board instructed the governors to consent to such issues until the close of the war, when the old instruction was renewed.[747] In 1764 the aid of Parliament was again asked; and the act of that year, which was also prepared by the Board of Trade, included all the colonies.[748]

It is thus seen that the Board constantly opposed bills of credit in the interest of commerce, but that its opposition was not very successful. The slowness of communication and the still slower methods of the Board made it difficult to disallow the acts creating paper money before third parties had acquired the bills, after which a disallowance was not expedient. Parliament was successfully applied to; but the legis-

---

[745] 24 George II, cap. 53, Pickering. *Statutes at Large*, vol. xx, 306.

[746] Bernard in a letter to the Board, in which he discusses the necessity of issuing more bills of credit and the consequent change in his instructions, says: "And it will be absolutely necessary that this power should be free from the exception to making the bills a legal tender: for I am satisfied the Assembly will not pass a bill with that exception." — Bernard to the Board, August 31, 1758, in New Jersey *Archives*, vol. ix, 133.

[747] New Jersey *Archives*, vol. ix, 147, 274.

[748] The chairman and two of the other five members of the committee to bring in the bill were members of the Board. See: House of Commons *Journal*, vol. xxix, 1027; 4 George III, cap. 34, Pickering. *Statutes at Large*, vol. xxvi, 103.

lation, acting as it did upon governors, was not satisfactory. It irritated the assemblies, but did not restrain them from issuing more bills when they saw fit
to do so. It is strange that the Board did not take
active measures to remove the primary cause of the
paper money issues by providing some adequate form
of circulating medium. Some such measure as the
establishment of a mint for America, or a bank, or
both, would have gone far toward solving the vexed
question.

Defense

In 1696 the most pressing colonial question was
that of defense; and as soon as the Board was organized, it began to consider the most effectual means for
the protection of New York. Its first report on the
subject, which appeared in September, 1696, stated
the quotas which had been assigned to each of the
colonies, and their failure to observe the royal order
on that point. The report adds:

> It is almost incredible that His Majesty's governor of New
> York in the middle of above forty thousand English that he
> has in his neighbourhood should say as he does, that he has
> but the four companies His Majesty sent, and are in His
> Majesty's pay . . . to rely on for the defense of that
> frontier, in case of any attempt from the French.[749]

The Board gave as its opinion that there was force
enough in America for purposes of defense and that
the colonies should protect themselves; and as the
power of the English was of little avail so long as it
was divided, the whole military power of the northern provinces should be united under one military

---

[749] Representation on the condition of the northern provinces, in New
York *Colonial Documents*, vol. iv, 227.

officer. The recommendation took the form of the Bellomont commission, which was discussed in another connection. In the meantime, however, Governor Fletcher, who had been asking for supplies, for presents for the Indians, and for recruits,[750] was not left unsupported. The Board recommended that his requisitions should be honored without delay,[751] and in a few months notified him that the supplies had been forwarded.

The above incident illustrates the position of the Board in providing for the defense of the colonies. Accounts were kept in its office of the military situation in the plantations, and the governors were constantly called upon for reports which would keep the records up to date. When a governor found that he must have military supplies in addition to those which his assembly was able to furnish, he sent a request to the Board or to one of the principal secretaries of state. No matter to whom the requisition was forwarded in the first instance, it was referred to the Board for consideration, since that bureau alone had the necessary information to pass upon it.[752] Upon the report of the Board, the treasury or the ordnance department furnished the supplies asked for, which might be guns, ammunition, clothing, intrenching tools, or even money. These were then forwarded to the governor of the province by the Board of Trade directly, or turned over by that body to his agent, who looked after their transportation.

---

[750] See the letters of Governor Fletcher during the year 1696, New York *Colonial Documents,* vol. iv, *passim.*

[751] Representation of the Board, October 14, 1696, *Ibid.,* 230.

[752] See the requests of Bellomont, Cornbury, and Hunter for supplies, in New York *Colonial Documents,* vols. iv, v, *passim.*

The commissioners of ordnance opposed these demands for military supplies, as they came unexpectedly, and there was no separate fund from which to defray their cost. This resulted in an effort to shift such charges upon the colonies. The supplies were furnished as they were needed, but on condition that the colony to which they were sent should reimburse the home government for their first cost and the expense of sending them. In 1702 supplies to the value of £3,388 were sent to Virginia in answer to an urgent request from Governor Nicholson, but they were ordered to be paid for out of the quit rents of that province.[753] Similar action was taken when other military stores were forwarded from England. Massachusetts failed to keep her promise to pay for some guns and ammunition which she received in 1704. When she applied for a new quota in 1742, the Committee of the Privy Council refused to furnish them until the old account of five hundred pounds was settled.[754] The agent agreed to pay this and the new supplies were granted.[755] In some cases the Board had officers appointed to care for the arms and the public stores which had been supplied, and the one appointed for Maryland received a salary of £200 a

[753] This could easily be done, as there was a considerable balance in the hands of the receiver-general in Virginia. A warrant was drawn for the amount, and the governor ordered to remit by bills of exchange, payable to the paymaster of the ordnance. See: C.O. 5, 1360, pp. 218-219.

[754] Cannon were also furnished in 1704, but apparently they were paid for by the home government. The stores of heavy ordnance asked for in 1742 amounted to £4,877 16s. 4d. The first application came before the committee, August 24, 1742, and was finally granted June 30, 1743. See: Privy Council Register, "George II," vol. viii, 224, 288, 457.

[755] Privy Council Register, "George II," vol. viii, 457.

year out of the permanent revenue there.[756]   In 1712 the Board attempted to secure a fixed annual allowance from which to defray the many calls for colonial supplies; [757] but as the war closed soon after, the old method of meeting each call, when it came, continued.[758]

The Board secured troops for the colonies, some of which were regulars sent from England, and some recruits enlisted in America. It also sent over competent engineers to superintend the erection of fortifications on the frontiers and about the harbors, of whom Colonel Romer is the best known, and the one upon whose reports the Board secured an appropriation of five hundred pounds for the erection of a fort in the Onondaga country.[759]   Additional sums were afterward sent over from England for the forts at Albany and Schenectady, although the colonies usually bore the charge of whatever fortifications they deemed essential to their own safety.

The colonies, however, would not, or possibly could not, erect and maintain permanent fortifications, nor did the Board expect them to do so. New York was the most important of the frontier colonies as far as

---

[756] Board to Governor Seymour, February 4, 1706, in C.O. 5, 726, pp. 242, 369.

[757] Representation of the Board, February 15, 1712, C.O. 324, 10, p. 1. There had been heavy demands for ordnance supplies from Virginia, Massachusetts Bay, Leeward Islands, and Nevis, but the Board had been informed that there were no funds available for such supplies for the plantations, hence this request.

[758] See the letter of the Board to Newcastle, February 20, 1730, in C.O. 5, 400, pp. 273-274, recommending that seventy-two cannon and five hundred muskets be sent to South Carolina.

[759] New York *Colonial Documents*, vol. iv, 305, 326, 334, 339, 487, 609, 676, and *passim*.

the French were concerned; it was necessary to maintain fortified posts in that colony, not merely for its own protection, but for that of the other northern provinces as well. The Board determined which posts should be made permanent and provided for the expense of erecting the proper defenses by appropriations from England, by sums given by the assembly of New York, and by contributions which it attempted to secure from the neighboring colonies,[760] but this last measure was not very successful. In 1700 the Board proposed to secure five thousand pounds from that source, but the colonies replied that they could not afford the additional charge after the heavy expenses of the last war.[761] The request for troops to man the defenses met with a similar rebuff, and the Board was never able to get the colonies to assist each other except in time of actual war.

The process of securing permanent defenses for a port is illustrated in the attempt to fortify the harbor at Cape Lookout. In 1755 Governor Dobbs wrote the Board of Trade a most glowing description of it; for a small sum it could be made a Gibraltar of defense and would furnish ample room for all the British navy in American waters. The secretary of the Board of Trade answered his letter quite promptly and asked him to have a careful survey made of the harbor and plans drawn for the necessary fortifications,[762] which, together with an estimate of the cost of

---

[760] See the representation of the Board, October 4, 1700, for a detailed estimate of the charges of the forts at Albany and Schenectady which should be borne by the various colonies, in New York *Colonial Documents*, vol. iv, 705-706.

[761] — *Ibid.*, 921-922.

[762] North Carolina *Colonial Records*, vol. v, 442-443.

the projected work, were to be sent to the Board, which would then be in a position to decide on the merits of the proposed defenses. The Board was thus very careful not to ask the government to pay for the erection of any forts until it was convinced that they were necessary and that they could be secured in no other way.

Even the forts which were erected by the colonies were frequently supplied with ordnance and stores at the request of the Board. In 1753 Governor Dobbs asked that such supplies should be furnished for the forts which the province of North Carolina had erected on Cape Fear River. A final answer was not given to this request for two years, when the Board reported:

> That although we are sensible that the frequent applications of this nature which have of late been made by the colonies in America bring a very heavy expense on this country nevertheless as the ordnance and stores prayed for in the said memorial are represented to us to be absolutely necessary for the security and defence of the Province of North Carolina and as His Majesty has been graciously pleased to indulge other of his colonies in the like request, we are humbly of opinion that His Majesty may be graciously pleased that such ordnance and stores as from the plan of the said fort and Mr. Dobbs' account of it shall appear to be absolutely necessary may be sent thither.[763]

A part of the Board's plans for defense turned upon the Indian alliances which will be discussed in another place. It has already been indicated that the plans for union and the attacks upon the charter and

---

[763] Representation of the Board, April 24, 1755, in North Carolina *Colonial Records*, vol. v, 399-400.

proprietary colonies were actuated by a desire to provide better defense for the colonies and to secure more effectual enforcement of the trade laws. From an imperialistic point of view the first of these was the more important, but the second afforded the more tangible argument for influencing commercial England.

In the period of peace which followed the close of Queen Anne's War, the Board had little to do in caring for the defense of the plantations, as the struggle for final control of the interior of the continent had not begun. About 1717, however, the Board received information that the French were settling on the Mississippi, and had opened communications between Canada and Louisiana. Letters were written to the governors of the chief colonies in America, directing them to learn the extent of the French operations, and to suggest the most effective means of preventing the English colonies from being enclosed.[764] This was the beginning of a western policy of the British colonial officials, which continued for nearly half a century.

The surest method of checking French or Spanish occupation of the back country was to expand the English settlements into that region as rapidly as possible, and so occupy the lands before their rivals. Here colonial defense fitted closely into the trade policy of the Board – an increase in population would further both. In 1720, South Carolina was ordered to be taken "Provisionally into the hands of the

[764] Letter of the Board to Governor Spotswood of Virginia, January 29, 1718, in C.O. 5, 1365, pp. 42-43; to Governor Shute of Massachusetts, March 16, 1718, in C.O. 5, 915, pp. 102-103.

Crown," ostensibly as a means of preventing the possible loss of that colony.[765]

The next year the Board advised Carteret that special inducements should be offered to settlers in the western counties of Virginia, in the shape of a ten years' exemption from quit rents and a remission of the customary registration fee for taking up land. As the settlements in question controlled the mountain passes, it urged that:

> If these passes are not soon secured, they may fall into the hands of the French, who are already situated nearer them than His Majesty's subjects are by their lodgments upon the Great Lakes which continue their communication from the River St. Lawrence to that of Mississippi, and it is very obvious of what fatal consequences such a neglect on our part must certainly prove to the British plantations which would be thereby perpetually exposed to the Incursions of the French and of the Indian nations in their interest; we cannot, therefore, but be of opinion that all possible encouragement should be given for the enlarging and extending of the British settlements toward the said mountains, as one of the most effectual means to prevent the growing power and further encroachments of the French in those parts.[766]

The Board also advised that forts should be erected to control the passes and that two companies of soldiers should be sent to Virginia to garrison them, adding that they were "of opinion and have long been

---

[765] Order in Council reassuming the government of South Carolina, August 11, 1720. "Their Excellencies, the Lord Justices in Council, this day taking into consideration the great importance of the Province of Carolina, both with regard to its own product, and as it is a frontier to His Majesty's provinces on the continent of America, and the eminent danger of its being lost in this critical juncture, by the confused state of its present government, are pleased to Order," etc. See: Privy Council *Register*, "George I," vol. ii, 463.

[766] Board to Carteret, July 17, 1721, in C.O. 5, 1365, pp. 231-234.

so that it will be impossible to improve or even preserve His Majesty's empire in America without sending a military force thither." [767] These recommendations did not find the secretary of state so enthusiastic
for westward expansion as the Board, for two years
later, in a letter to Lieutenant-governor Drysdale, the
Board said nothing had been done, and that it antici-
pated that the proposed remission of the quit rents
would "meet with very great difficulties at the treasury." [768]

In the meantime orders had been sent to Governor
Burnet of New York "to extend with caution the
English settlements as far as possible." [769] This Burnet did, and erected a fort at Oswego, to which the
French objected and in turn advanced their own out-
posts, which brought forth another warning from
the Board of the dangers from French aggression.[770]

Grants of land to prospective settlers in the back
country received ready encouragement from the
Board. In recommending that Mr. Purry should be
given a grant of forty-eight thousand acres in South
Carolina, it said that it had been the constant sense
that all the colonies, and especially the two frontiers,
should be peopled as rapidly as possible with white
inhabitants. The accession of new inhabitants could
not fail to increase the trade and commerce of the
kingdom and increase the revenues of quit rents. As

[767] Representation of the Board, July 17, 1721, in C.O. 5, 1365, pp.
232-233.

[768] Board to Drysdale, June 19, 1723, in C.O. 5, 1365, p. 246.

[769] Instructions sent to Governor Burnet by the Board in 1722. See:
Chalmers, George. *Introduction to the Revolt*, vol. ii, 52.

[770] Representation of the Board, April 6, 1732, in New York *Colonial
Documents*, vol. v, 932.

South Carolina was a frontier to both the French and the Spanish settlements, and was surrounded by a great number of Indian natives, the grant was favored, since "the well peopling of this province seems a necessary means for the defense and security of all our plantations on the continent of America." [771] Other grants met with the same favor, except when the land in question was claimed by different persons, in which cases commissions were proposed to mark the boundaries, so as not to retard settlement. [772] Backed by this constant support from the Board, the English settlements were pushed steadily westward until they began to cross the mountains. In 1749 the Board reported favorably on a grant to the Ohio Company of five hundred thousand acres on the condition that they plant a settlement on the banks of the Ohio River, and instructed the governor of Virginia to pass the grant, the settlement of which brought on war with the French. [773]

Up to the outbreak of formal war, the Board actively encouraged westward expansion. In 1752, in commenting on the unfair way in which the laws of

[771] Representation of the Board, May 26, 1732, in C.O. 5, 401, pp. 37-38.

[772] See the representation on William Keith's proposal for settling the back country, July 20, 1732. Keith and some associates planned to settle some thousands of families from Switzerland in the region back of Virginia, but Lords Baltimore and Fairfax had claims on the land. The Board proposed a commission to mark out the boundary. September 13, 1732, it advised Lieutenant-governor Gooch of Virginia not to make any further grants beyond the mountains until the claims could be determined. Gooch had written that he had permitted some settlements to be made. See: C.O. 5, 1366, pp. 86-88, 92.

[773] The original instruction was to pass a grant of two hundred thousand acres, but before it could be confirmed other petitions had been presented to the Privy Council; consequently the first instruction was referred back to the Board, where the grant was increased to five hundred thousand acres.

Virginia favored the large landholder, and discouraged the poor settler, it advised that every encouragement should be given to foreign protestants, that they
should be exempted from all parochial charges and
taxes for a term of years, not exceeding fifteen, and
advised that the ecclesiastical laws of Virginia be so
modified as to accomplish this result. These measures
were proposed as desirable means of encouraging the
rapid settlement of the interior.[774] Two years later
we find the Board urging that, as

> The settlement of the country west of the great ridge of
> mountains seems to us of the greatest consequence, as noth-
> ing can more effectually tend to defeat the dangerous de-
> signs of the French . . . therefore, all proper encour-
> agement should be given for the enlarging and extending the
> British settlements in this part of the country.

To this end it advised the remission of all fees and
quit rents for a period of ten years, as an inducement
to actual settlers to enter the region.[775] Thus up to

See the entries in the *Journal* for December 9, 1748, February 14, and February 21, 1749, in Board of Trade *Journal*, 56, 57.

[774] "The advantages and security arising from erecting settlements in
the interior parts of America, clearly mark out the good policy of giving
them all possible encouragement; it is therefore matter of surprise to us,
that Virginia, whose situation and circumstances not only admit, but call for,
an increase of inhabitants, should have established and acquiesced in
regulations, which from the very nature of them, have a very different
tendency and effect.

The success of the settlement of Spottsylvania and Brunswick where
foreign protestants were allowed to be exempted "from parochial charges
and taxes for a certain number of years, sufficiently point out the impro-
priety of such a system . . . and we are of opinion that it would be
greatly for the interest and advantage of the colony, if foreign protestants
were exempted from all parochial charges and taxes whatever for a term of
years, not exceeding fifteen from the time of their arrival in the province." —
Board to Governor Dinwiddie of Virginia, November 29, 1752, in C.O. 5,
1366, pp. 518-522.

[775] As the Virginia assembly had spent a considerable sum in advancing

the very outbreak of the French and Indian War the British Board of Trade was thoroughly committed to the policy of rapidly filling up the back country and pushing settlements across the mountains into the Ohio Valley. It even advised that the crown bear a portion of the cost of such settlements by waiving the land revenue for a time.

There is one apparent exception to this policy of extending the English settlements into the back country. The Board refused to favor grants of land beyond the Altamaha between South Carolina and the Spanish settlements, and in 1736 gave strict orders to the governor of South Carolina not to make any grants in that region, notwithstanding the inhabitants of his province insisted upon entering and settling upon the forbidden lands.[776] It even went so far as to have the settlers who entered the region in defiance of its orders forcibly removed, although a fortified post was held there.[777]

Why should the Board favor expansion toward the

the settlements in that region, the Board thought the crown could well afford to contribute a little in the form of a remission of land charges for a period of ten years, especially as it considered the total revenues would be enlarged by so doing. As a further inducement to settlers, the Board proposed that grants beyond the mountains should be limited to small quantities. Large plantations were not wanted, as they discouraged close settling. Population with small farms and few slaves was what was desired for purposes of defense. See: Report to the Committee of the Privy Council on western settlements and a request from the House of Burgesses that the quit rents be remitted in the region and that grants be limited, June 20, 1754, in C.O. 5, 1367, pp. 73-74.

[776] Additional instructions to Lieutenant-governor Broughton of South Carolina, December 3, 1736, in C.O. 5, 401, pp. 192-193.

[777] See the letter of the Board to Pitt, April 28, 1758, advising him that such action should be taken, and the letter from Governor Ellis of Georgia to the Board, January 28, 1759, informing it that Pitt's orders in the matter had been executed. C.O. 5, 646, N. 54; 673, pp. 44-45.

French and oppose it toward the Spanish frontier? Was it trying to prevent the settlement of that region so as to keep the colonists near the coast? Not at all! The object of expansion westward was to defend the settlements nearer the coast from the attacks of the French and their Indian allies, and so to occupy the back country that such dangers should be pushed farther and farther away. The settlements beyond the Altamaha were in a region occupied by Indians in alliance with the English, and there was danger that the encroachments of the whites might drive them over to the enemy.[778] Hence it was as good policy to check expansion there for a time, as it was to encourage it on the borders of Virginia. The whole western policy was turning upon the question of defense. The enemies to be feared were France and Spain, in the struggle the Indian tribes had to be reckoned with, and an expansion of the existing settlements was favored or opposed as it affected the question of defense. In the case of Virginia, western settlements strengthened the English position; but on the Altamaha, if they resulted in alienating the Indians and driving them over to the enemy, instead of being a source of strength, they would become an element of weakness.

During the ascendency of Newcastle the Board of Trade played a very minor part in colonial affairs. The war from 1744 to 1748 came at a time when the

---

[778] "We think it may be of very dangerous consequence" to allow the people to remain in a settlement "begun without His Majesty's authority" and in defiance of Governor Lyttelton's orders for them to remove. If they were not removed, it might have "very pernicious effects on His Majesty's interests with the Indians." — Board to Pitt, April 28, 1758, in C.O. 5, 673, pp. 44, 45.

Board was at the very lowest point to which it ever sank, but soon after the appointment of Halifax it was called upon to adjust the complicated accounts, which the northern colonies had presented as a result of the attempted invasion of Canada; [779] which work properly belonged to the treasury, but the necessary information for an equitable settlement of the claims was in the plantation office. In the French and Indian War the Board was frequently called upon to distribute subsidies which had already been granted, and to prepare estimates for future grants.[780]

It was during the administration of Halifax that the Board shows its greatest activity in matters of defense. The governor of each province was called upon for accounts of the arms and munitions of war which he had on hand, the strength and efficiency of the militia, and the troops and the moneys which were furnished for previous campaigns.[781] In September, 1753, the Board sent urgent orders to the governors to summon their assemblies without delay and prevail upon them to appropriate funds to buy presents for the Six Nations. The attempts of the Board to effect some form of union during the year 1754 have already been mentioned. As a temporary measure, however, Halifax secured a commission for Governor Sharpe of Maryland, by which he was made commander of all the forces to be raised in America.

---

[779] See the detailed report on these claims which was made, February 28, 1750, in New Jersey *Archives*, vol. vii, 383-400.

[780] See the correspondence between the Board and the secretaries of state, in North Carolina *Colonial Records*, vol. v, 805; Sharpe's *Correspondence*, vol. i, 119, 220, 359; New Jersey *Archives*, vol. viii, part ii, 205.

[781] North Carolina *Colonial Records*, vol. v, 738; Sharpe's *Correspondence*, vol. i, 81, 119, 352, 359, 435; New Jersey *Archives*, vol. viii, part ii, 217.

In the meantime the Board had been busily engaged supplying ordnance and military stores for such of the colonies as were in urgent need of them.[782] The question of providing for the safety of the frontiers was a pressing one, and when Braddock was sent over with a small army, the Board proposed that he should prepare a general scheme for defense.[783] In order that he might have all the information possible, the Board called upon each governor to state what forces he would need for his own protection and what fortifications should be erected on the frontiers of his province.[784] As the war went on, the Board secured the information and prepared many of the estimates for the operations of each succeeding year. It also passed upon the claims of the various provinces for pecuniary aid,[785] and did all it possibly could to urge the colonies to exert their best efforts to make the war a success.

The most cherished administrative plans of the Board were sacrificed in the interests of the war; the plans for a fixed civil list were abandoned, and the colonies were permitted to issue bills of credit in

---

[782] North Carolina *Colonial Records*, vol. v, 399-400.

[783] "We submit to you whether it may not be proper that General Braddock should be directed forthwith to consider and report his opinion in what manner the frontiers may be best defended; what number of forts it will be necessary to erect; of what size and strength; where those forts should be situated; what number of regular troops it will be necessary to have constantly kept up in America for garrisoning them and for the other necessary services; how these troops should be distributed and where stationed." — New York *Colonial Documents*, vol. vi, 960-961.

[784] New York *Colonial Documents*, vol. vi, 961.

[785] January 3, 1757, Pitt referred a number of memorials from Virginia and the Carolinas to the Board, and asked that body to advise him whether or not he should ask Parliament to appropriate money to repay them and to encourage them for the future. Extract from the Board of Trade Journal, North Carolina *Colonial Records*, vol. v, 805-806.

practically their own way. Possible disputes between
the governors and the assemblies were kept in abey-
ance, and the former were instructed to do all they
could to avoid antagonizing the lower house of the
legislature. The settlement of boundary disputes was
postponed and attempts made to secure a temporary agreement which should continue till the war
was over. In a word, the Board exerted itself to the
utmost to secure concerted action on the part of the
colonies. The quotas of men which each province
should furnish for the general defense were arranged
by common agreement in America, or by the Board
after consulting with colonial agents and the military
officers, they were then forwarded to the governors
and usually complied with by the assemblies.

Even as important a measure as an embargo was
laid by a circular letter sent out by the Board in October, 1756, which directed the governors to stop all
vessels laden with provisions, unless they were bound
for some port in the British colonies; in which case,
the masters had to give bond that they would not take
their cargoes into a French port and sell the provisions to the enemy.[786] A few months later this order
was modified by directions from Secretary Holderness not to apply the embargo to provision ships bound
for England.[787] The above incident, however, illustrates the important part which the Board of Trade
took in the actual execution of measures for colonial
defense.

---

[786] Circular letter from the Board, in New York *Colonial Documents*,
vol. vi, 162.

[787] Circular letter from Holderness, in North Carolina *Colonial Records*,
vol. v, 756.

Indian Relations

The problems presented by the presence of strong Indian tribes on the frontiers were closely connected with the plans for defense. The Board inherited its Indian policy from the old Committee of the Privy Council, and for many years it shows very slight changes. In its general outline the policy of the Board embraced three objects: to preserve the alliance with the Six Nations as a protection against the French and with the southwestern Indians as a barrier to the Spanish; to pit one group of Indians against another; and to preserve and develop the fur trade.

The method used to secure the first of these was to give the Indians presents from time to time, and the Board sent over large quantities of goods for this purpose. The Indians expected these presents regularly, but they were not given to the Iroquois on a large scale except in case of war, the arrival of a new governor, or the accession of a sovereign. On these occasions the Indians received presents amounting to hundreds of pounds, and the Board looked upon the outlay as one of the legitimate charges upon the crown. The assemblies adopted the same policy and added to the sums sent over from England for the purchase of goods.

The irregularity in sending these gifts sometimes strained the relations with the Indians, and in its report of 1721 the Board advised that regular sums should be set aside for this charge, instead of occasionally taking the necessary funds from the already overburdened civil list. In this way the Indians could also be kept more constantly in the English interest.[788]

The friendship of the southern Indians was cultivated even more assiduously than was that of the northern ones, and presents in large quantities were regularly given to the Indians on the borders of South Carolina and Georgia. From 1731 to 1748 these were paid for out of the expense money allowed for the soldiers stationed in those colonies, and according to Crockatt, the agent for South Carolina in 1751, amounted to £7,000 or £8,000 annually.[789] This charge did not appear as a separate item, consequently the question of the advisability of making the grants from year to year did not come before the Board. From 1748 on, however, requests for money for Indian presents were regularly presented, and, on the advice of the Board, £3,000 were regularly expended for this purpose.[790]

The Board also had plans for uniting the Six Nations more permanently to the British interest by erecting forts among them and by supplying them with missionaries. The latter plan was not carried out with sufficient energy to make it successful, as the

---

[788] Representation on the trade conditions in the plantations, September 8, 1721, in C.O. 324, 10, p. 413.

[789] According to Crockatt these presents were at first paid for out of the sum granted by Parliament to the trustees of Georgia, and afterwards charged "to Extraordinaries" in the expense accounts of the soldiers. See: C.O. 5, 385, no. 180.

[790] Colonel Vanderdusen stated to the Board, May 25, 1748, that the government had granted that amount for Indian presents. Crockatt also states that this sum had been paid annually since 1748. The records of the correspondence with Georgia indicate that such sums were given each year. See: C.O. 5, 672, pp. 52-58, 184; Board of Trade *Journal*, 56, p. 74; 63, January 21, 1755; 64, November 2, 1756; 66, February 21, 1758.

work of supplying and paying these missionaries was left to the Society for the Propagation of the Gospel, and consequently the ministers were not sufficiently well supported to induce able men to enter the field.[791] Another great obstacle to the success of the plan was the language difficulty, which few ministers were able to surmount.   Supplying the Indians with black- smiths and other artificers was a more practical means of securing their friendship and became of growing importance in the later measures proposed by the Board.

The colonies were left pretty much to themselves in directing their relations with the Indians, except so far as they might be influenced by the letters which were written to the governors.   Robert Livingston had been sent over as Indian commissioner, but his duties were so poorly defined that he never exerted a directing influence over the affairs of the Six Nations. The Board, however, was careful not to permit any action which might alienate the Indians.   This atti- tude is seen in its treatment of the claims of the Mohe- gan Indians and its refusal to grant a tract of land in the Mohawk country until it knew whether the In- dians were seated on any part of it.[792]

The whole treatment of Indian affairs was without any clearly defined general plan and was dictated by the exigencies of the moment until the administra- tion of Halifax.   During the war from 1744 to 1748 William Johnson had been appointed colonel of the Six Nations and supplied with large sums of money to be expended upon them.   Consequently he ac-

---

[791] New York *Colonial Documents*, vol. iv, 521, 755, 1038, 1074, 1077, vol. v, 271, 278, 297, and *passim*.

[792] — *Ibid.*, iv, 203-204, vol. vi, 42.

quired a great reputation among the Indians; and when the war was closed and he was no longer paid a salary and furnished with money to be spent on them, they began to complain. The Board realized the importance of the Indian alliance in the coming struggle with France and in 1753 took steps to redress their grievances. The conference at Albany has been mentioned in another connection, but it should be remembered that the purpose of the meeting was to concert affairs with the Six Nations.[793]

Up to 1753, however, the main feature of the Board's Indian policy was to bribe them with presents. As late as November 29, 1752, we find it using the following statement in a letter to Dinwiddie:

The friendship and affection of the Indians is certainly of the greatest importance to the security and advantage of the colonies, and we are sensible that the principal, if not the only, means of gaining and preserving that affection is by making them annual presents, by taking care that those presents are properly and honestly applied to the service by a religious observance of our publick engagements, and a fair and upright conduct in all the commercial dealings of those who traffick with them.[794]

When reports came of Indian attacks upon the Virginia settlers beyond the mountains, it advised Secre-

[793] New York *Colonial Documents*, vol. vi, 800; New Jersey *Archives*, vol. viii, part i, 156.

There is an intimation in a letter of the Board to Governor Dinwiddie that it had hopes that some general plan of union might be formed at this meeting. "It might have afforded an opportunity of concerting measures, and proposing some general plan for a mutual union, and concert for the general security and defense of the whole." — Board to Dinwiddie, July 4, 1754, in C.O. 5, 1367, pp. 105-106.

[794] C.O. 5, 1366, p. 577. This letter goes on to say that it was by such measures as these that the French had won the Indians away from the English, and it was only by similar means that they could be again secured.

tary of State Holderness that one thousand pounds should be granted to the Twightwees* and every effort made to win them over to the English cause, as they were the most powerful tribe in that section and so long as they were friendly the frontier was secure.[795]

The instructions which were sent to Governor Osborn in September, 1753, indicate that the Board was beginning to adopt a saner Indian policy; he was to summon the assembly at once and urge them to appropriate money for presents to the Six Nations. Similar letters were sent to the governors of the other colonies and presents were also sent from England. So far the policy is that which had been followed for years, except that it was a little more elaborate. The instruction regarding future purchases of lands, however, was new. He was to permit no more purchases of lands by private individuals, "but when the Indians are disposed to sell any of their lands the purchase ought to be made in his Majesty's name and at the publick charge." This doctrine was not unknown in America and was one of the measures proposed at the Albany Congress for the better regulation of Indian affairs.[796]

General Braddock had reappointed Sir William Johnson as sole superintendent of the Six Nations, with unlimited credit for such expenditures as he needed;[797] but in a few months Johnson and General

---

* The Twightwees are more commonly known as Miamis, but the former name is the one regularly used by the English.

[795] Report on the Indian situation, March 16, 1753, in C.O. 5, 1367, p. 25.

[796] New York *Colonial Documents*, vol. vi, 888; Pennsylvania *Colonial Records*, vol. vi, 59.

[797] New York *Colonial Documents*, vol. vi, 961.

Shirley clashed, and the former threatened to resign unless he was made independent of the latter's control. In the meantime the Board had decided to give Johnson a commission from the crown, "with such salary and allowance to be paid by the commander-in-chief of His Majesty's forces in America as to His Majesty shall appear most just and reasonable." [798] From this time (1756) on Johnson retained his position, and the Board regularly consulted him on all questions of Indian policy. At the same time that Johnson was appointed agent for the northern colonies, Edmund Atkins was appointed for the southern colonies,[799] and the Board thus adopted the plan of regulating Indian affairs by commissioners appointed by itself and paid by the crown.[800]

The many frauds practiced upon the Indians by the traders and their lawless conduct had long been a prolific source of trouble. Each colony had made its own regulations, no two were alike, and frauds forbidden by the laws of one were tolerated by those of its neighbors. The Board had contributed to this condition by its refusal to permit the colonies to restrict the Indian trade by law, and by its insistence that such trade should be free and open to every British subject who cared to engage in it.

One avowed object in appointing the Indian agents in 1756 was to secure definite information upon which a general plan for the control of the Indian trade

---

[798] Representation of the Board, February 17, 1756. A letter of the same date to Governor Hardy announces that the appointment had been made. New York *Colonial Documents*, vol. vii, 35, 37.

[799] Board of Trade *Journal*, 64, May 13, 1756.

[800] The salary of Johnson was six hundred pounds per year. See: C.O. 324, 17, pp. 57-59.

could be framed.   In 1757, Governor Lyttelton was informed that, although the regulations lately formed in that colony for the Indian trade were very proper and desirable, any measure of a single province,

> However proper in itself must be partial and local, and probably will be counteracted by the measures of another province, the people of which may carry on a trade with the same Indians.   We are of opinion that the only effectual method of conducting Indian affairs will be to establish one general system under the sole direction of the crown and its officers . . . and we hope soon to be enabled . . . to enter upon the consideration of such a plan; at present we have very imperfect information upon almost every point necessary to form a proper judgment.[801]

Thus questions of defense were forcing the Board to conclude that the home government should assume full control over trade among the Indians, that the operations of unscrupulous traders could be regulated in no other way; and until this was done, the frontier might be endangered at any moment by the wrongs done the Indians by irresponsible individuals.

The war had scarcely begun before the Board began to see that the westward movement which it had steadily favored for so many years was in danger of alienating the Indian allies.   Pennsylvania had proposed bounty lands for the officers and men who volunteered from that colony, such lands to be located in the western part of the province.   As some of the lands lay within the region claimed by the Iroquois under their treaty of 1726, the Pennsylvania authori-

---

[801] Board to Governor Lyttelton, of South Carolina, November 9, 1757, in C.O. 5, 403, pp. 200-203.   The letter concludes with the statement that there was no desire to disparage the action of the assembly in passing the law, and that the Board would be very glad to see it carried into execution as a temporary measure.

ties had been careful to secure permission from the
Indians for the proposed settlements. The Board,
however, entered the most emphatic objection to any
such grants, on the ground that they were contrary
to the treaty of 1726, that the Indians insisted they
would never give up their lands, that there was serious danger of arousing suspicions as to the good faith
of the English, and that there was plenty of land
within the province for such purposes without entering the Indian country.[802] Here was a new policy. A
province was forbidden to make grants of land within its own undisputed boundaries, if such lands were
included in an Indian reservation created by treaty.

In order to lessen the danger of losing the support
of the Indians in the struggle for the continent, the
Board set to work to remove all just grounds for complaint on their part; consequently, early in 1756, Governor Hardy of New York and Chief Justice De-
Lancey were instructed to secure a law breaking the
exorbitant grants of lands in the Mohawk country.[803]
The fact that DeLancey was appealed to shows that
the Board recognized the difficulty which would be
experienced in securing the desired law. The difficulties were even greater than it realized; but as
Johnson insisted that the chief complaint of the Indians was against the encroachments of the whites,

---

[802] Representation on land grants in Pennsylvania, December 11, 1755,
in C.O. 5, 1295, pp. 185-187. The paper concludes: Therefore we are of
opinion that at any time, but more particularly at present, when we ought
cautiously to avoid giving the least cause for jealousy or distrust to the
Indians, and religiously observe engagements with them, it would not be
advisable to attempt any settlement in the lands, which by the deed of 1726
are given by them to Your Majesty to protect for their use.

[803] Letters of the Board, in New York *Colonial Documents*, vol. vii,
77-79.

it continued to insist that the law should be passed. The assembly refused to comply, and in 1764 the Board sent a positive order to Governor Colden again to lay the demand before that body, and if the law were not passed, it threatened to apply to Parliament.[804]

Complaints of trouble between whites and Indians were coming in from other sources, and as Johnson had reported the Indians as considerably disaffected, the Board became very conservative in approving land grants. It had forbidden private purchases of the Indians, but even those made by the provincial authorities were in danger of becoming troublesome. In 1759, in a report on the dispute between Pennsylvania and the Indians over lands on the Delaware, it informed the Council that the "extensive purchases of land, made not only by the proprietaries of Pennsylvania but in other governments bordering on the Indian country, have long since occasioned disgusts and suspicions of injury in the minds of the Indians," and that this had been the chief cause of their defection to the French and the hostilities committed by them on the frontiers.[805] If these statements were true, the Board would have to solve a new problem of defense, and evolve an Indian policy different from that which had been followed during the last half-century.

---

[804] New York *Colonial Documents*, vol. vii, 377, 633, 673-674.

[805] Report on Franklin's petition relative to the dispute with the Delaware Indians, June 1, 1759, in C.O. 5, 1295, pp. 259-260.

In spite of the objections of the Board, settlers continued to enter the Wyoming Valley. The colonial officials made a pretense, at least, of preventing such encroachments, but without much effect. April 27, 1763, the Board advised that the same steps to remove the settlers should be taken

The success of the English in the war had aroused some apprehension on the part of the Indians that their lands were to be taken from them. These fears were increased by the grants in the Mohawk country and many new ones which were being made in the Ohio country. The Board early saw that these would alienate the Indians and might bring on a general uprising against the frontier settlements. Governor Fauquier of Virginia had informed the Board that the settlers on the Green Briar and the Kanawha were returning to their settlements. He was told in turn, that while the success of the war was assured,

> The difficulties arising from the claims of the Indians and their jealousy of encroachments exists in full force; and whatever may in any degree tend to alarm their suspicions and disappoint their hopes of the intention on our part to redress past and prevent future abuses, cannot fail of being attended with fatal consequences.

Hence if any Indians claimed the lands in that region, it would be very imprudent to encourage any new settlements; but if there was no difficulty of that kind, the settlements might continue, as "they would prove very valuable and be greatly for the benefit and security of the colony." The governor was ordered not to take any further steps in the matter, until he had informed the Board of any Indian claims in that part of the country and received its further orders.[806]

as were used in the case of settlements south of the Altamaha. Accordingly it proposed that instructions should be sent to the governors of Pennsylvania and Connecticut to appoint commissioners who should go to the region and send the settlers away. See: Representation of the Board, January 14, 1763, in C.O. 5, 1296, pp. 13, 16-17, 20-21.

[806] Board to Fauquier, February 17, 1761, in C.O. 5, 1368, pp. 12-15.

Early in 1761, it advised the king that,

In this situation the granting lands hitherto unsettled and establishing colonies upon the frontiers before the claims of the Indians are ascertained appears to be a measure of the most dangerous tendency, and is more particularly so in the present case, as these settlements now proposed to be made, especially those upon the Mohawk River are in that part of the country of the possession of which the Indians are the most jealous having at different times expressed in the strongest terms their resolution to oppose all settlements thereon as a manifest violation of their rights.[807]

As a result of this representation, the Board was ordered to prepare additional instructions to the governors on the question of new land grants, which were sent out before the close of the year. These instructions forbade each governor

Upon any pretence whatever upon pain of our highest displeasure and of being forthwith removed from his office [issuing] any grant or grants to any persons whatever of any lands within or adjacent to the territories possessed or occupied by the said Indians or the property possession of which has at any time been reserved to or claimed by them.

Here was a distinct announcement of a policy to recognize certain tracts as Indian reservations which should be protected from the encroachments of settlers. The governors were also instructed to issue a proclamation at once in the king's name

Strictly enjoining and requiring all persons whatever who may either wilfully or inadvertently have seated themselves on any lands so reserved to or claimed by the said Indians . . . forthwith to remove therefrom.[808]

---

[807] New York *Colonial Documents*, vol. vii, 473.

[808] Instructions to the governors of Nova Scotia, New Hampshire, New York, Virginia, North Carolina, South Carolina, and Georgia, December 2, 1761, in C.O. 324, 17, pp. 164-170.

They were also to prosecute all persons who should have secured any titles to such lands by fraud, and future purchases of Indian lands were to be made only by persons who had secured licenses for that purpose, which were to be obtained by application to the Board.[809]

The conclusion of the treaty of Paris placed the affairs of all the Indians of the greater portion of the continent of America in the hands of the Board of Trade, and that body began to realize the task which was before it. The ministry was anxious to have the government's policy in the western country determined at once, as the discontent of the Indians was known to be serious. The shadow of Pontiac's conspiracy already hung over the northern provinces. The root of the difficulty was the dispute as to what was Indian land and what was not. Johnson and other officers in America advocated the adoption of a boundary line between the colonies and the Indians on the west, and the prohibition of settlements beyond that line.[810] The Board was already committed to the policy of respecting the claims of the Indians and strictly forbidding encroachments by the whites, consequently it was led to believe that such a line was the

---

[809] Cf. the royal proclamation concerning America. Several of its provisions are identical with the instructions of 1761. *Annual Register*, 1763, pp. 208-213.

[810] See the letters of Johnson and Croghan in New York *Colonial Documents*, vol. vii, 560, 578, 602-607. These letters do not appear to have reached the Board until after the boundary line had been decided upon, nor is there internal evidence that they knew, when the letters were written, that the Board had committed itself to such a policy. Croghan's undated letter proposes a natural boundary, and that is what was adopted in the proclamation. Did he suggest the plan while Shelburne was making up his mind?

best way to give the Indians immediate satisfaction. Shelburne had scarcely assumed control of the plantation office when he was called upon to formulate a plan for the government of the acquired territory, to decide what governments should be established, and the military force necessary for the protection of the region.[811] June 8, 1763, the Board made its report, indicating the main features of the Proclamation of 1763. August 5, it reported particularly upon the Indian situation, advising that a royal proclamation should immediately be issued, establishing bounds for the Indian country and forbidding all settlements or grants within the limits of such region, but at the same time declaring "Your Majesty's Intention to encourage all such persons who shall be inclined to commence new settlements from your old colonies." [812] Here was a reasonably plain program: establish fixed Indian reservations, prevent encroachments upon them, and encourage and control the westward movement. The proclamation was prepared and finally transmitted to Halifax on October 4, 1763.[813]

It is evident that the rough bounds of the Indian country included in this proclamation were intended to be temporary. There does not appear to have been any idea of creating a permanent Indian region

---

[811] Shelburne was appointed, April 20, 1763. May 5, Egremont requested his opinion on the above questions. See: Fitzmaurice, E. G. P. *Life of Shelburne*, vol. i, 247-248.

[812] It also proposed that fairly liberal grants of land should be given to the officers and soldiers who had served in the late war on condition that they lived on the lands they selected. See: C.O. 324, 17, p. 270.

[813] C.O. 324, 17, pp. 273-275. See: Alvord, C. W. "Genesis of the Proclamation of 1763," Michigan Pioneer and Historical *Collections* (1908), for the best account of the origin of this proclamation.

in the interior of the continent. It was only intended to pacify the savages and remove their just grounds of complaint by checking the great wave of encroaching settlements. New settlements were to be permitted within the region, but only after the bounds of the Indian lands were clearly defined and their claims satisfied. As applications for licenses to buy lands from the Indians had been ordered transmitted to England for the inspection of the Board, that body found itself in serious difficulty. The information at its command was wholly inadequate to enable it to pass intelligently upon requests for land grants. December 20, 1763, it recommended that surveyors be appointed at once to survey the dominions in America, and for this purpose two departments, a northern and a southern, should be created with a surveyor-general in charge of each, and nominated a Captain Holland for one of these positions.[814]

In the meantime the Board was at work on a general plan for regulating the Indian trade. In fact it had announced as early as 1756 that it considered control directly by the crown as the only proper solution.[815] In the summer of 1763, Johnson, the other Indian agent, and some of the governors, received particular instructions to lay their ideas on the subject before the Board.[816] They did this rather freely,

---

[814] Representation of the Board, in C.O. 324, 17, pp. 317-318.

[815] The Board stated in its letter to Lyttelton in 1757 that one object in appointing the Indian agents was to secure data upon which it could formulate a general plan for the regulation of Indian affairs, commercial and political. C.O. 5, 403, pp. 200-203.

[816] These instructions were issued, August 5, 1763. Those to Johnson are in New York *Colonial Documents*, vol. vii, 535-536. Those to John Stuart, who had been appointed Indian Agent for the southern section of America, are in C.O. 5, 404, pp. 195-198.

and Johnson's letters, especially, are full of valuable suggestions.[817] He proposed that the whole matter should be placed under the control of a royal commission, as the task was too large for any one man; that carefully trained interpreters should be provided; and that trading should only be carried on under careful regulations. The plan was gradually taking shape in the fall of 1763, and was so far advanced by October 19, that Halifax informed Amherst that trade would be permitted only at regular posts and by those holding licenses.[818] At last it was completed and would have been presented to Parliament in the session of 1763-1764 to be enacted into law; but as it would require a considerable sum of money to put it in operation, and funds were hard to get, it was postponed until the next session, in the hope that money might be available by that time.[819] In the interval it was submitted to Johnson, Governor Colden, and other persons in America who were supposed to be competent to pass upon the measure.[820]

The proposed plan was so far in advance of any previous arrangement that it merits careful consideration. It was, as the Board said, a plan for

---

[817] Both his earlier and later letters contain valuable information and suggestions on this point. See: New York *Colonial Documents*, vol. vii.

[818] Letter of Halifax to Amherst, in New York *Colonial Documents*, vol. vii, 571. This letter raises the query whether the plan which was finally proposed was not largely the work of Halifax. As he had been at the head of the Board for so many years, had been responsible for the assertion in 1757 that Indian trade should be regulated by the crown, had no doubt given the matter considerable thought, and the more important under clerks and officers were his own appointees, it is more than probable that he is the father of it.

[819] Letter of the Board to Johnson, July 10, 1764, in C.O. 324, 17, pp. 407-421.

[820] New York *Colonial Documents*, vol. vii, 634, 661, 667-670.

The regulation of Indian affairs both commercial and political throughout all North America upon one general system under the direction of officers appointed by the crown, so as to set aside all local interfering of particular provinces.

The continent was to be divided into two departments, each under the control of a superintendent, or agent. The Ohio River was selected as the boundary between the two, but because some tribes under Johnson's control lived south of that line, the Board decided to arrange the jurisdiction by tribes and asked the agents in America for suggestions on that point.[821]

All provincial laws for the regulation of Indian affairs were to be repealed and the control centered in the superintendents appointed by the crown, who were to have charge of all questions of a political nature, such as peace and war, purchase of lands, making of treaties, and all other matters which required general meetings with the Indians. Each superintendent was to consult with the several governors in his department, and was to be appointed an extraordinary member of the council of each province. The Indian agents, however, were to be independent of all local control, and no military officer could interfere with the trade of any tribe without the consent of the head of the department in which it was located. The superintendents were to be assisted by deputies, two for the southern district and three for the northern, and in each of the tribes of the southern district the crown was to appoint a commissary, an interpreter, and a smith, all of whom should be sub-

[821] Letter of the Board to Johnson, July 10, 1764. New York *Colonial Documents*, vol. vii, 634.

ject to the control of the agent.   The religious life
of the Indians was to be under the care of missionaries, four for each district, who were to be appointed
by the Society for the Propagation of the Gospel and
were to reside where the superintendents directed.

Indian trade was to be carefully regulated under
the inspection and supervision of the superintendents;
but any person who wished to engage in it could do
so by securing a license from the governor of the
province from which he came, the fee for which was
only two shillings.   The license was good for one
year and specified the region in which the holder was
entitled to trade; and to insure the observance of the
laws regulating such trade, each person who engaged
in it was placed under bond.   The traders were not
allowed to charge exorbitant prices for their goods,
but the value of each article was to be agreed upon
in advance by the commissary, the representative of
the Indians, and the agent.   In the northern district
all trade had to be carried on at regular posts, which
were to be fortified and properly garrisoned, and in
both districts the traders were forbidden to sell rum
or rifled guns to Indians.   To protect the Indians
against the evils of debts, no trader was permitted
to give credit for a larger amount than fifty shillings,
and debts greater than that could not be collected by
law.

The intercourse of traders with the Indians required some well regulated arrangements for the administration of prompt justice.   For this purpose the
agents and the commissaries at each post were empowered to act as justices of the peace in both criminal and civil cases, and the testimony of the Indians

was put on the same footing as that of the whites in the courts of all the colonies. In civil cases involving sums not exceeding ten pounds, an appeal could be taken from the commissary to the agent for the department, whose decision was final. Civil cases which involved larger sums and the more important criminal cases were left to the regularly established colonial courts.

As the worst abuses of which the Indians complained had arisen from the sale of their lands, no private person or corporation was to be allowed to purchase any lands from the Indians, except where such lands were within the bounds of some colony; and even in that case, the purchase could be made only at a general meeting presided over by the agent and attended by the chiefs of each tribe claiming the land. Purchases of lands for the use of the crown were to be made in the same way, carefully surveyed in the presence of the Indians, and maps of the tracts so purchased were to be kept on deposit at the office of the agent. The agents were also directed to use their best efforts to secure a determination of the western boundary, so that the above regulations could be made effective.

An attempt was made to regulate the election customs among the Indians. In the southern district the members of each village of a tribe were to select, under the supervision of the commissary, a chief man. The chief men so chosen were then to meet with the commissary and select a chief for the tribe, who was to reside with the commissary. As far as possible, the same plan was to be extended to the northern department.[822] Some such arrangement seemed necessary as a means of knowing in all cases who was the legally chosen chief of each tribe, otherwise a tribe might refuse to be bound by action of the individual who styled himself chief.

The Board estimated that the cost of the establishment required by the proposed plan would amount to about twenty thousand pounds annually. This sum it proposed to raise by means of a tax upon the Indian trade, collected either in the form of an export duty on furs or as an excise tax payable by each trader at the various posts. The final determination of the method of collection was to rest upon the advice of the Indian agents as to which plan would prove the least burdensome to the traders.[823]

This plan met with the approval of Johnson and Governor Colden, although they suggested a modification of the regulation forbidding the sale of rum to the Indians. Their arguments were based upon the known desires of the Indians for liquor, its value as an article of trade, and the additional revenue which would be realized from its sale.[824] The Board endeavored for the next four years to get this plan instituted by act of Parliament, but never succeeded. Various reasons could be given for its failure on this point, but probably the most potent ones were opposition in the colonies and the lack of funds to finance the scheme. Finally in April, 1768, a circular letter to the governors announced that the whole plan

---

[822] Plan for the management of Indian affairs, in New York *Colonial Documents*, vol. vii, 637, clauses 1-13, 15-18, 23-39, 41-42.

[823] New York *Colonial Documents*, vol. vii, 639.

[824] Letters of Johnson and Colden. *Ibid.*, 661-666, 667-670.

had been abandoned.[825] As the Indian policy after that date lies outside the scope of this work, it is not necessary to follow it further.

Notwithstanding the changing personnel of the Board of Trade and the shifting ministries, there is a surprising continuity of policy toward settlements in the west. Up to 1754 the Board steadily favored them as the best means of defense against the French and the Spanish, except where such a policy endangered the friendly relations with very strong and dangerous Indian tribes. The exigencies of the French and Indian War compelled the Board to modify its former policy. Alliances and combinations among the Indian tribes had developed, and there was so much danger from their growing hostility to the advanced English settlements that westward expansion was hazardous at many places where it had formerly been encouraged. After the expulsion of the French and the acquisition of the Spanish claims east of the Mississippi, there was no longer need for the former rapid occupation of the interior. On the other hand, Indian tribes which had formerly been pitted against each other, now tended to unite for common purposes, and thus occupied the menacing position formerly held by the French. Westward expansion might endanger the peace and safety of the whole frontier, where formerly it was a means of defense. Hence the insistence of the Board that Indian claims be acquired by recognized authority before settlements were made.

The policy of the Board not only shows continuity,

825 Pennsylvania *Colonial Records*, vol. ix, 552.

it also shows progress.   As long as it was largely a question of pitting one Indian tribe or confederation against another, each colony could easily regulate the relations with its own Indians, with what assistance it could get from England.   But as the settlements spread into the back country and flowed together, Indian problems became national instead of local.   The Board recognized this change by limiting purchases of Indian lands, by the appointment by the crown of Indian agents, by insisting that treaties should be made under the supervision of these officers, and by proposing a national regulation of all commercial and trade relations with the Indians.   It had gradually arrived at the conclusion that the Indian was properly the ward of the state, and that it was necessary for the central government to protect him.

RÉSUMÉ

During the first seventy years of its history the Board of Trade had a somewhat checkered career: at one time it was the source of authority for all questions of colonial policy, its president exercising all the influence of a cabinet minister; at another it was merely an advisory body, whose recommendations were accepted or rejected as the secretary of state saw fit. Because of the periods of impotency and apparent indifference, the Board has frequently been set down as an inefficient bureau which could be ignored as an essential factor in colonial history. The foregoing account shows that such is not the case, that for more than one half of the period under consideration it was a decidedly active and influential organ of government, and that even during the decadent period it did some effective work.

The Board was no better and certainly but little worse than other parts of the British government, and periods of inefficiency in one are contemporary with similar periods in the other. In each case the cause of bad government must be sought in the personality of the men who were responsible for the conditions. This fact is most clearly illustrated in the history of the Board of Trade, for while its power and influence varied from time to time, the commission usually remained unchanged. The activities of the Board were not measured by its commission, but were dependent upon the will of the secretary of state for the Southern Department, who controlled it. If he gave it a free hand, it was a powerful body; but if he insisted upon interfering with its work and required that all questions of colonial management should be referred to himself personally, it at once lost its influence.

The history of the Board of Trade shows the effects of the gradual change which was taking place in the British government. Created in 1696 as a committee under the immediate control of the crown, it came naturally into the power of the slowly developing parliamentary executive. During the ascendency of Walpole and Newcastle, two men ran the government, or kept others from running it, and during that time Newcastle absorbed the chief executive powers of the Board of Trade and himself directed colonial affairs. Whatever inefficiency in the management of the colonies existed during that time must be charged to him, and to him must be given the credit for all important colonial policies initiated within that period, if any can be found.

With the downfall of Walpole there came into power a new school of active and independent men in the House of Commons who demanded a share in conducting the government. The old centralized parliamentary executive was broken, new men entered the administration and with them the executive functions had to be shared. In spite of the wishes of Newcastle, Halifax was given the presidency of the Board of Trade, and within a very short time that body again came into its own because of the personal influence he was able to wield. He first demanded and secured permission for the Board to act up to its commission powers, insisted upon an extension of those powers, compelled his colleagues to give his recommendations the same weight as though they came from a secretary of state, and finally secured the public recognition he craved by being admitted to the cabinet.

In its relations with the Privy Council the Board was a bureau of investigation, an advisory body, and a court of first instance. Through its correspondence with colonial officials and personal consultation with merchants and others familiar with conditions in the plantations, it gathered data, learned what was going on, and tried to discover the particular needs of each province; with this information before it, colonial policies were mapped out and orders were drawn to carry them into execution. In their final shape these were then laid before the Privy Council for ratification, where they were reviewed just as were other governmental questions before final action was taken.

The Privy Council was developing its committee system so as to give actual control of the government to those who were responsible to Parliament. The meeting with the sovereign ceased to be a deliberative body, and all matters of a controversial nature or which required investigation were referred to committees, that is council meetings to which the sovereign was not invited. These were not standing committees nor committees appointed for any particular service, but all matters were referred to what was in reality the committee of the whole, consisting of any three or more members of the council. Apparently, the clerks attempted to give to these committee meetings names descriptive of the work done, hence a most confusing list of committees was created, which even trained scholars have sometimes assumed to be divisions of the Privy Council. No such separate divisions existed, that there was but one committee – that of the whole – during most of this period; that even the so-called "Committee on Appeals from the Plantations" was not a separate and distinct committee, that it was only a council meeting to dispose of judicial matters, and that it by no means limited its activities to the consideration of appeals, but like all other committee meetings, disposed of whatever other business demanded attention. Furthermore it seems clearly established that there was no fixed personnel for the various committees suggestive of an actual division of the work of the Privy Council, except so far as the presence of the chief legal minds when judicial business was transacted may be construed to constitute such a specialization of duties.

In carrying out the limited functions permitted it, the Board encountered serious natural difficulties, among which were: distance and the absence of regular means of communication, even with the most accessible colonies; the niggardliness of the British government in supplying it with funds, so that dispatches had to be entrusted to masters of trading vessels and chance messengers to save postage; and last of all, lack of regular means of communication from one colony to another, causing delays if not more serious hazard to dispatches. These natural difficulties were greatly enhanced by the many years of warfare, which rendered communications even more precarious. To all this must be added the handicap of exacting commercial duties in no way connected with colonial government, but which absorbed the time and energy of the Board at critical times. Some of the difficulties were finally overcome by the Board's securing a regular packet service for the mails and free postage for its communications, thus enabling it to keep more closely in touch with the colonies.

The most serious difficulty in colonial government was one growing out of the gradual revolution which was taking place in the colonies due to the rising power of the assemblies. This movement had scarcely begun in 1696 when the Board was organized, but it developed rapidly and was almost complete by 1765. The assemblies, through their assumed power over what they chose to call a money bill, were able to usurp the chief legislative powers of the council by denying to that body the right to amend proposed financial measures, thus rendering it powerless to assist the governor in carrying out his instructions. With the council eliminated and with full control of the purse in their own hands, the assemblies proceeded to force the governors to sign forbidden legislation and to strip them of their executive functions. By designating officers by name in the appropriation bills the assemblies forced the governors to appoint such persons to office as were pleasing to itself, extraordinary and even ordinary executive duties were delegated to committees of the lower house, and finally the control of the military was assumed, so that the governors were reduced to little more than figureheads. Instead of being dependent upon the Board, they had become dependent upon the assemblies, whose speaker had acquired almost the powers of a local prime minister. As he was backed by the majority in the assembly, the governor had to consult him upon nearly all measures, and take his advice if he wished things to go ahead smoothly in his government. This extended in some cases to summoning, proroguing, and dissolving the assembly; hence there were many elements tending to develop in the colonies ministerial forms of government patterned strongly after that in England.

The Board of Trade was not ignorant of the political tendency within the colonies, nor slow to recognize the practically unworkable character of the imperial arrangement for governing them. With unerring foresight it picked out the most vital defect in the constitution and sought to remedy it by securing in each of the royal and proprietary provinces a fixed civil list which would render executive and judicial officers independent of the local legislatures. To secure this object it resorted to every means in its power; instructions to the governors, threats, reprimands from the sovereign, and even appeals to Parliament were all used in vain. The assemblies refused to be intimidated, governors could not starve, wars at inopportune times necessitated making terms with the assemblies and allowed them to increase their power. Ministers were too indifferent or too timid to supply the only other remedy and establish a civil list by act of Parliament. The Board had repeatedly demanded that such action be taken, ministers sometimes permitted bills to that effect to be introduced, threats of their passage were held over the colonial assemblies, but nothing was done until after the elimination of the French from the continent. At last the ministers appealed to Parliament and secured the desired legislation but encountered armed resistance in the colonies.

In dealing with the judges the Board was more successful. Judges had at first been commissioned only during the pleasure of the crown; but the instructions to the governors were ambiguous, and in the course of time it became the custom for governors to issue commissions during good behavior. Under Halifax the Board discovered the irregular practice, changed the instructions, and when all commissions fell vacant on the death of George II, forced the renewals to be made at the pleasure of the crown. This policy was very closely connected with the attempt to render the governors more independent of local control. As long as the judges were dependent upon the assemblies for their salaries, and held office during good behavior, they were absolutely independent of all control by the mother country. From an imperial point of view this was a serious situation, especially so in view of the numerous acts of Parliament regulating trade and navigation which had to be enforced in courts presided over by these judges, and the provision that they could be removed from office by the crown gave the empire its only measure of protection against an ignorant or partisan bench.

The Board of Trade had other important colonial

policies; such as, the development of some form of military union for purposes of defense, the reduction of all the colonial governments to one type by the resumption of the charters and the proprietary grants, and the rapid westward expansion of the population, especially on the French and Spanish frontiers. Its trade policy was not excessively narrow, but was intended to make the colonies and the home country mutually helpful to each other industrially. Each was to be a market and a source of supply for the other. To make such a condition possible the Board sought to engage the colonists in those enterprises which threatened the least competition with British industries, and at the same time would yield ample returns to the labor and capital invested. To this end it favored bounties, drawbacks, discriminating tariff duties, and the expenditure of money for popular instruction in new and promising enterprises. The Board itself seldom favored direct limitations upon colonial industries, except when it was forced to do so by those engaged in some English trade which appeared to be suffering from American competition. The value of the colonial market, however, was never underrated and every opportunity was taken to protect and expand it, especially that for English woolens. The importance of this last can hardly be overrated, and much of the naval stores policy of the Board was instigated by a desire to extend and safeguard the colonial wool market.

The power to approve or disapprove colonial legislation was the most important means of shaping the legal relations of the colonies to the mother country, of

securing uniformity of legal procedure, and of preventing unfair local and special legislation. In the exercise of this power the Board of Trade was not arbitrary or tyrannical, but acted with the judicial fairness
of a court of first instance. Each law was submitted to
a crown lawyer for his opinion as to its legal fitness,
was permitted a day in court for a public hearing and
argument from attorneys, was tested by members of
the Board as to its general fitness from an administrative point of view, and was finally recommended for
approval or disallowance. From that recommendation an appeal lay to the Privy Council, which could
reverse the action of the Board, but seldom did so.

Probably no part of our colonial experience has
had more permanent results than this constant sub-
jection of local laws to the review of the central government. The power of the Supreme Court of the
United States to declare state laws unconstitutional is
scarcely more than an American version of the constant practice of the Board of Trade. Even the
reasons for the disallowance of colonial laws, worked
out as they were as each specific case presented itself,
show a surprising similarity to the limitations upon
state legislation today. Prior to 1765 the limitation
imposed upon their legislative powers was not especially irksome to most of the colonies, and was generally submitted to by the mass of the population
with about the same grace that people today submit
to decisions of the Supreme Court which are adverse
to popular laws. In many cases the colonial legislatures hastened to remedy defective laws so as to make
them conform to the demands of the Board, thus in-

dicating their appreciation of the value of the general system. The cases of direct opposition and evasions of the royal veto are probably greatly overestimated and their importance exaggerated.

No doubt principles of government worked out under the administration of the Board of Trade have influenced later administration in many ways. The Indian policy of the Board by its very example persisted for many years, at least so far as its main features are concerned. And it is a significant fact that when the new American government acquired territories, that is colonies, of its own, it did not place the governors, judges, or territorial officers at the mercy of a local legislature, nor were unlimited financial powers conferred upon such legislatures, and all laws were subjected to a review and possible veto by the central government.

BIBLIOGRAPHY

In the following list no attempt has been made to compile an exhaustive bibliography, only those works being included which were directly serviceable in preparing this volume. With a very few exceptions, the list includes no material not specifically cited in the footnotes.

ALDEN, GEORGE H. New Governments west of the Alleghanies before 1780: in University of Wisconsin *Bulletin*, historical series, vol. ii, no. 1 (Madison, 1897).

ALVORD, CLARENCE W. Genesis of the Proclamation of 1763: read before the Michigan Pioneer and Historical Society, December 13, 1907, and reprinted from the *Proceedings* of that organization (Lansing, 1908).

    Contains new material on the attitude of important British officials toward westward expansion, 1760-1767.

AMES, HERMAN V. Pennsylvania and the English Government, 1699-1700: reprinted from the Pennsylvania *Magazine of History and Biography* (Philadelphia, 1900).

    Contains important extracts from the correspondence of Colonel Robert Quary.

ANDREWS, CHARLES McL. American Colonial History, 1690-1750: in American Historical Association *Report for 1898* (Washington, 1899).

    This article suggested some phases of the present investigation.

—— Colonial Self-government, 1652-1689 (New York, 1904).

    Has an excellent summary of colonial administration prior to 1696, written largely from the records in London. It also has a very good bibliography of the earlier period of colonial government.

—— British Committees, Commissions, and Councils of Trade and Plantations, 1622-1675: in Johns Hopkins University *Studies in Historical and Political Science* (Baltimore, 1908), vol. xxvi, nos. 1-3.

This is by far the most accurate and definite account extant of the growth of organs of imperial control during the seventeenth century. It also contains an excellent account of the evolution of instructions to royal governors during that period.

ANDREWS, CHARLES McL.   List of the Journals and Acts of the Councils and Assemblies of the Thirteen Original Colonies and the Floridas in America, preserved in the Public Record Office, London: American Historical Association's Public Archives Commission in *Report for 1908*, vol. i, Appendix D (Washington, 1909). .

An invaluable finding list for those who have occasion to use the London manuscripts. Ultimately this list will be completed for all the manuscripts dealing with colonial history.

BASSETT, JOHN S.   Constitutional Beginnings of North Carolina, 1663-1729: in Johns Hopkins University *Studies in Historical and Political Science* (Baltimore, 1894), ser. xii, no. 3.

BEER, GEORGE L.   Commercial Policy of England toward the American Colonies: in Columbia University *Studies in History*, etc. (New York, 1893), vol. iii, no. 2.

—— British Colonial Policy, 1754-1765 (New York, 1907).

Written entirely from original material, drawn very largely from the manuscripts in the Public Record Office in London, this volume has rendered all other accounts of the commercial relations of the American colonies to the mother country obsolete for the period it covers. It is somewhat deficient in its account of political relations and institutions.

BOARD OF TRADE Journal.   See Great Britain, Board of Trade Papers.

BRITISH MUSEUM. Additional Manuscripts, 32,692-32,884 (London).

These comprise a portion of the voluminous Newcastle correspondence and contain the letters which passed between Newcastle and Halifax, also some of the correspondence between Bedford and Halifax. Many of the letters are of great historical value. Only the originals in London were used. Transcripts are to be found in the Library of Congress at Washington.

BURKE, SIR BERNARD.   Genealogical and Heraldic Dictionary of the Peerage and Baronetage (London, 1899).

BURNET, GILBERT.   History of his own Time (London, 1857), 2 vols.

Is valuable for its account of the organization of the Board of Trade and its estimate of men.

CARROLL, B. R. Historical collections of South Carolina (New York, 1836), 2 vols.

CHALMERS, GEORGE. Introduction to the History of the Revolt of the American Colonies (Boston, 1845), 2 vols.

A strongly biased account of the rising power of the colonial assemblies, but very valuable for the extracts which it contains of documents not elsewhere in print. Needs to be used with caution.

—— Opinions of eminent Lawyers on various points of English Jurisprudence (Burlington, Va., 1858), 2 vols.

Largely devoted to the legal opinions of the crown lawyers on the laws enacted by the various colonies.

CHANNING, EDWARD. Century of Colonial History, 1660-1760, vol. ii of *History of the United States* (New York, 1908), 8 vols.

Has several pages devoted to a description of the Board of Trade and its activities, and probably the longest discussion of the royal veto to be found in any history of the colonies. It is an excellent account considering the amount of space allotted to these topics.

CHATHAM, EARL OF. Correspondence (London, 1838-1840), 4 vols.

COBBETT, WILLIAM. Parliamentary History of England (London, 1809-1813), vols. v-xv.

COFFIN, VICTOR. Province of Quebec and the early American Revolution: in University of Wisconsin *Bulletin*, historical series, vol. i, no. 3 (Madison, 1896).

C.O. 5. See Great Britain, Board of Trade Papers.

COLDEN, CADWALLADER. Letters: in the New York Historical Society *Collections* (New York, 1875-1876), vol. x, xi.

These letters are of especial value for the information they contain on judges' commissions and Indian relations, during the period from 1760 to 1765.

COXE, WILLIAM. Memoirs of the Administration of the Right Honorable Henry Pelham (London, 1829), 2 vols.

CROSS, ARTHUR L. Anglican Episcopate and the American Colonies (New York, 1902).

Of little value in this study, because it neglects the relations of the Bishop of London to the Board of Trade, not even indicating that the bishop was a member of the Board.

DICEY, ALBERT V.   Privy Council (London, 1887).
Of little help in understanding the committee changes of the eighteenth century.

DOYLE, JOHN A.   English Colonies in America (New York, 1882-
1907), 5 vols.

DU BOIS, W. E. BURGHARDT.   Suppression of the African Slave
Trade to the United States of America, 1638-1870 (New York,
1896).

EDWARDS, BRYAN.   History of the British Colonies in the West
Indies (London, 1817), 3 vols.

EGERTON, HUGH E.   Short history of British colonial policy
(London, 1897).

FITZMAURICE, EDMUND G. P.   Life of William, Earl of Shelburne (London, 1875-1876), 3 vols.

FROTHINGHAM, RICHARD.   Rise of the Republic of the United
States, sixth edition (Boston, 1895).
Institutional in its treatment. Shows a keen perception of the
fundamental changes in the colonial constitution in the first half of
the eighteenth century.

GREAT BRITAIN.   Calendar of State Papers, colonial series, America and the West Indies, 1693-1697, edited by J. W. Fortescue
(London, 1903-1904), 2 vols.
The condensed account of the calendared document was found so
unsatisfactory that the originals were resorted to as far as possible.

——— Board of Trade Papers. Manuscripts in the Public Record
Office (London).
These are the original manuscript records of the Board of Trade,
including the ones it inherited from earlier committees, and the ones
accumulated under its régime. The set of papers is very extensive,
including a great variety of material which has been recently reclassi-
fied or is now in process of reclassification, consequently the papers are
no longer cited as Board of Trade papers but as C.O. The Board of
Trade papers proper are regularly made up of what were known as
"entry books," and "originals." The "entry books" contain the official
copy of all the out-letters and frequently copies or condensations of
important in-letters. As the out-letters contain the record of the official
action of the Board in dealing with each particular colony, and as this
monograph is primarily a study of the Board's dealings with the
American territorial colonies, the "entry books" have proved of the
greatest value and have been gone over carefully. The bundles of
in-letters, known as "originals" have been consulted only so far as they

readily threw light upon the operation of the announced policy of the Board. On account of the nature of the subject under investigation, the in-letters were far less valuable than were the out-letters, as they throw comparatively little light upon the influences in England which were shaping colonial policy. But for any subject dealing with conditions in the colonies they are a veritable mine of information. The sets and volumes which were examined and to many of which citations have been made in the text are:

C.O. 5, 5, ONE VOLUME. AMERICA AND WEST INDIES. General correspondence with the secretary of state. Contains some especially valuable papers incident to Governor Burnet's quarrel with the Massachusetts assembly.

C.O. 5, 52, ONE VOLUME. Secret correspondence concerning a treasonable plot in America during the French and Indian War, apparently implicating Sir William Shirley and George Croghan.

C.O. 5, 293-299, SEVEN BUNDLES. NORTH CAROLINA. In-letters to the Board.

C.O. 5, 319, 323-325, THREE VOLUMES. NORTH CAROLINA. Entry books of out-letters.

C.O. 5, 358-376, NINETEEN VOLUMES. SOUTH CAROLINA. In-letters to the Board.

C.O. 5, 383-384, TWO BUNDLES. SOUTH CAROLINA. Unbound letters to the secretary of state.

C.O. 5, 400-404, FIVE VOLUMES. SOUTH CAROLINA. Entry books of out-letters.

C.O. 5, 644-648, FIVE BUNDLES. GEORGIA. In-letters to the Board.

C.O. 5, 672-674, THREE VOLUMES. GEORGIA. Entry books of out-letters.

C.O. 5, 714-721, EIGHT BUNDLES. MARYLAND. In-letters to the Board.

C.O. 5, 724-727, FOUR VOLUMES. MARYLAND. Entry books of out-letters.

C.O. 5, 751-753, THREE BUNDLES. MASSACHUSETTS BAY. Letters to the secretary of state.

C.O. 5, 970-977, EIGHT BUNDLES. NEW JERSEY. In-letters to the Board.

C.O. 5, 994-1000, SEVEN VOLUMES. NEW JERSEY. Entry books of out-letters.

C.O. 5, 859-890, THIRTY-TWO BUNDLES. NEW ENGLAND. In-letters to the Board, very largely from the governors of Massachusetts Bay.

C.O. 5, 907-923, SEVENTEEN VOLUMES. NEW ENGLAND. Entry books of out-letters, principally to the governors of Massachusetts Bay.

C.O. 5, 925-928, FOUR BUNDLES. NEW HAMPSHIRE. In-letters to the Board.

C.O. 5, 941-942, TWO VOLUMES. NEW HAMPSHIRE. Entry books of out-letters.

C.O. 5, 1114-1134, TWENTY-ONE VOLUMES. NEW YORK. Entry books of out-letters.

C.O. 5, 1257-1276, TWENTY BUNDLES. PROPRIETIES. In-letters from or concerning the proprietary and charter colonies.

C.O. 5, 1287-1298, TWELVE VOLUMES. PROPRIETIES. Entry books of out-letters.

C.O. 5, 1307-1330, TWENTY-FOUR BUNDLES. VIRGINIA. In-letters to the Board.

C.O. 5, 1358-1368, ELEVEN VOLUMES. VIRGINIA. Entry books of out-letters. This set and the one above were very helpful. They contain material dealing with westward expansion, trade policy, and treatment of colonial laws not found elsewhere.

C.O. 323, 2-25, TWENTY-FOUR BUNDLES. PLANTATIONS GENERAL. In-letters to the Board.

C.O. 324, 6-17, TWELVE VOLUMES. PLANTATIONS GENERAL. Entry books of out-letters. Transcripts of these two sets are deposited in the library of the Pennsylvania Historical Society at Philadelphia.

GREAT BRITAIN. Board of Trade. Journal, 8-74, 67 volumes.

This is the record of the proceedings at the Board meetings, and is of varying value. For most of the period covered by this monograph it furnishes an excellent index to the other Board of Trade papers, although a part of it was so badly kept that its usefulness is seriously impaired. In general it is not very valuable by itself, as many of the citations in it are unintelligible without the aid of the other records. Transcripts of the *Journal* have been made by the Pennsylvania Historical Society.

—— Board of Trade. Jamaica, vols. 66, 67. Entry books of out-letters.

The Jamaica correspondence shows that the island colonies sustained about the same relations to the Board as did those on the continent.

—— Board of Trade. Commercial Series I, vols. 10-47, 38 vols.

In-letters from various sources dealing with trade conditions and commercial relations, largely European, but including many colonial papers.

—— Board of Trade. Commercial Series II, vols. 640-654, 15 vols. Entry books of out-letters, many of which concern the colonies.

These two sets are an invaluable supplement to the general colonial correspondence. They are especially rich in material for a history of trade conditions during the colonial period.

—— Board of Trade. Miscellanies.

Ten bundles of in-letters and papers concerning the organization, business, and financial history of the Board, also four volumes of entry books of out-letters and matters affecting clerks, salaries, material, etc. Together these throw considerable light upon matters of organization otherwise difficult to determine.

GREAT BRITAIN. Historical Manuscripts Commission (London, 1895), fourteenth report, appendix, part x.

Contains extracts from the Dartmouth papers which afford a valuable check for the records printed in other collections.

—— Journal of the House of Commons (London, 1803), vols. xi-l.

The journal is especially valuable in showing the prominent part the members of the Board of Trade took in all affairs relating to the colonies, and the constant dependence upon these men for information of various kinds.

—— Privy Council Register, 1696-1765 (Privy Council Office, Whitehall, London).

WILLIAM III, vols. iv-vi.
ANNE, vols. i-vi.
GEORGE I, vols. i-v.
GEORGE II, vols. i-xviii.
GEORGE III, vols. i-iv.

These are the original manuscript records of the Privy Council and have not been transcribed or printed, although the portions dealing with the colonies are now available in printed form, under the title *Acts of the Privy Council of England*, colonial series, of which the first volume, covering the years 1613-1680, appeared in 1908. These have not been used in preparing the present volume for two reasons; in the first place, they were not available when chapters III and IV were being prepared, and in the second place, an examination of the original manuscripts was considered sufficient.

The *Register* is one of the most valuable records for the student of history, as it was kept with scrupulous care and contains information not recorded elsewhere. It is the only source which explains the relations of the Board of Trade to the Privy Council and its committees. It also contains the only accurate record of the crown's disallowance or confirmation of colonial laws.

—— Statutes at Large, Pickering edition (Cambridge, 1764), vols. ix-xxv.

GREENE, EVARTS B. Provincial America (New York, 1905).

—— Provincial Governor in the English Colonies of North America (New York, 1898).

These two volumes contain the best accounts extant of the rise of the colonial assembly and the relations of the colonies to the mother country. The copious footnotes and the carefully edited bibliographies also furnish a convenient guide to the sources and secondary materials which were most useful in preparing this volume.

GRENVILLE PAPERS. Edited by William J. Smith (London, 1853), 4 vols.

These volumes are valuable for the personal estimate they afford of Hillsborough and his administration. They also give reasons for certain political changes which affected the Board of Trade.

HAZELTINE, HAROLD D. Appeals from the Colonial Courts to the King in Council, with especial reference to Rhode Island: in American Historical Association *Report for 1894* (Washington, 1895).

HENING, WILLIAM W. Statutes at Large, being a Collection of all the Laws of Virginia, 1619-1792 (Richmond, 1821), 13 vols.

HILDRETH, RICHARD. History of the United States to 1821 (New York, 1849-1852), 6 vols.

HILL, WILLIAM. Colonial Tariffs: in American Economic Association *Reports*, vol. ii, 78-100.

HUTCHINSON, THOMAS. History of the Province of Massachusetts Bay, 1691-1750 (Boston, 1764-1828), 3 vols.

JENKYNS, SIR HENRY. British Rule beyond the Sea (Oxford, 1902).

KELLOGG, LOUISE P. The American Colonial Charter: in American Historical Association *Report for 1903* (Washington, 1904), vol. i.

This monograph contains the best discussion in print of the Board of Trade and its policy. There is a failure, however, to realize the great change after 1752, and the ministerial character and the Parliamentary influence of the Board is minimized to a greater extent than the facts justify. One of its best features is the account of the policy of the Board toward the charter and proprietary colonies.

LARNED, J. N. Literature of American History (Boston, 1902).

LECKY, WILLIAM EDWARD H. History of England in the Eighteenth Century (London, 1878-1890), 8 vols.

Its chief value for this study lies in its estimate of men and measures.

LEWIS, SIR GEORGE. Essay on the Government of Dependencies (Oxford, 1891).

Originally published in 1841.

LORD, ELEANOR. Industrial Experiments in the British Colonies of North America: in Johns Hopkins University *Studies in Historical and Political Science*, extra vol. xvii (Baltimore, 1898).

This is a very thorough study of the attempts of the Board of Trade to foster the production of naval stores in America, but does not show the continuous relation between that and the larger trade policy of the empire.

MAHON, LORD (STANHOPE). History of England from the Peace of Utrecht to the Peace of Versailles, 1713-1783 (London, 1858), 7 vols.

MACAULAY, THOMAS B. History of England from the Accession of James the Second (London, 1866), 8 vols.

McCRADY, EDWARD. History of South Carolina under the Proprietary Government, 1670-1719 (New York, 1897).

—— History of South Carolina under the Royal Government, 1719-1776 (New York, 1899).

MASSACHUSETTS. Acts and Resolves, Public and Private, of the Province of Massachusetts Bay (Boston, 1869-1896), vols. i-vi.

The notes in these volumes furnish much information on the relations of the colony to the Board, which proved most valuable in preparing the chapter on the treatment of colonial legislation.

MASSACHUSETTS HISTORICAL SOCIETY. Collections (Boston, 1894), sixth series, vols. vi-vii.

These two volumes contain the papers of Jonathan Belcher, Governor of Massachusetts and later of New Jersey. His letters give much information of the influences which a governor had to propitiate in order to hold his position. They also throw many sidelights upon the actual work of the Board of Trade.

NEW JERSEY. Acts of the General Assembly of the Province of New Jersey, from the surrender of the government to Queen Anne, on the 17th Day of April, in the year of our Lord 1702, to the 14th day of January, 1776, compiled by Samuel Allinson (Burlington, 1776).

—— Documents relating to the Colonial History of New Jersey 1631-1776, edited by William A. Whitehead (Newark, 1880-1902), 24 vols.

Aside from the regular correspondence between the governors and the Board, the personal letters from such men as Paris and Alexander give much information of the inner workings of colonial administration.

NEW YORK. Documents relating to the Colonial History of the State of New York, procured by J. R. Brodhead, vols. i-xi, edited by E. B. O'Callaghan, vols. xii-xv, edited by B. Fernow (Albany, 1853-1883), 15 vols.

This set of documents contains the most complete and voluminous extracts from the Board of Trade papers of any of the sets of colonial documents, and has been the chief source for New York and its relations with the Board. The documents are deficient, however, in material illustrating methods of procedure before the Board. Has an excellent index.

NEW YORK. Colonial Laws of New York, from the year 1664 to the Revolution, vols. i-iv (Albany, 1894).

NORTH CAROLINA. Colonial Records, published under the super-
_ vision of the trustees of the public libraries, by order of the General Assembly, collected and edited by William L. Saunders, vols. i-vi (Raleigh, 1885-1888).

> The complete extracts from the Board of Trade *Journal* of all entries which relate to North Carolina make an excellent supplement to the information contained in the other collections of printed documents.

O'CALLAGHAN, E. B. Documentary History of the State of New York, arranged under the direction of Hon. Christopher Morgan (Albany, 1849-1851), 4 vols.

OSGOOD, HERBERT L. American Colonies in the Seventeenth Century (New York, 1904-1907), 3 vols.

> One of the most painstaking and detailed histories of the colonies which have appeared. As it deals almost entirely with the period preceding 1696, it was of little direct assistance in the present study.

PALFREY, JOHN G. History of New England (Boston, 1895), 3 vols.

> The footnotes contain many valuable extracts from the Board of Trade papers, which are not printed elsewhere.

PENN, WILLIAM and James Logan. Correspondence: in Pennsylvania Historical Society, *Memoir*, vols. ix, x (Philadelphia, 1872).

PENNSYLVANIA. Archives, first series, edited by Samuel Hazard (Philadelphia, 1852-1856), 12 vols.

—— Archives, second series, edited by John B. Linn and Wm. H. Egle (Harrisburg, 1874-1893), 19 vols.

—— Colonial Records, 1683-1790 (Philadelphia, 1852), 16 vols.

—— Statutes at Large, from 1682-1801 (Philadelphia, 1896), vols. ii-vi.

> These sets of documents are valuable for the information which they give of the Board of Trade's treatment of colonial laws. The appendices to the statutes are also especially good in illustrating procedure.

PEPYS, SAMUEL. Diary and Correspondence (Philadelphia, 1855), 4 vols.

POWNALL, THOMAS. Administration of the British Colonies, fifth edition, wherein their rights and constitution are discussed and stated (London, 1774), 2 vols.

PRATT, DANIEL J. Boundaries of the State of New York (Albany, 1884), 2 vols.

Contains some documents not found in print elsewhere.

RAPER, CHARLES L. North Carolina, a Study in English Colonial Government (New York, 1904).

This was published in a less complete form under the name of *North Carolina; a Royal Province, 1729-1775* (Chapel Hill, N.C., 1901).

RHODE ISLAND. Correspondence of the Colonial Governors of Rhode Island, 1723-1775, edited by Gertrude S. Kimball (Boston, 1903), 2 vols.

Supplements the private correspondence in the Belcher and Talcott papers, and is of similar value.

—— Records of the Colony of Rhode Island and Providence Plantations in New England, edited by J. R. Bartlett (Providence, 1856-1865), 10 vols.

RIPLEY, WILLIAM Z. Financial History of Virginia, 1609-1776: in Columbia University *Studies in History*, etc., vol. iv, 1-170 (New York).

SEELEY, SIR JOHN R. Expansion of England (London, 1883).

SHARPE, HORATIO. Correspondence: in Maryland Historical Society *Archives of Maryland*, vols. vi, ix, xiv (Baltimore, 1888-1895).

These volumes are of especial value for the period of the Board under the presidency of Halifax. The letters of Calvert and Sharpe furnish many illustrations of the aggressive attitude of the Board toward the proprietary colonies.

SHEPHERD, WILLIAM R. History of Proprietary Government in Pennsylvania: in Columbia University *Studies in History*, etc., vol. vi (New York, 1896).

SMITH, WILLIAM. History of New York, from its discovery till 1732, with a continuation from 1732-1814 (Albany, 1814).

SMITH, W. R. South Carolina as a Royal Province, 1719-1776 (New York, 1903).

SOUTH CAROLINA. Statutes at Large, edited by Thomas Cooper and J. B. McCord (Columbia, 1836-1841), 10 vols.

SPENCER, CHARLES W. Phases of Royal Government in New York, 1691-1719 (Columbus, O., 1906).

A thoroughly conscientious piece of work, but on account of the limited scope of the investigation, it is lacking in perspective.

STANHOPE, EARL. Reign of Queen Anne until the Peace of Utrecht, 1701-1713 (London, 1872).

STEPHEN, LESLIE, and Sidney Lee. Dictionary of National Biography (New York, 1885-1900), 63 vols.

This was the chief source of information for biographical material used in chapter I. The articles not only give valuable information but afford, by means of references, a convenient guide to other sources.

TALCOTT PAPERS, correspondence and documents during Joseph Talcott's governorship of the Colony of Connecticut, 1724-1741, edited by Mary K. Talcott: in Connecticut Historical Society *Collections*, vols. iv, v (Hartford, 1892-1896).

The letters in these two volumes illustrate the attitude of the Board toward a charter colony, and also throw many sidelights upon methods of procedure.

TODD, ALPHEUS. Parliamentary Government in England (London, 1892).

TRUMBULL, BENJAMIN. Complete history of Connecticut, civil and ecclesiastical, to 1764 (New Haven, 1818), 2 vols.

WALPOLE, HORACE. Letters (Oxford, 1905), 16 vols.

—— Memoirs of last ten years of the Reign of King George II (London, 1847), 3 vols.

—— Memoirs of the Reign of George III (London, 1845), 4 vols.

Of these three works the letters have been of most service. They furnish a great deal of information on the reasons for cabinet changes and for changes in the personnel of the Board. They also throw light on the personal relations of the various officials to each other.

WEEDEN, WILLIAM B. Economic and Social History of New England (Boston, 1890), 2 vols.

WINSOR, JUSTIN. Narrative and Critical History of America (Boston, 1886-1889), 8 vols.

Its chief service for a study of this kind lies in the fact that it affords a convenient guide to the literature of the field.

INDEX

ADDISON, JOSEPH: 38

Admiralty: instructions regarding jurisdiction, 121-122; relations with Board of Trade, 121-123; protection of colonial waters, 122; protection of witnesses, 122

Admiralty Courts: 121-122

Agents, Colonial: Board of Trade clerks forbidden to serve, 70-71; governors must maintain, 156; value to colony, 266-267

Albany: forts, 323; congress, 340

Albemarle, Earl of: 151, *footnote*

Alderney (island): 95

Altamaha (river): 331

Amherst, Gen. Jeffery: 350

Andros, Edmund: 19

Anne, Queen: 86-88

Appeals: how considered, 88; action of committees, 95-96; effect on laws, 274-275; procedure, 275-276; Board of Trade considers, 276-279; committee considers legal questions, 280-281

Appointments: not controlled by Board of Trade, 111; influence of Bishop of London, 124; by secretary of state, 142-143; of provincial councillors, 124, 146; of colonial secretaries, 147-148; of colonial chief justices and attorneys-general, 148; of proprietary governors, 149; Board of Trade controls, 150; of judges, 152-153, 195-209; promotions, 152

Ashe, Edward: 60

Assembly, Colonial: rise and increase of power, 11, 158-179; encroachments, 13, 160; excludes councils from legislation, 165-174; Board of Trade tries to check, 172-173; transfers power to America, 173-174; seizes military power, 174; effect of increased power, 174; nullifies Indian policy, 175; judiciary dependent upon, 198-199; modifies laws, 262-263; causes revolution in government, 361-362. *Of Maryland* — controls money bills, 169; refuses appropriation for French and Indian War, 169-170. *Of Massachusetts Bay* — powers described, 167-168; Board of Trade warns, 178. *Of New Jersey* — disburses military grants, 166; controls money bills, 166; audits accounts, 166-167. *Of New York* — appoints treasurer, 160; controls expenditures, 160-162; amendments to money bills, 160-161; controls appointments, 163; in time of war, 165; refuses permanent revenue, 183; judges commissions, 202. *Of North Carolina* — controls money affairs, 171-172; permits no amendments to money bills, 172. *Of Pennsylvania* — power of council, 170; controls money affairs, 170; borrows money, 170-171; issues bills of credit, 171; corrupts governor, 171. *Of South Carolina* — controls appointments, 172; develops committee system, 172

Atkins, Edmund: 341

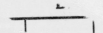